Spotlighting the Strengths of Every Single Student

Spotlighting the Strengths of Every Single Student

Why U.S. Schools Need a New, Strengths-Based Approach

Elsie Jones-Smith, PhD

 PRAEGER

AN IMPRINT OF ABC-CLIO, LLC
Santa Barbara, California • Denver, Colorado • Oxford, England

Library of Congress Cataloging-in-Publication Data

Jones-Smith, Elsie.
  Spotlighting the strengths of every single student : why U.S. schools need a new, strengths-based approach / Elsie Jones-Smith.
      p. cm.
  Includes bibliographical references and index.
  ISBN 978–0–313–39153–8 (hard copy : alk. paper) — ISBN 978–0–313–39154–5 (ebook)
1. Individualized instruction. 2. School improvement programs. 3. Multiple intelligences. 4. Academic achievement. I. Title.
LB1031.J63   2011
371.39′4—dc22   2011003124

ISBN: 978–0–313–39153–8
EISBN: 978–0–313–39154–5

15 14 13 12 11   1 2 3 4 5

This book is also available on the World Wide Web as an eBook.
Visit www.abc-clio.com for details.

Praeger
An Imprint of ABC-CLIO, LLC

ABC-CLIO, LLC
130 Cremona Drive, P.O. Box 1911
Santa Barbara, California 93116-1911

This book is printed on acid-free paper (∞)

Manufactured in the United States of America

Contents

List of Tables and Figures

Preface

The strengths movement is gaining increasing momentum not only in American society but also throughout the world. The strengths philosophy recognizes the talents young people bring with them into the school learning environment, and then it helps them to further develop and apply those strengths to new challenges. The strengths approach is in stark contrast to the deficit approach to education, which is the current paradigm used in education. The deficit paradigm concentrates on what is lacking in the student, as if focusing on what a student is lacking could somehow make him or her stronger or more academically capable. In contrast, the strengths approach looks for what is right in a student—what is working rather than what is not working. This approach in education requires an entire paradigm shift—from deficit to strengths.

It may take some convincing to get educators to change from their deficit educational paradigm because it has been in existence for so very long. Gallup asked this relevant question around the world: "Which would help you to be more successful in your life, knowing what your strengths are and attempting to build on your strengths or knowing what your weaknesses are and attempting to improve your weaknesses?" Most respondents in such countries as the United States, the United Kingdom, Canada, France, Japan, and China—virtually every country in Gallup's study—said they would choose to work on their weaknesses and try to make them better rather than to work on their strengths. Yet Gallup's studies of the top achievers in the world have revealed that they focus on applying their strengths rather than on trying to improve their weaknesses.

GUIDING PRINCIPLES FOR THE BOOK

There are several principles upon which this book is based. The *first principle* is that we learn and profit more from using our strengths than we do from trying to fix our weaknesses. We excel when we amplify, focus on, and develop our strengths. Fixing our weaknesses will only lead to a level of functional competency. The individuals who really succeed in life—Steve Jobs, Bill Gates, Warren Buffet, Michael Jordan, and Sister Mary Teresa—develop and capitalize on their strengths. Virtually all of the major achievements in human society were accomplished by individuals who used their strengths.

A similar situation exists with student academic achievement in our schools. Students develop to their greatest academic and personal potential when teachers and parents help them uncover and plan pathways to strengths development, strengths engagement, and capitalization. A strengths-based approach to learning promotes student achievement because it (1) builds students' sense of self-efficacy and increases their motivational level, (2) generates positive emotions that enhance students' problem solving and capacity for creating, and (3) helps students develop a wider repertoire of learning strategies and coping skills. Strengths development involves a process of awareness and identification of your strengths, integration of those strengths in your self-concept or self-picture, and strengths engagement to complete various academic and personal tasks or activities.

Schools help young people envision a future for themselves by examining how their strengths can be applied to the academic and personal challenges they encounter. They engage in a process that I call *strengths mapping for students*. Some strengths-mapping questions include: Tell me what you learn most easily in school. What subjects do you like the most? What do your teachers and friends compliment you about? Tell me about a time when you were in your strengths zone. What were you doing? Tell me about a challenge you have been able to overcome in your life. How did you overcome that challenge? What brings out the best in you? What strength do you rely on the most?

A *second principle* upon which this book is based is closely connected to the first one, and that is that self-knowledge is at the core of most learning. I do not maintain that just knowing what your strengths are will lead to academic achievement. However, I do maintain that schools must help youth become aware of their multiple intelligences, their learning strengths, and their own learning style preferences. Researchers have given this self-knowledge the label of metacognitive strategies. For instance, I learn best by understanding the concept behind specific subject matter. Other people learn from repetition, from breaking down the material into small steps. The point is that students must begin to unravel their own learning process so that they can achieve and apply what they have been taught. Self-knowledge also promotes young people's self-management skills. Students use information about their strengths to take increasingly more responsibility for their own learning. Students who understand their strengths learn how to recognize and to appreciate strengths in others.

The *third principle* emphasized throughout this book is that learning about our strengths is best conducted within the safe harbor of a trusted relationship—a parent, teacher, mentor. In fact, much of our learning throughout life—whether academic or personal—is relational. A trusted relationship causes us to relax our insecurities, fears, and doubts about whether or not we will ever master the academic discipline in question. Schools create a culture of achievement when they have caring teachers and administrative staff. The best teachers do more than instruct. They inspire students to achieve at their highest possible level.

The *fourth principle* stressed in this book is the metaphor of the seed and the garden. I am an avid gardener. In fact, much to my surprise my dahlias bloomed in late November. My neighbor called the blooming of my dahlias in November a miracle. The bloomings of some inner-city schools have also been labeled miracles of sorts. I use a garden metaphor throughout this book to examine the issues facing schools and to say that we get back what we plant. It all starts with a seed. I believe that every school in our nation—no matter how poverty stricken the area in which the school is located may be—can become a garden of hope and academic achievement for youth. Each school can bloom just where it is—whether it is located in the Promise Academy of the Harlem Children's Zone New York or in one of the prestigious school districts in Connecticut.

This book was written with the view that many teachers want to emphasize the strengths of their students—if they only knew how. The vast majority of teachers have been trained in the existing deficit-remediation model of education. For instance, in one of my introductory course on counseling for teachers, I had students role-play a teacher and a counselor with students who had been referred to a special program for a minor infraction of the law. If participants attended the four-week session, their records would be cleared. The teachers and counselors were excellent at identifying the students' problems, but not one knew how to use the adolescents' strengths as a means to establish a relationship with them or to help set them on a positive course for change. When I asked how they would they would feel if someone approached them with all of their weaknesses, they responded: "probably somewhat defensive," "maybe a little angry."

The book provides a blueprint for building a strengths-based school. It is rich in inventories that teachers and professors can use to discover and manage students' strengths within the classroom setting. For instance, Chapter 2 presents material on the strengths mindset, and I include the Strengths MindSet Questionnaire. Chapter 4 contains the Strengths Pyramid, while Chapter 5 has the Student Strengths Chart and Chapter 9 has the Teaching Strengths Checklist.

OUTLINE OF THE BOOK

The first three chapters of the book set the theoretical framework and rationale for strengths-based education. I analyze carefully the United States' current level of academic achievement in the world and compare it with other countries. The comparison is not in our favor. I introduce the concept of strengths mindset. Careful attention is focused on examining a scientific basis for our strengths. Thus I link strengths development to brain and relationship development. The rest of the book examines the five components of a strengths-based school.

Chapter 1 begins with the metaphor of living with buried treasures. Many people have gone through 12 years of education without any teacher or parent ever helping them to discover their strengths. This chapter defines what constitutes a human strength. It also examines the legacy of deficit-based education. In particular, the chapter details data on American academic achievement in comparison with other countries of the world. Without an educated, high-achieving workforce, the United States will find it increasingly difficult to compete with both the Western world and such emerging nations as China and India in an age of technology and computers. The consequences of the gathering storm in American education demand immediate attention. A rationale for a strengths-based approach to education is addressed.

Chapter 2 further explores the nature of human strengths. The concept of the strengths mindset for teachers and parents is addressed in detail and contrasted with the deficit mindset. A strengths-based mindset is critical for students, parents, and teachers, if American youth are going to be competitive on a global basis.

Chapter 3 covers brain development, emotion, and learning. I discuss human strengths as well-traveled pathways. Strengths are concentrated forms of brain energy, and when such energy is developed, strengths become our passions—thereby fueling us with a sense of life. The principles of brain-based education are analyzed in terms of strengths. This chapter provides the scientific, brain-based foundation for how educators and counselors can institute strengths-based practices in their schools.

Chapter 4 discusses Component 1 of a strengths-based school. I begin with developing the social-emotional component because children cannot be taught if they are upset. They must become emotionally ready for learning. Behavior is conceptualized as a garden of a child's or a young person's emotions. The chapter outlines 8 domains and 10 life skills frameworks for creating a social-emotional component for a school.

Chapter 5 provides information about Component 2 of strengths-based schools—the instructional or academic component. Educational systems are viewed as national gardens. The higher cognitive skills of a nation offer a path of continued economic development. The characteristics of strengths-based learning communities are presented. A strengths discovery and assessment program is outlined.

Chapter 6 focuses on Component 3, caring and empathic classrooms. The relationship between empathy and school connectedness is explored. Dimensions of school connectedness are analyzed. Techniques for developing a caring classroom are provided—for instance, the classroom wall of strengths.

Chapter 7 deals with Component 4, preventing failure in the strengths-based school. A number of prevention programs throughout this country are reviewed. Emphasis is placed on teaching students to stay in their strengths zones in order to accomplish their goals.

Chapter 8 introduces Component 5, increasing home, school, and community partnerships. No matter how desperate the economic situation of a community, there are always strengths in the people, in the community, and in the school. Research on the benefits of partnering with community organizations and businesses is reviewed.

Chapter 9 stresses the importance of teachers' understanding their own teaching strengths. This chapter is instructive because it presents educators with a rationale and a means for exploring teachers' strengths. Two self-report teaching strengths inventories are contained within this chapter.

Chapter 10 emphasizes the importance of creating a school vision for a strengths-based school. I present the idea a strategy for strengths mapping and developing a strengths-based coat of arms for a school and its stakeholders. The characteristics of effective schools are explored. Barriers to establishing a strengths-based school are considered.

Clearly, changes will have to be made in the American educational system if we are to be remain competitive with the rest of the world. This book outlines a strengths-based approach that is designed to help us to recover and maintain our competitive educational edge in the world.

Acknowledgments

Books are hardly ever written with just one person's efforts. In most instances, the seeds of a book have been planted long ago with the support of key supporters. I thank my parents, Richard and Geneva, for all that they have done to help me on my journey, and the teachers who encouraged me and saw strengths long before I recognized them in myself.

Special appreciation and gratitude go to Eli Jones, my brother, who put the figures contained in this book in final form. Knowing that he was working on the figures was extremely gratifying for me.

I also want to thank Debbie Carvalko for her immense insight and editorial review of the chapters contained in this book. Her encouragement was instrumental in getting the book written in a timely fashion. Her comments were extremely helpful. I also want to thank Deborah Bader for her careful copyediting of this book.

Finally, I dedicate this book to my son, Travis. May you capitalize on your strengths throughout your life.

1

Emergence, Growth, and Current Uses of Strengths-Based Educational Systems

Success is achieved by developing our strengths, not by eliminating our weaknesses.

—*Marilyn vos Savant (billed as the person with the highest IQ in the world; p. 228)*

LIVING WITH BURIED TREASURES

Ever since I can remember I have always been attracted to the notion of strengths—learning my own strengths as well as those of others. When I began teaching many years ago, I discovered that I could bring a smile to a discouraged kid's face simply by pointing out one or two of his or her strengths. We all want to be validated in some way. We all want to feel that we do something well, maybe even better than most people can do. What struck me most about my students and even many of my friends and professional colleagues was that few of them were knowledgeable about their strengths and about how to apply them to their own personal lives. It was as if they were all living with *buried treasures* inside of them—treasures just waiting for someone, anyone, to notice that they had. Sometimes the treasures were so deeply buried, so very often glossed over and minimized by themselves and others, that they were simply ignored or, at best, discounted—what I call lost treasures.

I began to wonder: How do people go through 12 years of K–12 and even college without any teacher ever pointing out the strengths that they have? And perhaps more important, what does it feel like living your entire life without any in-depth knowledge of your strengths? What does it feel like living your whole life believing that you do not have strengths? There's got to be pain somewhere. What do you feel deep down inside when you sit on your living room couch watching others exercise their strengths and get paid really well for them? Do you ever feel a little jealous when you hear a person say "I enjoy doing what I am doing so much that I would even do it for no pay"? Do you ever feel: Why can't that be me? Why am I just so, so ordinary?

Think back to your grammar school years. Was there ever a teacher who pointed out your strengths? If so, how did you feel about that teacher? Did you feel that the teacher cared about you? What about your report card? Did it ever mention your strengths in any way other than a letter grade? If you earned an A, well that was your strength, and if you earned a C or D, clearly that was a weakness that you had to work at until you brought it up to an A or a B. Invariably, strengths in the American educational system are limited to letter grades in only a few subjects. And if your strengths lie outside those subjects—oh well. You'll have to just work harder at improving your weak areas.

Consider the strengths that you really value and the strengths that are rewarded in American society. I value, for instance, relational strengths—those strengths that help me to connect with another human being, to understand his or her feelings, and to be able to communicate such understandings to that person. Under the heading of relational strengths, I place the category of nurturing strength. But you will not find relational or nurturing strengths on many American report cards. Much of parenting involves nurturing, but most schools do not assess a child's or an adolescent's nurturing strengths, even though most of them will probably need to have this strength if they are interested in raising a healthy family.

There is' not much room in the American educational system for creative strengths. In fact, creative strengths bring people from different parts of the world together. What am I saying? The limited strengths that we place a value on in schools typically continue for 12 years of a young person's life. Twelve years is a long time to wait for strengths outside the five traditional subjects to be recognized and acknowledged. For some people, the wait for someone to recognize their strengths constitutes a lifetime.

What is lost when a child's potential has no outlet for expression in his or her school? The earlier children's strengths are identified and nurtured, the greater the likelihood that they will be able to use their strengths to achieve in school and within their communities and the

---

YOUR STRENGTHS

Do you know what your strengths are?
Can you list your top two strengths?
Who pointed out your strengths and helped you to develop them?

---

less time there will be for them to fall between the educational cracks. I maintain that if a school does not engage a child during the first few years of school, the chance for doing so may be lost forever.

I think about such notables as Albert Einstein, who was held back in school and who was told by a couple of his teachers that he would never learn and make anything of himself. Albert Einstein is viewed as one of the world's most outstanding scientists and thinkers, yet somehow his school and teachers missed such talent early in his life. And consider Winston Churchill, who failed the same grade three times but who never gave up, and became not only England's most outstanding prime minister but also one of the most admired leaders of the world.

The concept of strengths is based in each person's unique biological and environmental makeup. It is founded on the concept of doing what he or she does well naturally. The concept of strengths far exceeds the concept of traditional academic skills (ACT/SAT test scores; reading, math, and writing skills) because it identifies a child's naturally occurring dominant patterns of thought, feeling, and behavior that can be applied in a productive fashion. At the same time, we must recognize that strengths can be applied not only to academic tasks but also to manage our weaknesses.

Most people are not aware of their greatest strengths because those strengths feel so "natural" to them. Further, our awareness and perception of strengths may be restricted because of distorted feedback that we have received from significant others—especially those closest to us, meaning our family, teachers, and friends. Moreover, our culture may shape or limit our views of our strengths. Our strengths may be developed or ignored. If strengths are not developed and applied, they may be rendered relatively useless. That is, our strengths can atrophy, much in the same way that a muscle, if not used, may wither. For instance, I once worked with a client who had a strength in music; but after 20 years of neglect, she had rendered the strength to be rather average-ordinary. When we fully develop our strengths and apply them, we attain a high level of success and happiness.

Strengths development takes place most easily within the context of a trusted relationship where you feel free enough to share your intentions regarding your strengths. Strengths development is an intentional process, and it matures best when you apply your strengths in as many different settings as possible. You must actively apply your strengths in the areas in which you want to achieve excellence. More will be said about the process of strength development in later chapters. Suffice it to say, however, that strength development is not simply about making a person feel good about something that he or she does well. It is much more than that. There is a biological base for strength development. It begins first in the brain. When parents and teachers focus on a child's or even an adult's strengths, they precipitate a brain response that first interprets that person's action/talk as positive, and then the person's brain alerts and mobilizes the rest of the body for positive constructive action.

Consider for just a second what happens when teachers and parents focus on a child's weaknesses. They send a different signal to the child's brain, and the signal is usually one of alarm, fear, anger, or retreat. Thus far, there is not a theory of human strength development; however, I offer a beginning framework to help both parents and educators learn how to influence their children's strengths development.

This book makes a clarion call to change the American education system from emphasizing what's wrong about students (their deficits) to stressing what's right about them—what they can do. I begin by describing what I mean by a deficit-based system, and then I move to examine the strength-based movement in education. I believe that helping students to identify their strengths and to apply their strengths to achieve their goals and to make contributions to society should be one of the primary goals of our educational system. Every child has a unique combination of strengths, which, when nurtured and engaged by parents and the schools, lead to their academic achievement and later success and happiness. Focusing on students' strengths and teaching them how to use such strengths to manage their weaknesses will, in the long run, lead to higher academic achievement for all students.

Focusing on students' strengths gives them hope. Hope can be a powerful motivator for students to achieve academically and interpersonally. As Karl Menninger once said:

Are we not duty bound to speak up as scientists, not about a new rocket or a new fuel or a new bomb or a new gas, but about this ancient but

rediscovered truth, the validity of Hope in human development—
Hope, alongside of its immortal sisters, Faith and Love?[1]

Hope is extremely important to students' academic achievement, and its importance is revealed in the Greek myth about Pandora. Pandora received a box (actually a jar) that she was forbidden to open. The box contained a number of evil curses. Pandora was told not to open the box. Unable to resist her curiosity, Pandora opened the box, letting evils escape into the world. Realizing what she had done, Pandora closed the box, trapping hope inside. Hope is what students need to achieve and to do well in life. Hope motivates students to keep trying even against great odds. Hope allows students to believe that they can and will learn.

You do not need any fancy new program about how to motivate students. Focusing on students' strengths is a powerful motivator that will keep students in school, whereas focusing on their deficits will lead to high dropout rates. The legacy of deficit-based education is low academic achievement, a sense of hopelessness, and dread of going to school. Most teachers do not know how to motivate students by helping them to identify and to marshal their strengths. In fact, most teachers do not even know their own strengths, let alone their teaching strengths.

Spotlighting the Strength of Every Student provides a clear rationale for why educators must change the current educational paradigm from deficit to strength based. I explain how and why a system that focuses on students' strengths, rather than on their weaknesses, motivates and enables them to be self-confident and goal directed, with a stronger sense of self-efficacy, self-control, and achievement. A major theme is that we usually find what we are looking for: If we look for deficits in young people, we will find them. If we look for youth's strengths, we will find them. What we look for in others has a great deal to do with the lens that we use.

THE AMERICAN EDUCATIONAL SYSTEM: DEFICIT BASED

The American educational system has traditionally been "deficit based," concentrating on where children fall short in abilities and focusing on those needs.[2] Yet researchers are beginning to question the deficit approach to education, primarily because so many of our youth are not achieving academically at the level that one might expect, given their comparative favored economic status.[3] Scholars and educators are recommending that American schools move toward a strength-based rather than a deficit-based educational approach.[4] The movement toward a strength-based educational paradigm is understandable, given the disappointing achievement of American youth.[5] For instance, despite the fact that the United States is the most powerful nation in the world and one of the richest nations on this planet, American youth are achieving educationally at a rate far below that for some impoverished and Third World countries—for instance, Korea and India.[6]

Without an educated, high-achieving workforce, the United States will find it increasingly difficult to compete with both the Western world and such emerging nations as China and India in an age of technology and computers.[7] Not only do we live in an age of a global labor market, where international corporations seek out the most talented and educated wherever they may live, but we also live in a world where our national monetary systems are all interrelated. California's Silicon Valley, which has been said to house some of this country's most talented thinkers, has a large percentage of such workers from nations outside the United States.[8] Few Americans know that Yahoo, Sun Microsystems, eBay, Intel, and Google were founded or cofounded by immigrants from Taiwan, Germany, India, France, Hungary, or Russia. From 1995 to 2005, 52 percent of Silicon Valley start-ups were founded by immigrants. A Duke University study reported that from 1995 to 2005, foreign-born entrepreneurs founded, or cofounded, one-fourth of the new engineering and technology companies in the United States, employing 450,000 workers in 2005.[9]

American schools are in deep trouble. American youth are not learning and achieving at the level they should, given that they live in the most powerful nation in the world.[10] Some Third World countries, such as India, are producing students who are achieving at a much higher academic level in math and in science than are their United States counterparts.[11] This book maintains that we must change fundamentally the educational paradigm that we use to educate American youth. The vast majority of American students are taught under the deficit paradigm. Using a deficit lens to teach young people does not encourage or motivate them to learn.

The importance of changing teachers' mindsets from deficit-based instruction cannot be overestimated. Although it is accurate that demographic variables are directly linked to student achievement, researchers have also found that the professional practices of teachers and the decisions that leaders make can be more significant than student demographic variables. In his 2006 book, *Results Now*, Mike Schmoker[12] maintains that "the single greatest determinant of learning is not socioeconomic factors or funding levels. It is instruction." Schmoker has asserted that when it comes to school improvement, "the simpler the better." School programs that have very concrete and focused action steps designed to improve student achievement in a limited number of specific goal areas stand a good chance of positively impacting learning.

THE LEGACY OF DEFICIT-BASED EDUCATION

Deficit-based education has left the American educational system in a mess that has resulted in spiraling low academic achievement for most grade levels, low high school graduation rates, low college graduation rates, and startlingly low achievement in math, science, and technology. For instance, a recent national report from *Education Week* and the Editorial Projects in Education (EPE) Research Center has found that the nation's high school graduation rate has dropped for the second consecutive year.[13] In 2007, the graduation rate was 68.8 percent, the most recent year for which data were available, whereas in 2006, the rate was 69.2 percent. What these figures mean is that 11,000 fewer students graduated in 2007 than in 2006. These figures are dismal when one compares the high school graduation rates for years gone by. At its peak in 1969, the United States high school graduation rate was 77 percent—some 8.2 percent higher than in 2010.[14]

Racial and ethnic gaps in high school graduation continue to persist. African American and Native American students from the class of 2007 graduates at a rate of 56 percent, a graduation gap of 26 percentage points dividing members of these minority groups from their white peers. On a national basis, 1.3 million members of the public high school class of 2010 did not graduate with a high school diploma, which amounts to a loss of 7,200 students from the U.S. graduation pipeline every school day, or approximately 1 student every 25 seconds.[15]

How does the U.S. high school graduation rate compare with that of other countries? According to a recent report, the United States has the

18th lowest high school graduation rate among the countries studied. The United States falls behind Canada, the Czech Republic, Denmark, Finland, Germany, Greece, Hungary, Iceland, Ireland, Italy, Japan, South Korea, Norway, Poland, the Slovak Republic, Switzerland, and the United Kingdom. The countries with a lower high school graduation rate are Luxembourg, Mexico, New Zealand, Portugal, Spain, Sweden, and Turkey.[16] We should consider a daily dropout rate of 7,200 students another chink in the armor against our destiny to remain a world leader.[17]

What are some of the real consequences of dropouts? The future of high school dropouts is dim. Based on current reports from the National Center for Education Statistics (NCES), the median income of high school dropouts is 40 percent lower than those who earn a high school diploma. Over the cost of a lifetime, a high school dropout earns on average $260,000 less than a high school graduate. Dropouts from the class of 2010 alone will cost the nation more than $337 billion in lost wages over the course of their lifetimes.[18] Dropouts are inclined to have higher unemployment rates than those who sat next to them in class and graduated. They tend to be in worse health, causing a great burden on our national health care system. Increasing the high school graduation rate by just 1 percent would save the United States $1.4 billion in health care costs.

High school dropouts constitute a disproportionately higher percentage of the nation's prison and death row inmates. Increasing the graduation rate and college matriculation of male students in the United States by just 5 percent could potentially lead to combined savings and revenue of almost $8 billion each year by reducing crime-related costs.[19] If the U.S. high schools and colleges were to increase the graduation rates of Latino (Hispanic), African American, and Native American students to the levels of white students by 2020, the potential increase in personal income would add more than $310 billion to the U.S. economy.[20] American high school graduation rates affect us all because the more people who graduate from high school, the safer, healthier, and more viable we become as a nation.

The report by the Center for Labor Market Studies at Northeastern University and the Alternative Schools Network in Chicago proposed a national reenrollment strategy for high school dropouts. The report stated: "Because of the widespread, pressing nature of the crisis and the large numbers of young people who have already dropped out, a national re-enrollment strategy should be a fundamental part of America's national education agenda."[21]

ACADEMIC ACHIEVEMENT, UNEMPLOYMENT RATES, AND NATIONAL SECURITY

Leading economic advisors and scholars have linked the United States' low academic achievement with such issues as the current unemployment situation in this country, this nation's competitive place within the global nations, and our very own national security. For instance, during the August 15, 2010, edition of ABC's *This Week with Christiane Amanpour*, Laura Tyson, who chaired the Council of Economic Advisers and the National Economic Council under President Bill Clinton, maintained that the persistent high unemployment rate could be traced to low college graduation rates and a high school dropout rate for American youth.[22] When compared with 22 countries in 2007 on what proportion of the population has graduated from college by the typical college graduation age in that country, the United States ranked 14th, with 36.5 percent having a college degree. Denmark, Finland, Iceland, Ireland, Japan, the Netherlands, New Zealand, Norway, Poland, Portugal, the Slovak Republic, Sweden, and the United Kingdom all ranked higher than the United States, while Austria, the Czech Republic, Germany, Greece, Hungary, Italy, Spain, and Switzerland all ranked lower.

American youth are competing for jobs on a global basis. As technology grows even more important in the coming decades, jobs in math, science, and computer technology may be outsourced to nations that have young people who perform significantly better in these achievement areas than do American youth. A *yearly dropout rate of 1.3 million students* does not bode well for American national security. Do we, as Americans, go to China or India to get engineers and scientists to design and man our space program, to create new military equipment, or to rebuild our national infrastructure?

Yet, the disappointing high school graduation rate may be only the beginning of the problem of low academic achievement for American youth. The NCES conducts studies to provide statistical data for international comparisons of education. The Trends in International Mathematics and Science Study (TIMSS) is conducted under the aegis of the International Association for the Evaluation of Educational

Achievement (IEA) and is supported by NCES. TIMSS is an assessment of fourth and eighth graders in mathematics and science that is conducted every four years.[23]

The results of the 2007 TIMSS reported that U.S. fourth graders' average score (529) was higher than the average mathematics scores of fourth graders in 23 of the 35 other participating educational systems and lower than the scores in 8 educational systems.[24] The educational systems that outperformed the United States in fourth-grade mathematics were Chinese Taipei, England, Hong Kong SAR, Japan, Kazakhstan, Latvia, the Russian Federation, and Singapore—all located in Asia or Europe. In 2007, the educational systems that outperformed the United States in eighth-grade mathematics were in Asia (Chinese Taipei, Hong Kong SAR, Japan, the Republic of Korea, and Singapore).

On the 2007 TIMSS science assessment, U.S. fourth graders' average score (539) was higher than the average science scores of fourth graders in 25 of the 35 other participating educational systems and lower than the scores in 4 educational systems (all of which were located in Asia).[25] The educational systems that outperformed the United States in fourth-grade science were Chinese Taipei, Hong Kong SAR, Japan, and Singapore.

In 2007, the U.S. eighth graders' average science score was 520. The educational systems that outperformed the United States in eighth-grade science were in Chinese Taipei, the Czech Republic, England, Hungary, Japan, the Republic of Korea, the Russian Federation, Slovenia, and Singapore.

A CATEGORY 5 WARNING FOR THE ACHIEVEMENT OF U.S. 15-YEAR-OLDS

The data for 15-year-old American students is even more dismal—suggesting that years of attending the American educational system, especially public school, may actually result in achievement declines relative to their international counterparts.

How do 15-year-old American students perform academically in comparison to international students on the Program for International Student Achievement (PISA)? PISA is a system of international assessments that measures 15-year-olds' performance in reading literacy, mathematics literacy, and science literacy on a triennial (every three years) basis.[26] Initiated in 2000, PISA is sponsored by the Organization for Economic Cooperation and Development (OECD), an international organization of 30 member countries and 27 non-OECD jurisdictions. It is the world's most comprehensive and rigorous comparison of international student achievement; participating countries make up nearly 90 percent of the world's economy.

Reading Literacy

PISA's 2006 reading literacy results were not reported for the United States because of an error in printing the test booklets, and so the United States' standing for 2006 is unknown. Therefore I report instead the findings for 2003. In 2003, the United States ranked 15th out of 29 OECD countries in reading literacy, and with a score of 495, came in near the OECD average of 500.[27]

Scientific Literacy

In 2006, the United States ranked 21st out of 30 OECD countries in scientific literacy, and the United States' score of 489 fell below the OECD average of 500.[28] U.S. students scored lower on science literacy than their international counterparts in 16 of the other 29 OECD jurisdictions and 6 of the 27 non-OECD jurisdictions. Approximately, one-quarter (24.4 percent) of U.S. 15-year-olds did not attain the baseline level of science achievement, which is defined as the level at which students begin to demonstrate the science competencies that will enable them to use science and technology in life situations.[29]

The U.S. students had lower scores than the OECD average score for two of the three content area subscales (*explaining phenomena scientifically* [486 versus 500] and *using scientific evidence* [489 versus 499]). The findings did not indicate a measurable difference in performance of U.S. students compared with the OECD average on the *identifying scientific issues* subscale (492 versus 499).[30]

When examining the performance of the highest-achieving students—those at the 90th percentile for science achievement—there was no measurable difference between the average score of U.S. students (628) compared to the OECD average (622) on the combined scientific literacy scale. Although the score of this elite group of American students was high, 12 jurisdictions (9 OECD jurisdictions and 3 non-OECD jurisdictions) had students at the 90th percentile with higher scores than the United States on the combined scientific literacy scale. Our best students score high on science literacy, but not as high as the high-performing students of some OECD countries.[31]

Mathematics Literacy

In 2006, the United States ranked 25th out of 30 OECD countries in mathematics literacy, and the average score of 474 dropped well below the OECD average of 498. Thirty-one jurisdictions (23 OECD jurisdictions and 8 non-OECD jurisdictions) scored higher, on average, than the U.S. students in mathematics literacy. More than one-quarter (28.1 percent) of American 15-year-olds performed below the baseline level of mathematics proficiency, which is the level at which students begin to demonstrate the kind of skills that enable them to use mathematics actively in daily life.[32]

What about the high-performing U.S. students? Did they score as well as a group of similar high-performing OECD students? When the performance of the highest-achieving students—those at the 90th percentile—the U.S. students scored lower (593) than the OECD average (615) on the mathematics literacy scale. "Twenty-nine jurisdictions (23 OECD jurisdictions and 6 non-OECD jurisdictions) had students at the 90th percentile with higher scores than the United States on the mathematics literacy scale."[33]

One conclusion that one might draw from these data is that while African Americans and Latinos may depress the average scores for U.S. students on the PISA, even our very best—those at the 90th percentile—score lower than a comparable group of students from nations within the OECD.

Problem Solving

In 2003, the United States ranked 24th out of 29 OECD countries in problem solving, and the average score of 477 fell 23 points below the OECD average of 500. Half of American students fell below the threshold of problem-solving skills viewed necessary to meet emerging workforce demands.[34] National surveys of American employers corroborate this finding; for instance, 46 percent of American manufacturers state that their employees have inadequate problem-solving skills.[35]

Equity in Achievement: Ethnicity and Immigration

In comparison to the OECD nations, the United States has an average number of students who perform at the highest proficiency levels, but a much larger proportion who perform at the lowest levels. When examined in reference to other OEDC nations, the United States is the only member country to have relatively high proportions of both top and bottom performers. Although American white students' average science score of 523 ranked above the OECD average, Hispanic American (439), American Indian and Native Alaskan (436), and African American (409) students all fell far below.[36] These groups scored similarly to the national averages of Turkey and Mexico, the two lowest-performing OECD member countries.

The difference between the science scores of two students of different socioeconomic backgrounds is higher in the United States than in almost any other country. While the existence of immigrant groups seemed to be correlated with lower average scores on various PISA literacy tests for the United States, this was not the case with some OECD nations. Four of the five member countries that have higher proportions of immigrants than the United States also evidence higher national scores than the United States.[37]

According to the Alliance for Excellent Education, Fact Sheet, March 2008, the United States has substantial disparities in student achievement across the nation, and international surveys reveal that the achievement performance gap between the most- and least-proficient students in the United States is the highest of all OECD countries. The Alliance for Excellent Education's Fact Sheet stated:

> Despite the myth that other countries achieve only because they have small, homogenous student populations, data show that many countries' schools successfully assimilate immigrant or high-poverty populations that are proportionately larger than those in the United States. American schools, on the other hand, do little to mitigate the barriers that these groups face (OECD 2007b). Moreover, the rapidly growing minority populations that represent a disproportionate share of America's lowest-achieving students are projected to make up more than half of the U.S. population by 2050 (United States Census Bureau 2004). Unless the United States begins to prepare *all* students for college and the modern workplace, America's disturbing downward trend will only get worse.[38]

Clearly, there are bright spots in the nation's 14,000 public schools. But when it comes to math and science, these school systems have shown little signs of improvement.[39]

THE GATHERING STORM: CONSEQUENCES OF THE AMERICAN CRISIS IN EDUCATION

There are dire consequences for American youths' low academic achievement in math and science. Equally as important, the world is taking notice of such low academic achievement. In its 2010–11 Global Competitiveness Report, the World Economic Forum ranked the U.S. number 52 out of 139 countries for math and science education quality. In prior 2008–9 and 2009–10 reports, the World Economic Forum ranked the United States number 48 for math and science education quality.[40]

In addition to a low competitiveness rating in math and science, the United States also fell in terms of *overall global* competitiveness. Switzerland takes the highest ranking in the Global Competitiveness Report 2010–11 released by the World Economic Forum.[41] The United States tumbled from its prior second place to fourth place, with Sweden rising to second place and Singapore to third place. The Nordic countries continue their high positioning in the ranking, with Finland (7th) and Denmark (9th) among the top 10, and with Norway at 14th. After falling in the rankings over recent years, the United Kingdom moved from 13th to 12th position. Several databases are used to calculate a nation's overall global competitiveness including publicly available data and the Executive Opinion Survey, a comprehensive annual survey conducted by the World Economic Forum together with its network of Partner Institutes (leading research institutes and business organizations) in the countries examined within the report.[42]

Recently, a National Academies study warned of a precarious economic future unless changes are made to STEM (science, technology, engineering, and math) education in the United States. The National Academies consists of five academies—the National Academy of Sciences (NAS), the National Academy of Engineering (NAE), the Institute of Medicine (IOM), and the National Research Council (NRC). These academies serve as advisors to the American government, namely Congress. The report, *Rising above the Gathering Storm*, was prepared pursuant to a request by a bipartisan group of senators and members of Congress who asked the National Academies to respond to the following question:

> What are the top 10 actions, in priority order, that federal policymakers could take to enhance the science and technology enterprise so that the United States can successfully compete, prosper, and be secure in the global community of the 21st century?[43]

The Executive Summary of the National Academies' original report began with the following statement: "The United States takes deserved pride in the vitality of its economy, which forms the foundation of our high quality of life, our national security, and our hope that our children and grandchildren will inherit ever-greater opportunities." But the report concluded that "without a renewed effort to bolster the foundations of our competitiveness, we can expect to lose our privileged position." Contained in the initial report were 20 specific actions that were intended to help assure that America could in fact remain competitive.[44]

Five years have elapsed since the original *Gathering Storm* report was written. While the National Academies' 2005 report outlined a struggling U.S. educational system, its second report was even more sobering, and probably should be read by every American who has a child in school or who loves this country. In *Rising above the Gathering Storm, Revisited*, the authors concluded that the nation's competitive outlook has worsened since 2005, when the first *Gathering Storm* report issued a call to strengthen K–12 education and double the federal basic-research budget. Even though there are intermittent bright spots, the report states that the nation's educational system has revealed little sign of improvement, especially in math and science. The National Academies buttressed this finding with data gleaned from the ACT College Readiness Report. According to this report, 78 percent of high school graduates did not meet the readiness benchmark levels for one or more entry-level college courses in mathematics, science, reading, and English.[45]

The National Academies' *Gathering Storm* committee concluded that a major driver of the future global economy and the creation of jobs will be innovation that comes from advances in science and engineering. To buttress this assertion, the committee cited Robert Solow,[46] who received a Nobel Prize in economics partly because of his work that showed that well over half of the growth in the U.S. output per hour during the first half of the twentieth century could be attributed to advancements in knowledge related to technology. Although only 4 percent of the nation's workforce consists of scientists and engineers, this group disproportionately creates jobs for the other 96 percent. The National Academies' report stated:

> When scientists discovered how to decipher the human genome, it opened entire new opportunities in many fields, including medicine. Similarly, when scientists and engineers discovered how to increase

the capacity of integrated circuits by a factor of one million as they have in the past forty years, it enabled entrepreneurs to replace tape recorders with iPods, maps with GPS, pay phones with cell phones, two-dimensional X-rays with three-dimensional CT scans, paperbacks with electronic books, slide rules with computers, and much, much more. Further, the pace of creation of new knowledge appears by almost all measures to be accelerating.

. . . It is not simply the scientist, engineer and entrepreneur who benefit from progress in the laboratory or design center; it is also the factory worker who builds items such as those cited above, the advertiser who promotes them, and the truck driver who delivers them, the salesperson who sells them, and the maintenance person who repairs them.[47]

In its Executive Summary, the National Academies' report lists a number of factoids that suggest that the United States is rapidly approaching a Category 5 warning in education. I have summarized a number of the key points that should make you stop and ponder what needs to be done to change the American educational system:

- Thirty years ago, 10 percent of California's general fund went to higher education and 3 percent to prisons. Today, nearly 11 percent goes to prisons and 8 percent to higher education.
- China is now second in the world in its publication of biomedical research articles, having recently surpassed Japan, the United Kingdom, Germany, Italy, France, Canada, and Spain.
- In 2009, 51 percent of *U.S.* patents were awarded to non-U.S. companies.
- Of Wal-Mart's 6,000 suppliers, 5,000 are in China.
- IBM's once promising PC business is now owned by a Chinese company.
- The legendary Bell Laboratories is now owned by a French company.
- Only 4 of the top 10 companies receiving United States patents last year were U.S. companies.
- The world's largest airport is now in China.
- In 2000, the number of foreign students studying the physical sciences and engineering in U.S. graduate schools for the first time surpassed the number of U.S. students.
- GE has now located the majority of its R & D personnel outside the United States.
- The legendary Bell Laboratories is now owned by a French company.
- China has now replaced the United States as the world's number one high-technology exporter.
- Eight of the 10 global companies with the largest R & D budgets have established R & D facilities in China, India, or both.
- In a survey of global firms planning to build new R & D facilities, 77 percent indicate that they will build in China or India.

- China has a $196 billion positive trade balance. The United States' balance is negative $379 billion.
- When MIT put its course materials on the World Wide Web, over half of the users were outside the United States.
- Japan has 1,524 miles of high-speed rail; France has 1,163 and China has just passed 742 miles. The United States has 225. China has 5,612 miles now under construction, and one plant produces 200 trains each year capable of operating at 217 mph. The United States has none under construction.
- Six of the 10 best-selling vehicles in the United States are now foreign models.
- Sixty-nine percent of U.S. public school students in fifth through eighth grade are taught mathematics by a teacher without a degree or certificate in mathematics.
- Ninety-three percent of U.S. public school students in fifth through eighth grade are taught the physical sciences by a teacher without a degree or certificate in the physical sciences.
- The United States ranks 27th among developed nations in the proportion of college students earning undergraduate degrees in science and engineering.
- Because of budgetary limitations, for the next five to seven years, the United States will be able to send astronauts to the Space Station only by purchasing rides on Russian rockets.
- An American company recently opened the world's largest private solar R & D facility, in Xian, China.
- The average American K–12 student spends four hours a day in front of a TV.
- Sixty-eight percent of U.S. state prison inmates are high school dropouts or otherwise did not qualify for a diploma.

To be fair, some mention should be made of government actions to improve our educational system. In partial response to the National Academies' two reports, President Obama has made STEM a priority as part of his administration's recent $4 billion *Race to the Top* competition, wherein states were encouraged to develop a comprehensive strategy to improve achievement in STEM subjects, partner with local institutions, and broaden participation of women and underrepresented minorities.[48] As a result, the winning states are taking decisive actions to embed improvements in STEM education into their overall educational reform plans.

In addition to STEM funding, the Obama administration has used the American Recovery and Reinvestment Act to invest heavily in education as a means to provide jobs now and to lay the foundation for long-term American prosperity.[49] The act targets $5 billion for early-learning programs, including Head Start, Early Head Start, child care, and programs for children with special needs.

- The act allots $77 billion for reforms to strengthen elementary and secondary education, including $48.6 billion to stabilize state education budgets.
- The Act makes provisions for $5 billion in competitive funds to increase innovation to close the achievement gap.
- The Act contains over $30 billion to deal with college affordability and to improve access to higher education.

A WAKE-UP CALL FOR THE AMERICAN EDUCATIONAL SYSTEM

Many of the problems in American educational achievement have been placed on African Americans, Latino Americans, and Native Americans. There is some basis for this claim. Members of these ethnic minority groups tend to score lower than white American students on most national achievement tests. A number of reasons have been cited for such low achievement scores, including hundreds of years of slavery, followed by decades of Jim Crowism, high crime rates, and the deterioration of the African American family in particular.

As relatively new immigrants to this nation, Latino Americans have faced their own set of challenges, including such factors as educational and employment discrimination, language barriers, and gang violence. Clearly, poverty is a major contributing factor to the low academic achievement of American students. According to *The Condition of Education 2010*,[50] one in six public school students now live in high-poverty schools. The report states that students who are enrolled in high-poverty schools not only perform persistently lower in math and reading achievement but also are less likely to attend four-year colleges in comparison to their counterparts in low-poverty schools. For the 2007–8 academic year, approximately 20 percent of all public elementary schools and 9 percent of public secondary schools were considered high-poverty schools. Some key findings on the relationship between school poverty and academic achievement include:

- For eighth-grade students in 2009, the reading achievement gap in low-poverty versus high-poverty schools was 34 points, on a 500-point scale, and the mathematics achievement gap was 38 points.
- For the 2007–8 academic year, school administrators reported that about 28 percent of high school graduates from high-poverty schools attended four-year colleges after graduation, compared with 52 percent of high school graduates from low-poverty schools.

- The NCES is the statistical center of the Institute of Education Sciences in the U.S. Department of Education. The full text of *The Condition of Education 2010* (in HTML format), along with related data tables and indicators from previous years, can be viewed at http://nces.ed.gov/programs/coe.

Yet, the problem in American education is more than just poverty statistics. Consider the educational achievement of students in India where poverty is much higher than in the United States. While we must acknowledge the devastating effects of such widespread social factors that have militated against African American and Latino American academic achievement, we must also move beyond having members of such groups claim victim status. Even if I may have been victimized, I refuse to see and live my life as a victim. Clearly, there are members within both groups who have excelled despite tremendous odds against them. We need to discover what factors break the cycle of low academic achievement for such individuals. I maintain that somewhere along the line, those who overcame the devastating effects of poverty found some adult person—teacher, parent, community person—who emphasized their strengths rather than their weaknesses, their possibilities instead of the limitations of their backgrounds.

Asian Americans, as the so-called model Americans, are not included in the low-academic achievement group. Routinely, Asian Americans outscore white American youth on national achievement tests. What causes such high academic achievement for Asian American youth, even though members of this group have also faced ethnic/racial discrimination and poverty? The answer that I have heard again and again from Asian Americans is that Asian culture has great respect for teachers and education, and this respect is translated into higher achievement scores. Therefore we have to look at cultural factors that may or may not contribute to American youths' academic achievement.

Parents' and students' demands for high grades also contribute to students' declining academic achievement. Repeatedly, I hear conversations from college and university professors about students' demands for As, even though they may not be able to write a grammatically correct paragraph, or they balk at writing a research paper longer than 10 pages. In some respects, American college students evidence a sense of entitlement to high letter grades (A). Some professors have claimed that 19-year-old American students use the leverage of their end-of-the-semester evaluation of professors, especially during tenure and promotion time, to enforce their demands for high grades. Students', and sometimes parents', demand for top grades and little academic work is part of the new academic culture in some public schools and in some colleges and universities.

Problems in academic achievement are not just limited to African Americans, Latino students, and students from impoverished economic groups. The achievement in suburbia is not all that it has been cracked up to be. As Andrew Coulson of the Mackinac Center for Public Policy located in Midland, Michigan, has stated: "The notion that America's public school problems are confined to inner cities, and that our wealthy suburbs produce world-beating high school graduates is a myth."[51]

CALLING FOR A LONGER AMERICAN SCHOOL YEAR

Factors other than race, poverty, and a culture of low educational achievement have also been listed as contributing to the low academic achievement of American youth. Educators have pointed to the difference in the length of the school year for American students and those from other nations. The United States has a much shorter year (180 days) versus 220 for South Korea. Research has found that teachers may spend up to six weeks reteaching what young people forgot over the summer. Therefore it seems reasonable to propose that American youth need a longer school year.

Charles Greenwood[52] has pointed out that the key to improving academic achievement, especially for minority children, is not just a simple matter of lengthening the school year. According to him, American students' academic achievement is highly correlated with the amount of actual instructional time. In white suburban school districts, teachers spend more time actually instructing students than is the case in inner-city schools. Using Carroll's[53] time-based model of school learning, Greenwood hypothesized that low-socioeconomic status students were at risk for academic delay and retardation because of their lower daily instructional engagement rates. Carroll's time-based model maintained that the degree of learning was a function of (a) the time spent learning and (b) the time needed to learn. In general, the time spent learning was defined as the time allocated for instruction and the time within it wherein the student was engaged. Greenwood found that the time spent for learning was less for minority children in school.

But the problem may be much deeper than just lengthening the school year or even spending more time actually teaching—even though I believe that these are critical factors. Structural changes need to be made in the educational paradigm we use to teach our youth—from a deficit-based paradigm to a strength-based one. The present educational system was designed for an agrarian age and then modified for an industrial age. We are far beyond both of those ages; yet our basic educational system has remained the same.

USING A STRENGTHS APPROACH TO IMPROVE EDUCATIONAL ACHIEVEMENT

What's different about the strengths-based approach to education? The strengths-based approach to education identifies what students do best so that those abilities can be developed to pull up other areas where they may need a boost. Strengths-based schools are designed to educate youth who can compete successfully with other youth throughout the world. The strength-based school model maintains that poverty, single-parent homes, and other factors do not necessarily constitute barriers to academic achievement. They are simply life challenges, hurdles over which the schools, parents, and the community work collaboratively to help young people to take their places of leadership in the world. The strengths-based model reframes and redesigns how schools address challenges to student achievement.

THE STRENGTHS MOVEMENT

The strengths movement has gradually gained momentum across this nation. It represents a shift from emphasizing individuals' weaknesses to focusing on their strengths. The dominant theme is that people gain more from improving their strengths than from stressing their weaknesses. This theme represents a departure from psychology's medical model, which concentrates on remediating a person's medical disorder primarily through the "talking cure" and medication.

Criticizing psychology's focus on pathology, in 1999 Martin Seligman, then president of the American Psychological Association, made a speech about psychology's love affair with individuals' weaknesses. He stated: "The most important thing we learned was that psychology was half-baked, literally half-baked. We've baked the part about mental illness, about repair of damage. The other side's unbaked, the side of strengths, the side of what we are good at."[54]

Seligman's point about psychology's love affair with what's wrong with a person rather than what's right with him or her is well taken and supported by other writers. During a tour related to his book *Go Put Your Strengths to Work*, Marcus Buckingham reported that when participants were asked "Which [building on strengths or fixing weaknesses] do you think will help you to be the most successful?" only 37 percent of the respondents answered "building on your strengths," while 63 percent answered "fixing weaknesses." Moreover, when asked "When you talk with your manager about your performance, what do you spend the most time talking about?" only 24 percent mentioned their strengths.[55]

Our obsession with human frailty and with perfecting human weaknesses is ingrained within us from early childhood. When young people are not good at something in school, it usually becomes the focus of both the teacher's and the parents' attention. Instead, it might be more beneficial for parents to figure out what strengths caused a child to earn an A than to emphasize a C letter grade. Once parents have identified the strengths that led to an A, they can help their child use those strengths to pull up the C to a better grade.

Most people give only lip service to the power and value of focusing on strengths. In fact, go to any school, and the principal or teacher might eventually mention the need to develop students' strengths, but little actually gets done on expanding them. Consider, for example, a typical cumulative record for the average student. Such a record usually reports test scores, attendance, and poor or disruptive behavior. Students' strengths may be mentioned only "in passing." Schools simply do not know how to go about instituting a schoolwide or district-wide program on students' strengths.

Yet success in school or in life is not all about high SAT scores and As in courses. In *The Millionaire Mind*, Thomas Stanley[56] reported the results of his survey of nearly 1,000 families that had built a net worth of $1 million or more, without having inherited it or attained it through anything except their own efforts and work. Wealthy people are not always the smartest in the class. In fact, the smartest might land a job paying $79,000–80,000 a year, while a high school graduate who focuses on developing a business based on his or her strengths might end up earning millions. For instance, Bill Gates, the billionaire, never completed college. He dropped out to work on a company in his garage that eventually led to Microsoft.

Stanley's research revealed that *success is more internal than external. Wealth first comes from within.* People who do well have an inner set of beliefs—a mindset—that helps them achieve no matter what hand they are dealt. The important contributions of education for Stanley's wealthy respondents were:

- Learning to fight for your goals because someone labeled you as having "average or less ability."
- Determining that hard work was more important than genetic high intellect in achieving.

The strengths movement is a wave of change that has swept across academic and professional disciplines. Corporations, psychology, psychiatry, universities, law, and sports have become part of the strengths movement. The Gallup Organization has completed some of the most compelling research on strengths. Gallup's research began in the 1980s at the organizational level. Some key findings were: (1) The probability of success was 86 percent greater for managers with a strengths approach. (2) Gallup research on employee engagement revealed that employees who said that they had the opportunity "to do what they do best every day" have a 44 percent higher probability of success on customer engagement and employee retention.[57] Peter Drucker, author of *The Effective Executive,* has indicated that a person should waste as little effort as possible on improving low areas of competence. It simply takes too much energy to improve from incompetence to mediocrity than it takes to improve from first-rate performance to excellence. Mr. Drucker stated: "Unless, therefore, an executive looks for strength and works at making strength productive, he will only get the impact of what a man cannot do, of his lacks, his weaknesses, his impediments to performance and effectiveness. To staff from what there is not and to focus on weakness is wasteful—a misuse, if not abuse, of the human resource."[58] Two of Drucker's major principles in *The Effective Executive* are:

- *Effective executives build on strengths – their own strengths, the strengths of their superiors, colleagues, and subordinates; and on the strengths in the situation, that on what they can do.* They do not try to build on weaknesses. They do not begin with the things they cannot do.
- *Effective executives focus on the few major areas where superior performance will produce outstanding results.*

As a result of Gallup's research and that of Peter Drucker, some of the world's foremost corporations, such as Wells Fargo, Intel, Best

Buy, and Accenture, have indicated their commitment to becoming an explicitly strength-based organization. And new managers at Toyota must now attend a three-day Great Manager training program that demonstrates how to spot the strengths of their subordinates.

In addition, the strengths movement is part of the positive youth development (PYD) shift that began during the early 1990s as a response to the single-issue programs for adolescents (substance abuse, violence, school failure, teenage pregnancy). Educators and policy makers were encouraged by the role of resiliency in helping at risk youth to overcome their life challenges and assume positive adult roles in their community.[59] The field of PYD views young people as resources rather than problems. PYD consists of a set of strategies that programs or schools can use to help guide youth on a successful transition to adulthood.

Dennis Saleebey's book *The Strengths Perspective in Social Work*[60] represents the contribution of the social work profession. My article "The Strength-Based Counseling Model,"[61] published in *The Counseling Psychologist*, was one of the first to present a theory of strengths-based counseling. Since my 2006 publication, 15 books have been written on strengths-based counseling or some form of strength-based education.

A TIPPING POINT HAS BEEN REACHED IN THE STRENGTHS MOVEMENT

Strengths-based education is an idea that will only continue to gain momentum, especially as younger teachers begin to fill professional roles in schools. When I searched the Internet in 2006 for articles on strengths-based counseling and strengths-based schools, there were few articles that emerged. Currently, there are thousands of articles on the Internet on strengths-based school improvement, helping teachers to understand their own teaching strengths and the like. The field has just taken off.

To understand the importance of an idea that has finally arrived, I have borrowed concepts from Malcolm Gladwell's 2002 book *The Tipping Point: How Little Things Can Make a Difference.*[62] Gladwell uses knowledge about how social epidemics develop to explain how an idea or philosophy (in this case, strengths-based education) becomes ripe for public adoption. A tipping point becomes that moment when an idea, trend, or social behavior crosses a threshold, tips, and spreads like wildfire. The strengths perspective is a current movement within education, psychology, counseling, and even business management that has reached a critical tipping point so that it can no longer be ignored or dismissed.

Why do so many different disciplines and professions see power in the strengths-based movement? The answer is simple. The strengths approach works better than the deficit perspective. Strength-based schools challenge fundamental educational assumptions about motivating students, developing their educational strengths, engaging them in the classroom, and assessment and managing their academic performance. Americans have a need to improve urban education by fundamentally rethinking and reshaping the basic paradigms we use in our schools.

SOME RESEARCH ON THE STRENGTHS APPROACH IN EDUCATION

Although strengths-related research in education is just in its beginning stages, some of the findings are quite compelling in improving children's, adolescents', and college students' academic achievement. In 2003, the president's New Freedom Commission on Mental Health called for a basic transformation of the nation's approach to mental health care. In the report, *Achieving the Promise: Transforming Mental Health Care in America*,[63] the commission outlined two principles for a successful transformation: services and treatments must be consumer and family centered, building on strengths; and care must focus on coping with and building resilience to face life challenges. In the book *Investing in Children, Youth, Families, and Communities: Strengths-Based Research and Policy*,[64] coeditors Maton, Schellenback, Leadbeater, and Solarz state that there now exists an impressive body of research to support the hypothesis that strength-based approaches to individuals, families, and communities are effective in fostering resiliency, improved physical health, and overall positive outcomes.

Maura Sellars[65] used a strengths-based philosophy to help students who were performing poorly in English to improve their achievement. An important part of the study was designed to increase eight- and nine-year-old students' knowledge of their own learning strengths. The theory was that if a teacher could increase students' knowledge of their own strengths, they would be able to use such knowledge to help them in areas in which they were not performing well.

A small group of 27 students who had been identified as low achievers in English were introduced to a program that promoted their self-knowledge as learners. Students took an instrument (The Multiple Intelligences Profiles by McGrath and Noble[66]) to identify their strengths based on Gardner's[67] multiple intelligences domains. Not only did students increase their knowledge of their learning strengths, but also they used this knowledge to negotiate their learning environment and to identify strategies that worked for them to improve their performance in other academic area. One surprising result of that study was that as students learned more about their strengths, they also took more responsibility for their learning.

Studies suggest that strength-based educational programs positively influence such factors as student optimism, strengths awareness, self-confidence, self-acceptance, goal-directedness, affirmation of others, sense of control, fewer disciplinary actions, timely class attendance, academic self-efficacy, and awareness of others' strengths (Austin;[68] Cantwell;[69] Clifton and Anderson;[70] Gillum;[71] Norwood;[72] Anderson, Schreiner, and Shahbaz;[73] Turner;[74] and Williamson.[75]

Donald Austin[76] used a strength-based approach with freshman students at La Sierra High School in California. According to him, students have demonstrated several benefits of the strengths intervention. At the high school, student conversations about their strengths became common, and discussions between troubled students and administrators now begin with the identification of their strengths.

Some of the general findings of the Gallup Organization's *Strengthfinder* are:

- College students who learned their strengths and how to apply them evidenced increased self-confidence, direction, hope, and altruism.[77]
- Strength-based teaching strategies increase students' levels of academic engagement, objective test scores, and quality of a public speech.[78]
- When students identified their strengths and talents, they perceived that they had more control of their academic futures than those who did not know their strengths or talents. Further, students who actively developed their strengths were more likely to establish learning goals and to have a growth mindset than were those whose talents were identified but not developed.[79]

CURRENT USES OF STRENGTHS-BASED SYSTEMS

More than 65 universities and colleges have adopted the strengths perspective. Princeton has established its own Center for Health and

Well-Being. Azusa Pacific University created a Center for Strengths-Based Education. Even major league soccer has a strengths-based coaching course that reinforces good soccer maneuvers instead of bad ones. If you are a coach taking this course, you will learn how to pass out "green cards," which focus a child's attention to an especially good pass or tackle he or she has executed rather than the traditional yellow and red cards.

In Michigan, the juvenile justice system is shifting to a strengths approach to individuals who come into contact with the legal system.[80] If young people break a law in Ingham County, Michigan, even before their day in probate court they will be asked to fill out a Strengths Assessment for Juvenile Justice, responding to such questions as: Have you made any good changes in the past? What is your first step to get out of this trouble? Who will be the first person to notice this step?[81]

In British Columbia, Principal Charlie Coleman was the American School Curriculum and Development's Outstanding Young Educator because he was able to change a low-achieving Khowhemun Elementary School to a high-performing school using a strengths approach.[82] After just four years as principal, Coleman found that students' scores on the British Columbia Performance Standards increased from 66 percent of students meeting or exceeding expectations in reading and 65 percent meeting or exceeding expectations in mathematics to 83 percent in reading and 88 percent in math. When Coleman was asked what some of the key strategies were that he used to improve student performance, he responded:

> We changed our focus from a needs-based approach to a strengths-based approach. At every staff meeting we start with the agenda item "Kids First." I use that time to tell good news about individual students or accomplishments of a whole class. This positive energy is contagious, and now staff members are eager to share their own good news at the start of every staff meeting. In addition, whenever we meet as a school-based team or to do an IEP for an individual student, we start with students' strengths. Then we look for strategies to help the student use these strengths to solve some of the problems he or she faces.[83]

In New Jersey the Purnell School,[84] a private, all-girls school, offers the award-winning Affinities Program, which grew out of the belief that building on a student's strengths is the best way to help her grow into the person she was meant to become. At Purnell School, girls learn their strengths and use them to map out their future. Sometimes girls who come to Purnell come with specific challenges to overcome, and Purnell helps each girl to find out how she can meet those challenges in healthy and productive ways.

In Tucson, Arizona, school districts have engaged in strengths-building training and coaching for schools. In Indianapolis, Indiana, there is a school called the Key Learning Community, which is a multiple-intelligences school.[85] The school is a K–12 public school that offers educational opportunities across all eight intelligences. Students are taught how to use their strengths in their major projects each semester. Also in Indiana, Culver academies, which consist of private college boarding schools, provide a systemic whole person, strength-based approach to building character strengths and positive emotions in the academic, athletic, wellness, arts, and spiritual life programs.

During 1999, Lincoln East High School (located in Lincoln, Nebraska) began an innovative education program that integrated a strength-based philosophy throughout the entire school. Initially, Lincoln East's teachers, staff, and administrators took StrengthsFinder, which is a web-based talent assessment tool created by the Gallup Organization. Beginning in the 2001–2 academic year, students in the ninth grade took the Gallup StrengthsFinder and participated in classroom activities to help them learn more about their talents. Students and faculty have focused on developing a common language to describe their strengths, and innovative ways to encourage themselves.

RATIONALE FOR A STRENGTHS-BASED APPROACH TO EDUCATION

The strengths perspective represents a shift in psychological theory from an emphasis on pathology to the positive attributes of people. There is an increasing emphasis on what is working in people's lives rather than on what is not working. Some of the key ingredients of the strengths perspective include hope, resiliency, gratitude, spirituality, and transcendence. Strengths-based schools have an abundance and gratitude mindset. Students are encouraged to embrace an attitude of resilience and a belief that they can accomplish their dreams. The entire school adopts a persistent search for strengths in students, teachers, school staff, and parents. All involved share a common vision.

In contrast to the deficit paradigm, the strengths perspective maintains that spending most of their time in their area of weakness will only improve young people's academic skills to a level of average. It will not produce academic excellence. The theory is that students' strengths awareness contributes to their increased confidence, which in turn leads to a greater sense of self-efficacy and motivation to excel. This position is supported by research conducted by the Gallup Organization, which conducted years of research on top achievers, and it found that the highest achievers:

- Spend most of their time in their areas of strength
- Focus on developing and applying their strengths and managing their weaknesses
- Use strengths to overcome obstacles
- Invent ways of capitalizing on their strengths in new situations
- Have learned to partner with someone to tackle areas that are not strengths

THE STRENGTHS-BASED SCHOOL

Five major components are outlined for a strengths-based school: (1) Component 1—the social-emotional curriculum, (2) Component 2—the academic curriculum, (3) Component 3—the caring school, (4) Component 4—prevention, and (5) Component 5—Increasing home-school partnerships. The book draws from brain-based research, positive psychology, multiple intelligences theory, and my own theory of strength development in children and adolescents.

Youth differ in their strengths as well as in the degree to which they understand and know how to apply their strengths to academic achievement and to other areas of their lives. Young people are more motivated and happier when learning about their strengths. Moreover, strength-based schools establish professional learning communities that are learner centered rather than authority centered. They teach youth how to use their strengths to achieve academically and to change negative emotions.

In 2009, Gallup began a partnership with America's Promise Alliance to track the hope, engagement, and well-being of students in Grades 5 through 12 across the United States. A web-based survey is administered. The data collected provide insight into what is happening in schools and also give a perspective on teacher quality and school climate.[86] Thus far, Gallup's survey has revealed that more than half of the students in the schools in the United States are hopeful—a measure regarding how students think, feel, and act in their lives. The remaining students indicate that they are stuck or discouraged and lack the ideas and energy they need to succeed in school. These students are disengaged learners.

A number of reasons exist for changing to strengths-based education. Focusing on young people's strengths:

- Helps students to become aware of their own talents and strengths, thereby improving their own self-understanding
- Assists students to achieve academically and creatively by using their strengths
- Encourages students to become involved in schoolwide strengths-based philosophy
- Motivates and engages students to become active learners and to do their very best
- Promotes student engagement at school and in their own learning

Moreover, strengths-based programs have a number of positive influences on the entire functioning of the school. Such programs:

- Positively influence factors such as student optimism, hope, self-confidence, self-acceptance, goal-directedness, affirmation of others, and sense of self-control
- Reduce school disciplinary actions
- Increase timely class attendance
- Promote a sense of student academic self-efficacy
- Heighten young people's awareness of others' strengths

The next chapter discusses the strengths mindset versus the deficit mindset. It also provides some basic definitions of strength, and strength categories are provided.

The Strengths Mindset: Understanding the Nature of Strengths

THE CONCEPT OF STRENGTHS

The concept of strengths is not as simple as it first appears. Everyone has strengths, right? Do you know your own strengths? If so, how did you come to know what your strengths are? If you do not have a clue as to what your strengths are, what has kept you from knowing them? Whom do you blame—yourself, your parents, your teachers? Did your parents and teachers encourage you about developing your strengths? To what extent do you use your strengths to achieve your goals? If you are a parent, do you know your children's strengths? Can you identify the strengths of family members, friends, or coworkers? What did you say in a job interview when the interviewer asked you to describe your strengths?

Most people do not know the answers to the questions presented above about strengths. Most of us spend the majority of our lives trying to correct or to improve our weak areas, but this is a strategy that has a low payoff—both in our personal lives and in the educational world. You excel primarily by maximizing and emphasizing your strengths, rarely by fixing your weaknesses. Yet, parents and schools put the *spotlight* mostly on students' weak areas rather than on the areas of their strengths.

Your greatest potential for growth is in the area of your strength. Does this make sense? Of course it does. Shaquille O'Neal is perhaps

---

YOUR KNOWLEDGE ABOUT STRENGTHS

Do you know the strengths of the children you teach?
Do your students' deficits get in the way of seeing their strengths?
Do you know how to nourish your children's/students'
    strengths?

---

one of the greatest centers in the history of basketball, but he had difficulty making foul shots. When the coach focused primarily on his foul shots, it took Shaquille off his game; his scoring plummeted, and the team lost. If he wanted to win, the coach had to use a different strategy. He focused on Shaquille's greatest strength—his movements in the paint under the basket hoop. There Shaquille blocked out all who dared to come into the paint, and he score a great deal with his seven-feet, two-inch husky frame. His team won the NBA championship title because the coach switched from focusing on correcting Shaquille's poor foul shooting to his spectacular strengths under the basket in the paint.

Remember that your greatest potential for growth is in the area of your strength. A similar situation exists for schools and educating American youth. Too much time is spent on detailing the problem areas of students' development, and insufficient time is spent teaching students how to maximize their strengths.

DEFINITION OF STRENGTH

Aspinwall and Staudinger[1] have noted the difficulties involved in defining human strength. According to these researchers, one reason that psychology was entrenched in the predominant medical model of repair and healing was that defining the desired or adaptive direction of change is easier if the goal of such a change were to return to a prior state of normality. *Strength* can be defined as that which helps a person to cope with life or that which makes life more fulfilling for oneself and others. Strengths are not fixed personality traits; instead, they develop from a dynamic, contextual process rooted deeply in one's culture. Our strengths are the lenses we use to process information, to experience others, to view time and structure, to accommodate or to make change in our lives, and to communicate with others.

Clifton and Anderson[2] have defined strength as specific qualities that enable and empower an individual to do certain things quite well. What kinds of qualities lead to strengths or to strengths development?

- Behavior patterns that help you to be effective
- Thought patterns that make you efficient in the execution of certain tasks
- Beliefs that help you to succeed
- Attitudes that reinforce and sustain your hope, optimism, and effort
- Motivations that cause you to take certain actions and to maintain the energy needed to move forward or to achieve goals.

Buckingham and Clifton[3] have defined strength as a "consistent near perfect performance in an activity." Strengths are made up of talents, knowledge, and skills. According to Buckingham and Clifton,[4] talents are naturally recurring patterns of thought, feeling, or behavior. In contrast, knowledge consists of the facts and the lessons learned. Skills are the steps of an activity.

Research conducted by Gallup has resulted in an important discovery. People who focus on their weaknesses and remediate them are only to achieve able average performance at best. In contrast, they benefit more and are able to reach higher levels of excellence if they use comparable effort to build upon their talents and strengths. In interviews with over 2 million people from all walks of life, Clifton and Harter[5] found several consistent characteristics of high achievers. The top achievers not only recognize their strengths but also use them to achieve their goals. In contrast, those who are average or mediocre are usually not able to identify their strengths. Clifton and Harter[6] found that:

- High achievers excel because they both develop and apply their strengths more fully.
- High achievers build their lives around their strengths. They spend most of their time in their areas of strength.
- High achievers search for ways to apply their strengths to various activities or achievement tasks.
- Highly successful people learn to play to their strengths and to manage or minimize their weaknesses.
- High achievers do not necessarily have more strengths than others. Instead, they simply have developed their strengths more fully and have learned to apply them to new situations. They invent ways of capitalizing on their strengths in new situations.

In contrast to Buckingham's and Clifton's position that strengths represent near perfect performance, I maintain that you do not have to have such performance. There are gradations of strength. A person may have strengths in carpentry, but that does not mean that whatever the person makes using his or her carpentry skills is near perfect in performance. For many people, perfection lies in the eyes of the beholder.

Moreover, strength development is a lifelong process, with peaks and valleys. Consider, for example, a great writer, such as William Shakespeare or Ernest Hemingway. Their writing ability fluctuated as a number of variables in their lives changed, including their state of mind, the topic about which they were writing, and their health and age. Whereas some writers become better writers as they age, others begin a process of decline. Yet, even with the decline, there is unmistakable strength in their writing. A similar analogy pertains to artists. The value of Picasso's paintings varies according to the stage of life in which he painted his works.

Psychologists have verified that high achievers do not necessarily have more talents than other people, but they have developed their capabilities more fully and have learned to invent ways of capitalizing on their strengths as they approach unfamiliar or challenging tasks.[7] Moreover, high-achieving, task-oriented people are significantly more likely to access thoughts about their personal strengths and to suppress thoughts about their weaknesses after a failure. Consequently, they rebound relatively quickly from failure experiences and reengage in their achievement-oriented tasks. In fact, their motivation and task persistence *increases more readily* after a failure than following a success. Commenting on this unexpected finding, Dodgson and Wood stated, "Focusing on strengths holds the potential for a relatively adaptive response to life's slings and arrows.[8] If we teach our children and our students to identify and to use their strengths to deal with life's challenges, they become more resilient. They come to believe that they have whatever is needed within them to deal successfully with adversity."

Culturally Bound Strengths

Strengths are almost inevitably culturally expressed. Characteristics regarded as strengths in one culture may be viewed as weaknesses in another culture.[9] Ethnic groups may be said to have particular cultural strengths.[10] A strength for one culture may be its emphasis on the family, whereas the strength of another culture may be its ability to save and to engage in profitable commerce. The importance of strengths differs among cultures. For example, in cultures labeled as individualistic, autonomy is highly valued. Conversely, in cultures described as collectivist, relational skills may be emphasized more. Helping professionals are faced with the challenge of learning and understanding both individual and cultural strengths so that they can address the needs of diverse clients.

Contextually Based Strengths

Human strengths have contextual dependencies as they involve interaction with a material environment or with human contexts.[11] Strengths are developed within a given situation containing certain contextual characteristics that may either promote or retard the human strength.[12] During war, for example, certain character strengths, such as courage or cowardice, may be exemplified. Therapists must consider the contextual situation confronting clients. A client's behavior might be considered a strength in one setting and a liability in a different social context. For instance, studies have found that clients who evidence internal control beliefs and problem-focused coping may become highly dysfunctional under conditions of high constraints, such as poor health. Furthermore, in some non-Western cultures, pessimism is adaptive rather than dysfunctional because it increases active problem solving.

Developmental and Life Span-Oriented Strengths

Strengths are developmental in that they require a certain level of cognitive, physical, and emotional maturity or experiential development.[13] Strengths are age related because young children's actions cannot be interpreted in terms of strengths such as courage. Strengths are both malleable and changeable. They can be learned or taught. An individual's strengths may unfold or blossom over his or her life span. Strengths are also incremental, so that one strength provides the foundation for achieving another.

Adaptability and Functionality

A person's ability to apply as many different resources and skills as necessary to solve a problem or to achieve a goal may be considered a human strength. Charles Darwin's[14] work on the origin of species first highlighted the importance of a person's ability to adapt to change. Darwin stated that individuals' ability to adapt to change equals their chances of survival. Strengths may be conceptualized as part of the human adaptational system.[15] From this perspective, people are biologically prepared to develop strengths. Researchers have characterized human strengths as critical survival skills that allow people to right themselves.[16] Strengths develop as individuals move toward external adaptation. Humans are self-righting organisms engaged in an ongoing adaptation to the environment. More recently, researchers have begun to study the critical significance of a person's ability to apply in a flexible manner as many different resources and skills as required to solve a problem or to work toward a goal.

Normative Quality and Enabling Environments

Strengths also have a normative quality because they exist in comparison with other, often less developed states. For example, the strength of courage exists in contrast to cowardice. Each society develops norms for what are considered human strengths. Individuals' violations of strength norms may cause societal sanctioning and rebuke. Moreover, each culture or environment contains enabling and limiting conditions that assist or thwart individuals in their progress along the strength hierarchy.[17] Social class structures may prevent individuals from achieving particular strengths. Each society tends to establish situations, events, or structures to help individuals move from one strength level to another. Cultures provide role models and parables that indicate the desired strength (e.g., Jackie Robinson, patience and skill; George Washington, truth and honesty). Some Asian cultures have priests or Buddhist levels for wisdom, expertise, or warrior skills.

Each environment has attributes that affect well-being. Some social, cultural, economic, and political environments exert a negative effect on a person's strength development, while others have a positive influence. Poverty environments tend to delimit the strength of individuals and entire communities. Hence, strength development is a process influenced by heredity, environment, and an interaction of these two forces. The social and economic attributes of environments can build strength if they have positive effects on individuals' lives.

PARADOX OF STRENGTHS

You often take them for granted and do not see them as being especially distinctive or great.

You often are not able to see or are blind to your own strengths.

You can use your strengths to surmount your weaknesses.

Transcendence

Human strengths can also have qualities of transcendence, as they can be used to resist a force or attack, whether mental or physical. Many studies on resilience emphasize the importance of a person's ability to transcend life circumstances. Strengths help one transcend and improve personal (e.g., being physically handicapped or learning disabled) and societal challenges (e.g., living in poverty or having parents with substance addiction or mental illness). Strengths may develop from a need to find meaning and purpose in our lives so that we seek people, places, and transformational experiences that help us feel a connectedness with the world.

Polarities

Strengths often develop from polarities. Human existence is characterized by polarities such as happiness/sorrow, autonomy/dependency, and health/sickness.[18] Human strengths may develop from the coactivation of negative and positive human states. Youth, for instance, is a time of physical prowess; thus young individuals work hard to compete athletically, but they are not typically wise. A shift in polarity occurs as we age, so that age is associated with a loss in physical functioning but a gain in wisdom.

THE PARADOX OF STRENGTHS

Strengths have an almost inherent paradoxical quality. They are sometimes born from the paradox of adversity. That is, we become stronger by confronting adversity, by trying to master it, rather than by running away from or denying it. One is reminded of John Wolfgang von

Goethe's (1749–1832) statement: "What does not kill me makes me stronger."

STRENGTHS SUMMARY

- Strengths can be defined as that which helps a person to cope with life or that which makes life more fulfilling for oneself and others.
- *Strengths are incremental, so that one strength provides the foundation for achieving another.*
- Strengths develop as part of our human driving force to meet our basic psychological needs (e.g., safety, belonging, and self-esteem needs).
- Strengths are not fixed personality traits; instead, they develop from a dynamic, contextual process rooted deeply in one's culture.
- Strengths are almost inevitably *culturally expressed*. Characteristics regarded as strengths in one culture may be viewed as weaknesses in another culture.[19]
- Strengths often develop from polarities such as happiness/sorrow, health/sickness.

STRENGTH CHARACTERISTICS

Strengths consist of our attitudes that sustain our efforts to achieve at high levels. They are the beliefs that empower us to succeed and to strive toward perfection. Some characteristics of strengths are:

- You must be able to do it consistently.
- You must derive some intrinsic pleasure from the strength activity. A strength energizes and motivates you to work toward achieving something. It enables optimal functioning or performance of an activity on your part.
- Your strengths are enduring, and they are picked up easily and quickly.
- You have rapid learning in your strength area—look for what comes easily.
- Your greatest possibilities for growth are in the areas of your greatest strengths.
- Your yearnings to achieve something and the positive activities that bring personal satisfactions reveal hidden strengths.
- Your strengths enable your optimal functioning in life.
- You experience "strength flow," or you have achieved excellence without conscious thought or without trying hard to do so.
- You excel only by maximizing your strengths, never by fixing your weaknesses.

STRENGTH INDICATORS

Notice your yearnings.
What do you enjoy doing the most?
Describe a successful day in your life.
Describe key achievements in your life.

HOW DOES THE CONCEPT OF STRENGTHS DIFFER FROM ACADEMIC SKILLS?

The concept of strengths is based on what a person does best naturally. In contrast, traditional measures of ability, such as IQ and academic aptitude, deal with a limited number of skills, usually math, English, or science. Strengths reflect your dominant patterns of thought, feeling, and behavior that you use in order to achieve your stated goals. Academic skills may not reflect a person's dominant patterns of thoughts or feelings. Because a student does well in an academic subject does not necessarily mean that the academic area is a strength for him or her. I recall a student who could perform well on a test in class in math, but who in no way could consider math his strength area.

STRENGTH ESTRANGEMENT

Strength estrangement can be defined as the lack of awareness of one's talents and strengths; of if such awareness exists, the lack of direction (or floundering) in using one's strengths to achieve desired goals or to bring about happiness. It is also defined as an individual's alienation from his or her natural talents such that a disruption of the bond between these talents and the individual takes place. One goal of counseling is to help individuals locate the source of the strength alienation and to help them restore it to a desired place in their lives to deal effectively with everyday life issues. Strength estrangement predisposes some people to experience a state of unspecified unhappiness. They may ask themselves, "Why am I unhappy? I've got everything going for myself." Addiction to chemical substances can cause strength estrangement.

MANAGING WEAKNESSES

The mantra for strength development is to promote strengths and manage weaknesses that may sabotage our strengths. The goal is to learn how to use your strengths to manage your weaknesses. The strengths perspective maintains that spending most of your time in your area of weakness will improve your weakness only to a level of average.[20] It will not produce excellence. This position is supported by more than 30 years of research conducted by the Gallup organization on top achievers. The highest achievers:

- Use strengths to overcome obstacles
- Have learned to partner with someone to tackle weaknesses

We often focus on our weaknesses, as if fixing what is weak is actually going to help us become excellent. Weakness fixing prevents failure, while strengths building promotes excellence. According to Peter Drucker,[21] we should waste as little time and effort as possible on improving areas of low competence. It takes much more energy to improve from incompetence to mediocrity than it takes to improve from first-rate performance to excellence. Instead of trying to make our weaknesses our strengths, we should bring the area of weakness to *functional competence*. We might not be good in math or science; however, we can bring our skills in these areas up to a level of functional competence. The concept of functional competence is similar to Winnicott's notion of the "good-enough mother." As Drucker[22] has stated: "Unless, therefore, an executive looks for strengths and works at making strength productive, he will only get the impact of what a man cannot do, of his lacks, his weaknesses, his impediments to performance and effectiveness. To staff from what there is not and to focus on weakness is wasteful—a misuse, if not abuse of the human resource."

MINDSETS AND STRENGTHS

Our lives are not determined by what happens to us, but how we react to what happens; not by what life brings to us, but by the attitude we bring to life. A strengths-based mindset causes a chain reaction of positive thoughts, events, and outcomes. It is a catalyst that creates extraordinary results. This approach is needed in education and in our everyday lives.

In the book *Mindset: The New Psychology of Success*, Carol Dweck[23] maintains that people develop mindsets as they age. A mindset is defined as a fixed mental attitude that predetermines a person's responses to and interpretations of life and situations. The two mindsets she outlines are fixed mindset and growth mindset. According to Dweck, a fixed mindset was partly responsible for the downfall of Enron. She explains that Bobby Knight, the infamous basketball coach had a fixed mindset, whereas legendary UCLA coach John Wooden a growth mindset. Dweck asserts that intelligence is not fixed; it can be changed. It is only our mindset that holds us back. To support her point, Dweck gives an example from her background that involved a teacher who seated the children in her class according to their IQ scores. The teacher had a fixed mindset; she believed that intelligence was immovable for each person.

A dominant theme in Dweck's book is that if we believe we cannot learn and that our abilities are limited, then they will be. Our limitations in life are learned rather than imposed upon us. Children accept impositions from their families, teachers, and the society at large.

I maintain that there are two additional types of mindsets: a deficit mindset and a strengths mindset. These two mindsets have a major impact on how we view the world, ourselves, and others. Our major institutions and organizations are constructed on one of these two perspectives. Most of us are not consciously aware of the mindset that we carry around with us and teach to our children. Our mindsets are the gorillas in the room with us, either enabling or limiting what we can do in life.

DEFICIT-BASED MINDSET

Our obsession with human frailty and with perfecting human weaknesses is ingrained within us from early childhood. When young people are not good at something in school, it usually becomes the focus of both the teacher's and the parents' attentions. Sometimes high student achievement in one area is ignored and emphasis is placed on the low-performance area. Yet, it might be more beneficial for a teacher or a parent to figure out what strengths caused a person to earn an A rather than to emphasize trying to improve a C grade in another subject. Once a teacher has identified the strengths that led to an A, he or she can help the youngster to use those strengths to pull up the C to a better grade.

Typically, the deficit mindset is focused on what is missing, what is lacking, or what is wrong with a situation or a person. If you have ever had a friend who is deficit based, you know the type. You ask her how the party was, and she recites every negative thing that she remembers about it. "Well, it was okay, but this was missing, or this was lacking." She hardly remembers any of the reasons that she was one of the last guests to leave the party. Deficit mindset people are difficult to be around because they complain and complain. Sometimes it takes a near-death encounter or something that really shakes them up to see the positive in life. Deficit mindsets find it hard to obtain a life partner because they are focused on what the person is lacking rather than on what the person has to offer.

DEFICIT MINDSET PARENTS

Deficit mindset parents are hard to live with if you are their child. They ignore the two As on your report card and then spend a half hour lecturing you about the B and C you received. When I think about Michael Jackson's covering his eyes and almost crying as the reporter asked him if his father ever abused him mentally or physically, I know that for Michael, Mr. Jackson had a deficit parenting mindset. His father claims that he never psychologically or physically abused Michael, but what his father actually says matters little. Michael felt abused, much in the same way that I felt loved by my parents all my life.

If you dread having your mother come to visit you because she has something to say about most of what you do, you have been raised from a deficit parenting mindset. I recall one client telling me that each time his mother criticized him, it felt like a ton of bricks on his chest. Another talked about how hard she had tried to get her father's approval, but he always most often seemed to dangle his approval in front of her like a piece of expensive candy or a much desired gift. Just when she thought her father's approval was within her grasp, he would suddenly snatch it from her, and the entire process would start all over again. All her life she felt that she had never earned her father's approval; and all her life she had sought it and felt lacking because he withheld it from her. Key issues involved in deficit-minded parenting are children's lack of some desirable quality and/or parental disapproval, criticism, and disappointment with them as people. Parents with this mindset have a tendency to interact with their children as if they are not good enough.

DEFICIT MINDSETS FOR TEACHERS

Schools, mental health agencies, and social services have a long history of focusing on children's deficits and their problem behaviors. What is the deficit mindset in education and in human services? Deficit models maintain there is a certain set standard of behavior and that whenever youth deviate from these norms, they are defective. Using the deficit approach, both school and mental health interventions then focus on fixing that which is in need of repair, sometimes inadvertently reinforcing a focus on the individual's dysfunction. Deficit models tend:

- To label youth negatively, such as conduct disordered
- To focus on reducing risk rather than on increasing protection for youth
- To ignore the paradox of adversity, that is, a youth's strength or growth in dealing with adversity
- To use a problem-focused approach to working with children rather than a possibility approach

Teachers who have a deficit mindset are inclined to use red ink to correct your paper and append to it loads of notes, even when they give you an A. Few deficit mindset teachers inspire youth to visit them once they have graduated. Such teachers fail to understand that teaching is a process of establishing a relationship with a student, one that is built on mutual respect and understanding. Deficit mindset teachers want to just focus on getting students to understand the academic subjects, such as reading, writing, and arithmetic. They neglect to understand that a great deal of learning has to do with students' emotions and feelings about their class, their classmates, and their estimates of their own academic ability. For such teachers, teaching is all about cramming the facts down the throats of students. There is little thought of engagement of students so that they are motivated to learn.

Teachers who operate from a deficit mindset tend to have low expectations for students, especially, if they are from a different cultural or ethnic background. Somehow, they are clueless that Derek knows that the teacher does not want to listen to what he has to say because she does not think he is smart. The teacher fails to understand that Derek gets a knot in his stomach when she frowns at him as he speaks or when she cuts him off right in the middle of answer to call on one of her brighter students. Derek knows better than the teacher understands that she does not expect very much from him, given his background.

Deficit mindset teachers hand out endless reams of dittos and then master dittoes of exercises that they have used without variation for the past five years. Not infrequently, there is a negative classroom climate, and students spend a good bit of their time wishing for the bell to ring. You know this if you have been in a deficit mindset class. The teacher's favorite class picks are the honor students, the ones with the high IQs.

THE STRENGTHS MINDSET

Some people seem to be born with a mindset that allows them to deal with life successfully, whereas others struggle with learning this skill. Why do some people seem to crumble from their adversities, while others grow stronger? Although each person is different, there are clearly mindsets that separate the winners from the losers, the strong from the weak. When people possess the mindset of resiliency, they are able to deal with their life experience so that they are not defeated. *Young people can be taught that they have a choice in how they view difficult or traumatic events in their lives.* Their lives can change from one of beating the odds to changing the odds.

What is the strengths mindset? The strengths mindset is a resilient mindset. Such a mindset consists of positive attitudes that sustain your optimism and your efforts toward achievement and excellence in your areas of talent. It involves behavior patterns that make you effective and beliefs that empower you to succeed. The strengths mindset helps you to become or stay motivated to take action and to sustain the energy necessary for your life journey. It represents a positive way of perceiving the world. You look for the opportunity that exists, even in a negative situation. You adopt the sentiment that behind every crisis lies an opportunity.

Consider for a moment some elements of a strengths mindset. Some questions to ask yourself about whether or not you have a strength or a deficit mindset are: Do you fight change or embrace it? Do you know your strengths? Do you use your strengths, talents, and skills with confidence, or do you shrink from using them?

There is also another side of the strengths mindset. The strengths mindset acknowledges and understands the weaknesses within the self. The strengths mindset does not run away from acknowledging one's own weaknesses. Do you know, acknowledge, and accept your imperfections or weaknesses? Do you know how to manage your weaknesses so that they do not sabotage your strengths?

I can remember working with one client who had exceptional strengths in several areas. When he was firing on all cylinders, there was no stopping him. But he never learned how to manage his weaknesses. On the contrary, his limitations seemed to trip him up right at the time that he was perched for success. "I kept promising myself that I wasn't going to engage in that behavior again," he lamented. "But there I was again doing the very thing that I had promised myself I would not do any more." An important issue for this young man was to learn how to take steps to prevent his demons, his weaknesses, from interfering with his strengths.

Ernest Hemingway once said, "The world breaks everyone, and afterward some are strong at the broken places." Your weaknesses can trip you up like a pair of skates left in a driveway; they can prevent you and others from appreciating your strengths. The goal is to learn how to use your strengths to manage your weaknesses. Focusing on your weaknesses rather than your strengths is not an appropriate way to go.

THE STRENGTHS MINDSET AND HOPE

Another key component of the strengths mindset is hope. Snyder and Lopez[24] have defined hope as the process of thinking about one's goals and one's motivation (agency) and ways to achieve those goals (pathways). According to Jevne and Miller,[25] hope can be defined as looking forward with both confidence and sureness to something good. When we hope, we anticipate that something we want to happen can indeed happen. Typically, hope is experienced in relationship to someone or to something. There are at least two levels of hope: a specific and a general hope.

When you believe that you and others have strengths, you have hope—hope that you can affect your own life positively and hope that others can achieve their dreams. You know, for example, that there is one thing in life that you do well—no matter what else your life looks like. When you are down in one of life's trenches, you can get out if you will get a visual picture of yourself using your strengths. I remember working with one client who was extremely depressed. He had tried several sales jobs and failed. He had lost interest in his exercise program, and the woman who was a part of his life for several years had left him. I knew that he had been an excellent boxer and had won many medals participating in this sport. Boxing was one of his strengths that he had tucked away for the past several years.

"I want you to do something for yourself," I said.

"What?" he asked, half expecting that he had to do something difficult that he did not want to do. "I want you to remember when you boxed your most difficult fight and you won." Even as I asked him to do that, I saw a smile come over his face, a smile that I had not seen in weeks. We then engaged in a visual imagery of his boxing a difficult fight and winning.

"How did winning that fight feel?" I asked. "You can do it again, you know. You can win at life again."

When you recognize or recall your strengths, you elicit hope in yourself. You bring forth a mustard seed of faith in your ability to deal constructively with the activity or life circumstance in which you find yourself. Hope lingers in the strengths mindset, even when things do not look promising. Hope encourages you to get up another day and "put out the garbage of life."

According to Jane Gillham and Karen Reivich,[26] optimism and hope are associated with a number of positive outcomes. For instance, optimists have greater success at academics, on the job, and on the playing field. Optimists report less depression and anxiety, and they indicate greater marital satisfaction, better health, and longer lives. In addition, optimists are more persistent, and persistence results in solutions. Optimists take better care of themselves. There is mounting evidence that pessimism is a risk factor for people.

Recent research suggests that both genetic and environmental factors predispose a person to think optimistically. For instance, Gillham and Reivich[27] cite one study that estimated that about 25 percent of the variability in optimism can be attributed to genetic factors. Environmental factors also contribute to pessimism, especially negative events that are chronic or traumatic. Parenting is another environmental factor that assumes a central role in the development of hope and a basic trust in the world. Children who are raised in a safe environment are able to trust others, and therefore are inclined to view the world with more hope than those raised in unsafe environments.

Similarly, teachers influence young people's sense of hope and optimism by the feedback they provide to them. We have all heard about the blue birds and the red birds, and what it meant to be placed in either one of these groups for children. Do children ever get over being a red, low-performing bird in class? Do they ever forget how they were categorized and packaged to begin their journey in this world? I think not.

Children who have hope and optimism tend to experience positive outcomes in their lives. These outcomes stem from the belief that they can control good outcomes in their lives. They have positive expectations rather than negative ones. Positive expectations are built on the belief that good things will happen to you. There is the expectation that your behavior will be effective (Bandura's theory of self-efficacy[28]); hence, you become optimistic. Both self-efficacy and optimism are important components in young people's development of resiliency, which increases their sense of hope.

In contrast, low hope is a sign of clinical depression and power mental health. One in five adolescents is estimated to experience an episode of depression by the end of high school. Both parents and teachers need to be concerned about depression among youth because it is associated with a great deal of suffering. Adolescents who experience depression may also feel social rejection and isolation from their classmates. In addition, depression can also lead to substance abuse and suicide among youth. Because depression is a recurrent disorder, it continues from adolescence to adulthood, where parents run the risk of transmitting their depression to their children.

Strengths-based schools create hope and optimism in youth. Such schools understand that education is not just about academics. It is about much more. As Robert Fulghumn[29] stated in his book of essays, "I learned all I needed about life in kindergarten." Students face a number of storms as they navigate from kindergarten to 12th grade. They might ask: "Will l ever learn my times tables?" "Why can't I read?" "Does my teacher like me?" We can endure a great deal when we have hope that things will get better—that the storm we are experiencing will pass.

The strengths mindset maintains that all children and families have strengths, if we take the time to discover them. Even the most troubled youth have strengths and talents that can be used to their benefit. When children have learning difficulties, teachers' uncovering children's strengths reduces their anxiety and prevents their developing low self-esteem. Strengths keep children afloat when they are struggling to control and manage their weaknesses. A young person's ability to perceive bad times as temporary (gaining perspective) is a strength. If we

---

STRENGTHS MINDSET AND GARDENS

Who provides the water and sunshine for your garden of strengths?

How is your garden pollinated with encouragement to grow?

- By talking and listening to friends?
- By the love of a friend?
- By having time alone in a special place?

---

are to build high optimism and hope in youth, parents and educators must help young people to focus on ways in which they are connected to others and larger group and community goals.

THE STRENGTHS MINDSET AND OUR INVISIBLE GARDENS

Each of us has an invisible garden. Our gardens are constantly being planted, nurtured, or left to their own survival instincts. Other people, such as parents, teachers, and friends, sometimes sow seeds or weeds in our gardens. When the ones closest to us sow seeds that blossom into fruits or flowers, we feel good about ourselves. When they plant weeds in our gardens, we tend to feel less good about ourselves. Weeds can sometimes challenge even the most beautiful garden of roses, dahlias, and daisies.

Each of us is an invisible sower into our own lives as well as into the lives of others. Everything that grows, including our feelings about ourselves and our strengths, starts off as a tiny seed hidden from view. The soil of every garden is different. It is easy to plant in gardens that have rich, dark brown soil. It is more difficult to plant in gardens that have challenges, gardens to which we have to add nutrients.

When I first started gardening, I was amazed that adding Miracle-Gro could produce beautiful flowers on land that otherwise seemed barren. I remember the conversation with my neighbor about why her plants look so much happier than mine. "Add a little Miracle-Gro," she advised. Helping people—both young and old—to develop their strengths in life is like adding Miracle-Gro to their gardens. Sure, they might have been able to have flowers in their garden, but adding Miracle-Gro cuts down on the time between seeding and harvesting.

Gardens need water and sunshine. These are the gifts from others whom we meet along the way in our journey. When we use growth-producing seeds to plant in other people's gardens—by saying or doing things that encourage them to strive for their best in life—we also plant seeds in our own garden. Conversely, when we plant weeds into others' gardens, we also plant weeds into our own lives.

Gardens need water and sunshine. These are the gifts from others whom we meet along the way in our journey. When we use growth-producing seeds to plant in other people's gardens—by saying or doing things that encourage them to strive for their best in life—we also plant seeds in our own garden. Conversely, when we plant weeds into others' gardens, we also plant weeds in our own lives. Important questions are:

- What seeds have been planted in your garden?
- What are the strongest seeds in your garden?
- Which seeds in your garden do you value the most?
- What seeds in your garden have you planted and nourished with care?
- What seeds have you harvested in your life?
- What seeds remain hidden in you, waiting for the right time to emerge?

Gardens are not exempt from insects, infections, and outside attack. Try hard as I did, the squirrels seem to always get up earlier than me to bite off the side of one of my tomato plants. I bought some tomato plant spikes, and this seemed to catch the squirrels off guard for a few days—that is, until I found a couple of them foraging my tomatoes on top of the fallen silver metal tomato spike. Despite the ongoing tug of war, I have enjoyed eating some tomatoes from my wonderful garden. I simply accept the fact that the squirrels and I will be battling it out in my garden. I will not stop planting tomato seeds. Just as gardening involves protecting what is growing and harvesting what has ripened, you must safeguard and shield the strengths in you, in your loved ones, and in students from outside damage—from negative life forces and summer thunderstorms.

OUR GARDENS OF STRENGTHS

Everyone has an invisible garden. We are at our best when our gardens contain rich, fertile soil that produces beautiful flowers and wonderful fruits.

We are at our worst when our gardens are dry and overgrown with weeds.

Gardening entails cutting back and weeding. Sometimes we become overwhelmed by putting too much in our gardens. Everything is crowded. There is little space for any plant or strength to grow in. What strength needs pruning or shaping in you? Are there strengths that you regret having cut out of your life?

GARDENS INVOLVE NOTICING WHAT IS THERE

I like waking up in the morning and discovering that a new flower has said hello to the world. Sometimes when I have been very busy writing, I walk downstairs to my garden and discover a host of daffodils. I murmur to myself: "When did they start blossoming? I didn't notice any small blossoms on the stem."

Learning to look for another person's strengths—be it your partner, child, or friend—involves a process of noticing what is there. I had lunch with an old friend whom I had not seen for a few years. Nora is an attractive woman in her late 50s. As we renewed our friendship over dinner, Nora began to report on each of the important people in her life and indicate how they were not meeting her needs and expectations. One of her long-standing friends had not invited her to a house-warming party, and she felt slighted. Her son and daughter-in-law had stopped coming over on Sundays, and therefore she did not see her grandchildren as much as she used to see them. Worse yet, her son sent her a Mother's Day card two days late. Her husband remembered her birthday only after one of her girlfriends mentioned it to him.

Nora has pictures in her head about what a good son, a good friend, a loving husband, and so on should say, think, feel, and give to her. Each day she searches her experiences for instances wherein those she comes into contact with fail to meet her ideal pictures. She has mastered the recipe for the deficit mindset, for depression, and for life-long disappointment—if she does not change the lens that she uses to view the world. We tend to focus on what we lack rather than on what we have. We notice what is missing rather than what is there right in front of us.

When we narrow our vision to focus only on the gap between what we want and what we have, we miss out on quite a lot. The deficit mindset misses out on quite a bit because it fails to notice what is there. It fails to acknowledge life's gifts that lie amidst our pain. Nora was so hurt from not getting her Mother's Day card on time that she failed to notice that her son had remembered her. I remember one Mother's Day that I had forgotten to send my mother her card on time. I called her all apologetic. What sticks out in my mind is how she tried to comfort me. "It doesn't matter," she said. "You called, and I'm happy about that. I'm happy with or without a card, and I will feel grateful for it whenever it gets here." I was relieved that what really mattered to her was that she knew that I loved her with all my heart.

As humans we tend to have a mindset that is rarely satisfied with what it has at the moment because it is always yearning for some ideal created within the movies or within a culture. All too often our eyes scan our lives for what we want, failing to see what we are being offered. Such noticing awareness is a critical step in retraining ourselves to be truly open to the gifts the universe is offering to us. How many presents have you left unwrapped because the person was late getting it to you or because you have failed to even notice their presence? I tried to nudge Nora to open her eyes to notice the many gifts in her life and to abandon the ideal images that caused her to devalue the many presents life was offering to her. Nora had simply to open her eyes to see how many gifts she had to unwrap. She had to notice what is good and what is working in her life. Her life was not disappointing: it is her mindset that caused the unhappiness and disappointment.

The strengths mindset notices what is happening and what life is offering. Act Three of Thornton Wilder's play *Our Town*, takes place at a gravesite. It is raining. Joe Stoddard, the undertaker, enters to tend to proceedings at a new grave, Emily's. Sam Craig, her cousin, also enters. Although he had gone out west to live, he had returned to Grover's Corners to attend Emily's funeral. As they talk, Stoddard tells him Emily died having her second child. The dead then begin to speak with one another. Mrs. Gibbs tells Mrs. Soames that Emily died in childbirth. Mrs. Soames says: "I'd forgotten all about that. My, wasn't life awful—and wonderful."

Mrs. Soames reminisces about Emily's wedding and about how beautifully she read the class poem at graduation. Mourners arrive at Emily's grave and sing "Blessed Be the Tie That Binds." Emily appears wearing white, and she says hello to her mother-in-law, Mrs. Gibbs. As one of the newest among the dead, Emily feels uncomfortable and nervous. She expresses a wish to return to life to visit for just one day, any insignificant day. Observing the funeral company, she says she never realized in life how troubled many people are.

Nevertheless, she expresses a wish to return to life for a little while. Mrs. Gibbs says she can but suggests that she not do so. But Emily reassures Mrs. Gibbs, saying that she plans to return to a happy day, not a sad one. "Why should that be painful?"

The stage manager answers, saying, "You not only live it; you watch yourself living it." He also says she will see the future. Mrs. Gibbs points out another reason Emily should not return: the proper activity of the dead is to forget all about life and to think only of what is coming next and to prepare for it. Emily says she cannot forget—and so she returns to the day of her 12th birthday. First, she sees the routine of life going on as usual—Howie Newsome delivering milk, Constable Warren telling how he rescued a man lying in snowdrifts, Joe Crowell delivering newspapers. Next, she sees her mother and father, who are surprisingly youthful to her and who are preparing to give her gifts.

As Emily greets her mother good morning, her mother tells her to eat her breakfast slowly. Mrs. Webb gives her a dress that she had to "send all the way to Boston" to get. Her father and Wally also have gifts, but Emily cannot go on any longer and breaks down, saying she did not realize how much the little things of life—things she did not notice before—really matter. Emily returns to that insignificant day in her life that she could hardly remember, and finds that life was so beautiful.

Emily returns to the cemetery and addresses Mrs. Gibbs:

"They don't understand, do they?"
"No, dear. They don't understand."

One memorable line of the play is Emily's question: "Do any human beings ever realize life while they live it?—every, every minute?" Or, one might ask: Does life sort of just slips through our fingers, used up by negative judgments and deficit mindsets?

The stage manager says almost everyone is now asleep in Grover's Corners. As he winds his watch, he notices that it is eleven o'clock. He tells the audience to get a good night's sleep. And life goes on, mostly unnoticed, viewed from deficit lens that count only what is missing.

TYPES OF STRENGTHS GARDENS

Reflect on what type of strengths garden you have at this point in your life, in the lives of your children, loved ones, or students. Is it the type of strengths garden that you want? If the answer is yes, how do you plan to maintain and enhance it? If the answer is no, how do you plan to change the situation?

- *A neglected strengths garden*: You have not thought about your strengths in years. In fact, you are not even on speaking terms with your strengths. You rarely acknowledge or use them to accomplish goals that mean something to you. Some parts of your garden are not growing very well, and you have few clues how to turn things around.
- *A secret strengths garden*: Only you and a few others in your life know about your secret strengths garden. You keep your strengths separate from what you do on a daily basis. For instance, you write poetry at night, but share it with only a few.
- *An abundant strengths garden*: Your strengths bring real satisfaction and happiness to your life. You are engaged in using or in developing your strengths on a regular basis. You use your strengths to accomplish your goals and to provide meaning and purpose to your life and to the lives of others.
- *A formal strengths garden*: The world recognizes your strengths because you have excelled so far above the crowd. You have established formal procedures for getting in touch with your strengths garden. For one thing, the displaying or sharing of your strengths with the public costs something—usually a great deal of money. These are the artists, the actors, the athletes, the writers, the scientists, and so on who have soared above the rest.
- *A deficit garden*: This kind of garden is one in which you are always thinking about what flowers or vegetables you would like to add or take out rather than appreciating and taking notice of what you have. The flowers and vegetables that once brought you joy and happiness are taken for granted and no longer catch your eye or bring a smile to your face.

STRENGTHS MINDSET FOR PARENTS

Parents have parenting mindsets that affect their children deeply as they are raising them and throughout their lives. Neither of Melissa's parents had much formal education to talk about—her father had a sixth-grade education, and her mother had a ninth-grade education. Yet when she wanted good advice—even good professional advice—she picked up the telephone and called one of them, instead of one of her many friends with PhDs. Sometimes she would try to convey to her father what her parents had given her and how try as she might she could not seem to give that to her daughter—no matter how hard she tried.

She recalled an incident where she was having difficulty with physics and she told her father that she might fail. Her father's parenting mindset was one of encouragement. First, he tried to convince her that she was not going to fail. Second, he reassured her that even if she did fail, what mattered to him was that she had done her best. She never felt pressured to get an A, yet she worked diligently to achieve all that she was capable of achieving. Mindsets of encouragement are extremely important for children to do well in school. Parents must also know their children's strengths and how to nurture them.

Parents who adopt a strengths mindset in parenting their children sit with their children and help them to make a list of their strengths. To help children identify their strengths, parents ask them such questions as: What makes you really happy? When do you feel the best about yourself? What kinds of activities do you like doing or participating in the most? What energizes you? Friends are an important part of your children's lives. Encourage them to find friends who share some of their strengths. Friendships based on the sharing of similarity of interests stand a greater chance of lasting than those based on popularity.

STRENGTHS MINDSET: TEACHERS AS SOWERS OF STRENGTHS

For youth to succeed and to reach their maximum potential, it is essential that educators and parents recognize their assets, capabilities, talents, and strengths. Strength-based approaches challenge teachers to build healthy relationship with young people, emphasize engaging them in the planning for their own success, and create opportunities for them to be involved and engaged in their communities. Teachers with a strengths mindset use students' strengths to motivate them for change. Their mindset is growth oriented. They look for the good in students, the hidden potential, rather than seeds for their failure or dark side.

Teachers who hold a strengths mindset believe that what they do and say in the classroom really matters to kids. They understand that their approval, disapproval, encouragement, or criticism may have a profound impact on their students' lives and how they respond to the learning process.

In addition, teachers who evidence a strengths mindset believe that when students are aware of their strengths, they will be more motivated to set goals, achieve at a high level, and complete the choices they make. The strengths mindset teacher is keenly interested in the talents and strengths students bring to the classroom. As Weick et al.[30] have pointed out, "People do not grow by concentrating on their problems. ... The effect of a problem focus is to weaken people's confidence in their ability to develop in self-reflective ways." Similarly,

Loehr and Schwartz[31] have noted that when individuals have feelings of deficit, such feelings influence their attention and limit their possibilities rather than enable them to devise creative ways of growing.

Teachers who manifest a strengths mindset actively seek to engage students in the learning process. They understand their own strengths as teachers and know how to use those strengths when working with youth. A strengths-based approach to teaching sees student engagement as a critical part of learning. Teachers with a strengths mindset understand the connection between motivating students by helping them to feel good about themselves. As Ryan and Deci have written, intrinsic motivation is facilitated by a sense of competence, facing "optimal challenges," feeling a sense of choice and self-directedness about the activities in which one is engaged, supportive relationships, and "freedom from demeaning feedback." (p. 70).[32] By helping students to identify their strengths and further nurturing them, teachers motivate students to become engaged in the learning process. They encourage students when they help them to unfold their strengths in life.

Teachers who have a strengths mindset manifest high expectations for their students. A sports analogy clarifies the significance of expectations. When Pete Sampras, the famous tennis star, was asked to explain his skillful ability to raise the level of his game at crucial times in a match, he said that his fans expected such from him. A similar situation exists in the classroom. When teachers expect more from their students, they step up to the plate and perform better. Teachers who are committed to maximizing their students' potential set high standards and high expectations in their classrooms.

There is a difference between standards and expectations. Whereas standards are what you want students to achieve, expectations are what you believe will take place. High teacher expectations will work if you assert them in positive and affirming manner. Search yourself to answer honestly if your classroom climate is positive or negative. Is your class a place where students feel comfortable asking for help without feeling stupid or inferior? Do your students feel accepted and liked by you?

During my early days teaching as a substitute teacher in an inner-city school, I ran into a situation that demonstrates the importance of expectations. I began by introducing myself and telling the students that I respected them and that I wanted them to respect me. In fact, I knew that they might act up in school, but in reality they came from homes that if I made a telephone call to their home, they would be in a great deal of difficulty. So the message to them was that I understood that the bottom line was that they came from good families who valued them and an education. "Some of you will become doctors and lawyers," I continued, and as I made this comment, I saw visible smiles come over their faces and the clowning around that had taken place just prior to the bell quieted down. I had instilled a positive belief and expectation within them with just a few words.

The class clown was determined not to lose his position of power in the class. Therefore when the class was over, I pulled him aside and talked with him. "Look in my eyes," I said. "Do you think that I want the best for you? Do you think that you can achieve in my class?"

He peered deep into my eyes, as if to say: Who's this woman? I continued by telling him that I needed his help and by asking him if I could count on him in class. I substituted for a few days at the school, and one day while talking with another teacher during the changing of classes, the student came up to me and said, "Hi, Ms. Smith. What are we going to be doing today?"

Observing the student's behavior, the other teacher said: "Hey, she comes here for a couple of days and you suddenly change? What's up with that?" The teacher continued by saying, "I saw her laying into you the other day. If I had done that . . . "

The student interrupted. "There's a difference, Ms. So and So. I can look in her eyes and know that she wants the best for me. You don't know me like that."

"I don't know you like that. Like what?"

"You just don't know me like that."

That night I went home and looked in the mirror to see if I could see the same thing that the student had seen in me. How could he see that deep down inside I cared about him, and I believed that he could achieve?

When you communicate your positive expectations to your students, you must also convey to the students that they can meet your expectations, that they will be rewarded for doing so, and that you will do all that you can to help them achieve. More will be said about teacher expectations later in this book. But remember that teacher expectations are extremely important.

Weeding the Educational Garden

Every school has weeds. Educational leaders must continuously remove weeds from their school garden, if children are to achieve academically and mature emotionally. In effective schools, teachers and principals become vigilant for persistent weeds with deep roots that destroy the school's academic garden and the learning motivation of young people.

Some deep-rooted educational weeds include low teacher expectations for student achievement, poor and inadequate school curriculum, teachers who cannot teach and who have little understanding of how to establish caring classrooms, substandard school discipline, and school violence. Strength-based education is designed to weed out deficit-based educational thinking and ineffective school issues.

THE SETTLING MINDSET

Many people decide to settle in life or to follow the path of least resistance. Therefore, in addition to the strengths and the deficit mindsets, there is also a settling mindset. The settling mindset tries to convince a person to stick with a job that pays well, even though he or she is unhappy in that job. The settling mindset also resides in far too many classrooms. I remember during my early years of teaching how one of my fellow teachers and I had a difference of opinion about one child. Through my lens, the child was creative and full of energy that could be harnessed for major achievements.

The lens the other teacher used viewed him as a problem, someone who talked too much, who did not do well in math, and who was always coming up with a different way of seeing things than most of the kids in her class. Some years later when I ran into the student as a young adult, I was amazed at what he was doing with his life. He was in the entertainment industry, and even as a relatively new entrant into that field, he was happy, talking about meeting people whom I had only seen on television, and excited about what he was doing with his life. Where I had hoped to hear just that he had graduated from college and obtained a "good-paying" job, he had simply leap-frogged over some of the more academically capable students in his class.

As I listened to his telling me that he knew early that he was not going to spend a great deal of his life studying "dead facts" in some professor's classroom, I wondered what the other teacher would say about him now. He was earning more than seven times what either one of us was earning as educators. Yet it was not just the money. It was the passion and the utter conviction that he knew what his real strengths were at an early age and that he had the good sense to apply them to achieve success.

While listening to my former student, I recalled the five-time Grammy winner, Lionel Ritchie, talking about how disappointed his father was that he had not become an accountant or a teacher—something that would give him a steady source of income. "Playing in this band can't provide you with a steady source of income, Lionel." Well, we all know that Lionel Ritchie focused on his strengths, music, and singing, and that focus has brought him happiness, fame, and millions more than what he would have earned as the accountant that his father wanted him to be. So many times we encourage young people, our loved ones, and those with whom we come into contact with to have a "settling mindset."

The "settling mindset" is a variation of the deficit mindset, and it goes something like this:

"Jada, you have a lot of talent. We both know that . . . But let's be realistic. An Oprah Winfrey you are not. Why don't you . . . "

When you hear the "why don't you" phrase, you know instantly that it is the beginning of a settling offer. "Why don't we get realistic about your future? You need to be able to support yourself . . . get a job like the rest of us." Although the person has good intentions, most of the settling mindset focuses on having you fit into someone else's view of the world.

Teachers create the climate within their classrooms. As a teacher, you have the power to be a tool of torture or an instrument of inspiration. You can choose to humiliate, hurt, or heal your students. Your response to students will determine if a situation becomes an unmanageable crisis or an opportunity for a teaching moment (Table 2.1).

REACHING PAST THE THORNS AND THE DEFICITS

A major theme throughout this book is that parents and teachers need to help young people discover their strengths. Yet before you can begin to do this, you will have to recognize and acknowledge your own strengths. Strength acknowledgment within yourself sets up the basis for another life force—strengths recognition in others. Recognizing strengths in others without seeing strengths in ourselves leads to depression and unhappiness—some measure of the feeling "everyone has something going for him or herself except me." In addition to our strengths, we all have thorns—much in the same way that the beautiful

Table 2.1   Summary of Deficit and Strengths Mindset

Deficit Mindset (-)	Strengths Mindset (+)
Demoralizes youth and erodes their confidence	Empowers youth, increases their beliefs in themselves, and gives them hope
Reduces motivation and aspirations to achieve	The best approach to help students persist and to become motivated
Focuses on past failures and sets up negative expectations (failure expectancy)	Emphasizes the present and the future and sets up positive expectations for achievement (success expectancy)
Notices only what is missing, what youth do not have	Notices what is there and searches for youths' and others' strengths
Focuses on problems—the thorns in people, what could go wrong	Focuses on possibilities—the roses on the end of stem containing thorns; emphasizes what could go right

Note: Copyright © Elsie J. Smith.

rose has thorns on its stems. My own backyard garden has roses on both sides, and each time I brush up accidentally against my roses, I am reminded that they, like people, also have thorns that can hurt. Despite the thorns, I would not think of getting rid of my beautiful roses. In keeping with my garden analogy, I offer the paradox of the rose (I have shortened the inspirational poem for the purposes of this book; the author is unknown).

> One of the greatest gifts a person can possess . . .
> is to be able to reach past the thorns and find the rose within others.

The point is that many of us fail to water our own roses. We put the responsibility on others to water our roses. In doing so, we place our happiness in their hands rather than in our own hands.

STRENGTHS-BASED/DEFICIT MINDSET QUESTIONNAIRE

Now that you have read about the deficit and strengths mindsets, in what group would you place yourself? When you look at yourself in the mirror, do you tend to see your imperfections, what you do not have? Or do you say to yourself, "You look good girl." "You handsome man." Do you choose to emphasize the parts on your body that you would like to change, or do your eyes naturally travel to your better features? When you look at your partner, what do you really see—the fact that he or she has gained more pounds than what you consider ideal? Or do you see his or her kindness, thoughtfulness, and love for you? Mindsets are a choice. On the Strengths Mindset Questionnaire, items 1, 2, 3, 5, 10, 11, 14, and 15 are oriented toward a strengths mindset; and items 4, 5, 6, 7, 8, 9, 12, and 13 are oriented toward a deficit mindset (Table 2.2).

Table 2.2   The Strengths Mindset Questionnaire

Directions: Using the numbers listed below, indicate the extent to which each statement below is either true or not true of you.

Very Untrue of Me				Very True of Me		
1	2	3	4	5	6	7

1. ____I am aware of the strengths I have.
2. ____I know how to apply my strengths to achieve my goals in life.
3. ____Even when others become discouraged, I believe I can find a way to solve the problem.
4. ____I have no idea what to do with my life.
5. ____I tend to look for the best in people.
6. ____Although I don't tend to look for the worst in people, it always seems to surface.
7. ____Some children come from such impoverished backgrounds that it is impossible to teach them.
8. ____Schools should focus primarily on helping students to improve their weak academic areas.
9. ____The current emphasis on students' strengths is a lot of fluff and leads to a watered-down academic curriculum.
10. ____Every student, no matter how poor, has strengths.
11. ____The best predictor of student persistence in college is the student's own motivation/desire to persist.
12. ____The best predictor of student persistence in college is the student's SAT scores and high school grades.
13. ____Top achievers spend most of their time working on their weaknesses.
14. ____You become more successful in life by knowing what your strengths are and attempting to improve them than by knowing your weaknesses and attempting to build upon them.
15. ____You tend to focus on what is right with people, rather than on what is wrong with people.

Note: Copyright © Elsie J. Smith.

HOW TO CHANGE FROM A DEFICIT TO A STRENGTHS MINDSET

It is not easy to change from a deficit to a strengths mindset. So much appears to be second nature and natural to you. You might even say to yourself: "But this is how I have always seen myself or the world. I am not about to change now." There are several steps one can take in this change process.

Step 1: Listen to the voices in your head. Do these voices reflect a deficit or a strengths mindset? Do you have a tendency to notice the good that is present in a situation, or do you focus your attention on what is missing or what is wrong? In determining what kind of mindset you have, use the analogy of the bucket that is found in Tom Rath and Donald Clifton's[33] book *How Full Is Your Bucket?* Everyone has a bucket and a dipper. In each interpersonal encounter, we can use our dipper either to fill or to dip from others' buckets. A person who has a strengths mindset seeks to fill both hi or /her own bucket and those of others.

Step 2: Make an intentional choice regarding how you will view yourself, others, and the world. You can choose how you interpret, react, and respond to the circumstances of your life. You can choose to focus on your strengths or weaknesses.

Step 3: Use your strengths mindset voice to bolster your courage or to interpret the events of your life. When you are faced with doubts about whether you can really write that novel or poem, talk directly to the deficit voice, which is usually based in lack and fear.

Step 4: Tackle your life challenges or problems with your strengths.

Step 5: Do not spend your life trying to improve your weaknesses. Focusing on weaknesses rather than managing them reduces the effectiveness of our real strengths. Managing our weaknesses includes: using our strengths to develop new ways of solving problems; partnering with others; delegating to others; learning the skills and/or knowledge required; and developing new techniques to use our strengths in positive ways.

Step 6: Spend most of your time developing and using your strengths to achieve your goals and purpose in life.

PARADIGM SHIFT IN EDUCATION

The strengths-based approach in education represents a paradigm shift. A significant part of this shift involves moving away from the prevailing philosophy of deficit remediation and toward one in which assessment of students' strengths provide the foundation for learning. As Kuhn[34] pointed out in his classic *The Structure of Scientific Revolutions*, paradigm shifts bring about a change in worldview, such that people see things differently than they did previously. The strengths perspective in education brings about a major shift in how teachers view students and how parents see their children. Students also learn to see themselves differently and with greater confidence. Likewise, they also learn to see others differently, within a context of strengths that transcend gender and race.

I maintain that a strengths-based approach to education holds a great deal of promise for helping students to fulfill their potential and to achieve excellence in the educational environment. Preliminary research has indicated that strengths develop best within a context of supportive relationships.[35]

SUMMARY

The strengths mindset encourages us to look for positive potentials in even the most challenging youth. It adheres to the belief that there are "no disposable kids." At the heart of strengths-based parenting and teaching is that every person has strengths. When parents and teachers focus on youths' strengths and resources, children feel they are worthwhile.

Instead of focusing on children's and families' weaknesses or deficits, strengths-based educators and practitioners collaborate with children and their parents to discover their strengths. The strength approach maintains that all children and families have strengths, if we take the time to discover them. When children have learning difficulties, teachers' uncovering children's strengths may help to reduce their anxiety and prevent their developing low self-esteem. Strengths keep children afloat when they are struggling to control and manage their weaknesses. If American youth are going to be competitive on a global basis, a strength-based mindset is critical for teachers, students, and parents.

3

Brain Development, Emotion, and Learning

This chapter lays the foundation for (1) brains-based education and (2) strengths development theory. The first section of the chapter focuses primarily on the brain and on how what happens to children influences the development of their brains.[1] Emphasis is placed on translating our knowledge about the brain into brain-based teaching.[2] Therefore, I examine some principles of brain-based education for teachers. I maintain that strengths-based education is facilitated when teachers have a thorough understanding of the brain. The second section of the chapter discusses my theory of strengths development with emphasis placed on the brain as well on as such psychological areas as personality development. Young children's development of strengths is conceptualized as well-traveled brain pathways.

THE BRAIN AND ITS STRUCTURE

The brain is a wonderful garden. It contains beautiful vines, and numerous flowers that reflect our senses and multiple intelligences. How a brain develops depends on the interplay between the genes a child is born with and the experiences that he or she has in life. Early childhood experiences have a critical impact on the architecture of the brain and on the nature and extent of adult capabilities. Such early interactions do not simply create a context for brain development. Rather, they directly influence the way the brain is wired. Hence every interaction a parent or a caregiver has with a very young child helps to wire that child's brain.

Infants come into the world with billions of neurons, which are largely unconnected to each other.[3] Almost immediately after birth, an infant's brain begins to form trillions of connections and pathways between the neurons. These connections and pathways are critical because they permit the infant to see, hear, smell, learn, and reason. The brain cells or neurons need to be activated, and the connections between neurons are either weak or they have not have not yet been formed.[4] As the neurons form synapses, they begin firing, which may be described as sending electrical impulses and layering the networks in the brain. First, the brain makes the networks that are necessary for survival (such as heartbeat, breathing, etc.). These survival functions are controlled by the hindbrain and midbrain.

As the infant ages, brain neurons are connected to corresponding patterns of nerve circuits, neural circuits, neural networks, or neural pathways throughout the cortex of the brain. A child forms neural pathways as a result of neuron activity which consists of propagation of electrical stimuli or nerve impulses along the neural junctions or synapses.[5]

Neural tissue can be modified when new synapses grow and develop via a process known as synaptogenesis. Neural brain tissue has the capacity to change or learn, and this capacity is known as *neuroplasticity*.[6] Neuroplasticity forms the structural basis for the function of learning and retention of learning or memory. Learning occurs by strengthening existing connections. As professor of neuroscience at New York University Joseph LeDoux[7] has maintained, new synaptic connections formed by practice, training, and experience are not created as entirely new entities, but rather are added to preexisting connections. Added connections resemble new buds on a branch rather than new branches.

Some early milestones in brain growth are: (1) at 4 months, the infant's brain responds to every sound produced in all the languages of the world; (2) at 10 months, babies can distinguish and produce the sounds of their own language, and they tend to stop paying attention to the sounds of language that are foreign; and (3) by 12 months, babies will point to a dog in a picture book when a parent says: "Point to the doggie in the picture." By age three years, a child's brain has formed dense connections.[8]

The Brain's Pruning Process: "Use It or Lose It"

The brain operates on a "use it or lose it" principle, meaning only those neural connections and neural pathways that are frequently activated are retained.[9] In the same manner that careful weeding is critical to creating a beautiful garden, getting rid of unnecessary neurons and connections is essential for those sculpting our brain pathways. Brain connections that are not used consistently are pruned or discarded, thereby enabling the active connections to become stronger. According to Dr. Harry Chugani,[10] professor of pediatrics, neurology, and radiology at Wayne State University School of Medicine, the synaptic connections in the brain that are the most used become the strongest. In the words of Dr. Harry Chugani, a professor of pediatric neurology at Wayne State University: "It's like a highway system. Roads with the most traffic get widened. The ones that are rarely used fall into disrepair."[11]

Part of raising and educating kids involves helping them to develop their own brain paths and eventually to orchestrate their own learning. In the book *How the Brain Talks to Itself*, author Jay Hams[12] tells a story about one of his friends (Nandor Balazs) who used to teach at Cornell University. Balazs told him that at Cornell after a few academic buildings have been built, the administration permits students to make their own paths to the new buildings. Following students' construction of their own natural paths to new buildings, the administration paves walkways among garden beds and trees by following the already established pragmatic paths. Teachers need to first examine students' natural paths of learning and to build upon these paths.

After age 10, the pruning process proceeds at a fairly rapid pace. The hard-wired areas of the brain, such as the brain stem, which controls involuntary functions such as breathing, experience few changes.[13] The most striking pruning takes place in the cerebral cortex, where approximately 33 synapses are eliminated every second—indicating that the developing brain responds continually to family and school conditions that either promote or hinder learning.[14] How well children and young people learn has a great deal to with the extent and nature of their brain connections.

As pruning increases after 10 years of age, those synapses that have been reinforced because of repeated experience tend to become permanent. Conversely, the synapses that were not used often enough in the early years tend to become eliminated. Thus the types of

---

OUR STRENGTHS AND OUR BRAINS

Our strengths represent brain energy that has become focused or located in specific parts of our brain.

experiences children experience in the first three years of life influence how their brains will be wired as adults, and accordingly what their talents, skills, and strengths will be.

Learning requires the construction of patterns, which are made from young people's making connections. The brain is a pattern-seeking device. It searches for patterns to understand the environment. Learning involves input to the brain from different intelligences.

Strengths as Energy Emitted by the Brain

In addition to the process of brain development just described, there is a more direct link between strengths and brain development. *I propose that strengths are a form of energy emitted by well-traveled pathways of the brain.* We learn in most basic introductory science classes the concept of energy. *Dorland's Medical Dictionary for Health Consumers*[15] defines energy as the power "which may be translated into motion, overcoming resistance, or effecting physical change, the ability to do work. Energy is recognized by the symbol E. Gibbs free energy (G) is equal to the maximum amount of work that can be obtained from a process taking place under conditions of fixed temperature and pressure. Kinetic energy is the energy of motion. Nuclear energy is the energy that can be freed by changes in the nucleus of an atom (as by fission of a heavy nucleus or fusion of light nuclei into heavier ones with accompanying loss of mass). Potential energy is energy that is at rest or not manifested in actual work." All of the definitions have been presented to identify two characteristics of energy. Energy is (1) the capacity for work or vigorous activity, vigor, and power, and (2) the capacity of a physical system to do work.

Our strengths are a form of energy that is first developed as a result of brain neuronal activity and the establishment of brain pathways by our interaction with the environment and significant others. Every strength that a human develops exists initially in the form of potential energy. This potential energy needs to be refined and further developed in terms of the capacity of a person's physical system to do work.

STRENGTHS AS THOUGHTS

Every strength exists as a thought about your own capability or someone else's capability to perform an activity or work.

Just as energy permits us to do work, our thoughts are a form of energy that permit us to accomplish work. The work that we perform, whether it is singing a song or playing the drums, represents a change in our energy states—from potential energy to actual energy.

Every strength exists as a thought in someone's mind, either in the mind of the person who possesses the strength or in the mind of the person who perceives the strength in that person. Every thought has its own energy. Consider, for instance, what takes place when only one person within a family experiences depression or depressive thoughts. The entire household frequently catches thoughts of depression—or as I might say, senses this thought energy. The American Psychological Association states in one of its publications on depression that depression is contagious within a family. There is even a television commercial that suggests that depression is contagious.

When we are around positive people, we sense and incorporate their positive energy; therefore, we feel good about ourselves. When we are around people who complain all the time, we may feel unhappy, depressed, or defeated in some way, even though we are not the person who is doing the complaining.

Every strength begins with a thought, a belief. Every strength exists as a thought about someone's capability. Every human strength carries with it its own source of energy. For instance in India, for years leaders practice meditation as a way to achieve energy and insight into life. In its more developed form, this energy is often experienced as positive energy—as one's passion for life. As Bruce Lipton,[16] renowned cell biologist has stated: "Cells are shaped by where they live." In other words, it is the environment. We control what our cells do, be it consciously or unconsciously. The environment of the cell is even more important than the genetics behind it. Identifying a strength as early as possible is critical because early brain connections can develop and expand much more rapidly than they can in later life.

Our brains emit signals that allow us to recognize that we can do some things better or more efficiently than other people can do the same things. In this respect, strengths development always has a perceptual and a conceptual basis. For instance, "I have a beautiful voice. I can sing better than most other people." "I can run faster than most people." Our brains may also emit signals to others about our strengths. For instance, a teacher may recognize a student's strength even before he or she does.

Strengths development is a process in which we experience our capacity to do work in a specific area—complete complex mathematical calculations, discover a new chemical element, write a beautiful play that the world loves. Strengths development is inevitably comparative in nature. We compare our capacity to do work with those around us or in the rest of the world.

A later section of this chapter deals with strengths zones, which are developed when a person has a strong talent in one area. Many of our strengths zones are interrelated. I describe and outline 11 strengths zones primarily in terms of how teachers might come into contact with these zones with students in their classes. The fact that no one person has the capacity to perform all 11 strengths zones at a high level speaks to the limitation of our human brains.

What Is Brain-Based Education?

Brain-based learning has come to represent a comprehensive approach to teaching that uses current research from neuroscience. Brain-based education pays attention to how the brain learns naturally. Its foundation is built on what we know currently about the structure and function of the human brain at different developmental stages. Brain-based education takes place when teachers purposefully engage strategies to teach based on how our brain works in the context of learning.[17] Such learning is founded on the structure and function of the brain. Educational techniques that are brain based use the latest neuropsychology research on the brain. Brain-based learning encompasses such educational concepts as:

- Experiential learning
- Learning styles
- Multiple intelligences
- Cooperative learning
- Movement education

HUMAN STRENGTHS AND ENERGY

Every strength carries with it its own source of energy, which we often experience as our passion.

Human strength energy almost always begins as positive energy.

Key researchers from major universities have taken knowledge about how the brain processes and retains information and incorporated that knowledge into books about learning. As a result, these scholars have proposed new theories of teaching and learning based on neuropsychological findings. Some noted scholars in brain-based education include Marian Diamond[18] at the University of California at Berkeley, Howard Gardner[19] at Harvard University, Renate and Geoffrey Caine,[20] and Eric Jensen.[21]

Core Principles of Brain-Based Education

Brain-based learning is taking what we know about the human brain, about childhood development, and about learning and combining this information in intelligent ways to connect with and excite students' desire to learn. This school of thought maintains that as long as the brain is not prevented from fulfilling its normal processes, learning will take place. The core principles of brain-based learning are:

Principle 1: The brain is a parallel processor. Our thoughts, intuitions, predispositions, and emotions function simultaneously and interact with other modes of information. Both hemispheres work together. Edelman[22] found that when more neurons in the brain were firing at the same time, learning, meaning, and retention were enhanced for the learner.

Principle 2: Learning engages the entire physiology. The physical health of children, meaning the amount of sleep they get each night and the kind of nutrition they have, affects the brain. We are holistic learners with the body and the mind interacting. All people are physiologically programmed, and they have cycles such as sleep cycles that must be honored. A child who does not get sufficient sleep each night will have difficulty absorbing new information the next day. Fatigue or sleep deprivation will hinder the brain's memory.

Principle 3: Learning is developmental. Whereas some students can think abstractly, others think primarily on a concrete level. It is important that schools and families help youth to build the necessary neural connections by exposure, repetition, and practice.

Principle 4: Each brain is unique. We are all products of our genetics and experience. The brain works more efficiently when facts and skills are embedded in real experiences.

Principle 5: Every brain perceives and creates parts and wholes simultaneously. While some people think more easily inductively, others find deductive thinking more comfortable. We should use both deductive and inductive thinking. The brain loves storytelling because you give the information, ground the meaning in structure, provide for emotion, and make the content meaningful.

Principle 6: Learning always involves conscious and unconscious processes. The brain and body learn physically, mentally, and affectively. People communicate with body language. Teachers should examine how they treat students and how they permit them to treat each other because it makes a difference in their learning and desire to learn. It also makes a difference in how the physical environment is organized.

Principle 7: The search for meaning is innate. People are naturally programmed to search for meaning in their lives and in their learning. Scientists believe that this principle is survival oriented. The brain needs and automatically registers the familiar, while it simultaneously looks for and responds to additional stimuli. For schools, this means that the learning environment should provide stability and familiarity. On the other hand, the classroom must also supply novelty, discovery, and challenge. Teachers' lessons need to be exciting and meaningful and offer young people a variety of choices. Ideally, students will find among the choices provided an opportunity to use their strengths in completion of the assignment.

Marian Diamond[23] found that animals in an enriched environment that were in lighted cages, were given more attention, and were given a chance to play in the fields or to jump over hurdles, evidenced a greater degree of brain cell growth. When Diamond compared the brains of rats in an enriched environment with those that had been in dark cages, had been isolated, and had not had the opportunity to engage in play, the rats from the enriched environment showed cortical changes, a larger number of gial cells, and a greater number of connections. Children need to be placed in enriched classroom environments that give them time and opportunities to make sense of their experiences. They also should be given a chance to reflect, to see how things relate to each other.

Principle 8: Emotions are critical to learning. The usual form of communication within our brain is the electrical-chemical-electrical process between neurons. Our emotions trigger the chemicals that activate axon-synapse-dendrite reaction.

Principle 9: Learning is enhanced by challenge and inhibited by threat. Survival is the brain's priority—often at the expense of higher order thinking. Stress should be kept to a manageable level. Teachers should have high but reasonable expectations.

Principle 10: The search for meaning takes place through patterning. Teachers should link learning to prior knowledge and use the know-want to know learning cycle.

Principle 11: Our brains organize memory in different ways. Retrieval of information learned depends upon how the information was stored. Relevancy is central to both storage and retrieval of information. Teachers should connect to what students already know and to what they have interests in.

Principle 12: The brain is a social brain. The brain develops better in concert with others. Students retain information better when they have to talk with others about it. They retain such information longer and more efficiently. Teachers should use small groups, discussion teams, pairings, and question-and-answer sessions.

Multiple Intelligences and the Brain

The theory of multiple intelligences is also related to strengths-based schools and students. Howard Gardner[24] of Harvard University has maintained that people have unique strengths and weaknesses in each of eight types of intelligences. Gardner viewed intelligence as "An intelligence is the ability to solve problems, or to create products, that are valued within one or more cultural settings" (Gardner, 1983/2003, p. x)[25]

The first two intelligences are typically valued in most schools, the next three are usually associated with the arts, and Gardner called the last two of the original seven "personal intelligence."Gardner added an eighth intelligence, naturalistic intelligence. Gardner's intelligences are:

1. Linguistic intelligence (word smart) involves sensitivity to spoken and written language, the ability to learn languages, and the ability to use language to achieve goals. Examples of people who use this intelligence are poets, writers, and the like.
2. *Logical-mathematical intelligence* (number/reasoning smart) consists of the capacity to analyze problems logically and to carry out mathematical operations, and the ability to calculate and to carry out complex mathematical operations. Examples of people who use this intelligence are scientists, mathematicians, accountants, and engineers.
3. *Musical intelligence* (music smart) involves a person's skill in the performance, composition, and appreciation of musical patterns. Examples of people who use this intelligence are musicians and critics.

4. *Bodily-kinesthetic intelligence* (body smart) involves using one's whole body or parts of the body to solve problems. Examples of people who use this intelligence are athletes, dancers, surgeons, and craftspeople.
5. *Spatial intelligence* (picture smart) entails the potential to recognize and use the patterns of space. Examples of people who use this intelligence are sailors, pilots, painters, and architects.
6. *Interpersonal intelligence* (people smart) is the capacity to discern the intentions, motivations, and desires of others. This intelligence allows people to work cooperatively with others. People must be capable of noticing differences in other people's mood, motivation, feelings, and intentions. Examples of people who use this intelligence are teachers, social workers, actors, and politicians.
7. *Intrapersonal intelligence* (self-smart) or the ability to understand yourself, to appreciate yourself, and to have a working model or theory of yourself. It involves the ability to act upon the knowledge you have about yourself and to plan and direct your life based upon such knowledge. Examples of people who use this intelligence are theologians, psychologists, and philosophers.
8. *Naturalist intelligence* helps people to recognize, categorize, and draw upon certain features of the environment. It involves a description of the core ability with a cultural framework. Naturalist intelligence deals with sensing patterns in and making connections to different features in nature. Using this same intelligence, people who have an enhanced sense of this intelligence are usually interested in other species, the environment, and the earth. They may have a strong affinity to animals, or they may show unusual interest in subjects like biology, zoology, botany, geology, meteorology, paleontology, or astronomy. People with naturalistic intelligence are keenly aware of their surroundings and changes in their environment, even if these changes are at minute or subtle levels. Primary examples of notable people having naturalistic intelligence include Rachel Carson and Charles Darwin.

Despite Gardner's research, the shift to teaching for multiple intelligences is a difficult one for most schools. According to Gardner, our schools and culture focus most attention on linguistic and logical-mathematical intelligence. Americans tend to value highly articulate or logical people. In fact, the other types of intelligences that Gardner mentioned are often the first ones to be eliminated from schools—namely, the creative arts.

One advantage of the theory of multiple intelligences is that it provides eight different potential pathways to learning. For instance, if a teacher is having difficulty reaching a student using linguistic or logical methods of instruction, the theories of multiple intelligences and strengths-based education suggest several other ways in which the material might be presented to promote effective learning. The theory of multiple intelligences gives hope to some students labeled learning disabled because now their "outside-the-box" talents may be recognized. Whenever teachers are engaged in instruction, they might consider connecting with their students using words, numbers or logic, pictures, music, self-reflection, a physical experience, naturalistic or a social experience.

Experience Memories and the Brain

Brain research has indicated that personal relationships, especially healthy attachments, are critical to the development of a healthy brain in young children. CAT scans have revealed that children process information first through their emotions.[26] It is believed that all learning is driven by emotions and that young people tend to remember information that is the most emotional. Children's genes start the process of brain development; however, as they age, their life experiences assume a large role. Babies' brains need stimulation. Their best learning comes from interacting with parents—singing, talking and reading to stimulate their senses.

Although genetics influence strongly the original programming for the number of connections, the child's sensory experiences assume a dominant role after birth. Sensory areas form about 50 percent of the brain. At the University of Southern California's Institute for Creative Technologies, researchers are exploring effective combinations of visual, auditory, and other sensory functions to provide an integrated learning experience that is based on the natural connectivity of the brain.[27] Jacquelyn Ford Morie and Josh Williams maintain that to tap into the emotional learning systems of young people, teachers must engage as many of their senses as possible. These researchers point out that each sense holds a proprietary "memory location" within the brain.[28] When teachers use multiple sensory inputs as part of their teaching, they elicit within young people's brains a wider degree of neural stimulation. Such elicitation of senses creates stronger memories because so many senses are involved, and such memories enhance the learning experience.

The hippocampus, a central part of the limbic system, is responsible for both storage and retrieval of all loosely linked memories. The limbic system provides emotional meaning to fragmented memories.

EXPERIENCE MEMORIES

"Tell me and I forget. Show me
  and I remember.
Involve me and I understand."

—Chinese proverb

When children have increased positive emotional connections with learning, they are more highly motivated. Research has found that people tend to remember emotionally salient events better than those perceived as being emotionally neutral.[29]

If children have excellent neurological equipment, they will most likely master appropriate developmental tasks, even if they receive mediocre nurturing. Yet children who have marginal genetic abilities may need more stimulation.

Children who are raised in a caring, stimulating environment grow a larger brain. Research with experimental laboratory animals has revealed that a neglected brain is 20 to 30 percent smaller than normal. A parent's love and activity also increase the brain's weight, number of neural connections, and its eventual complexity and raw intelligence.[30] Parents change the way their children's brain is wired if they spend just 20 pleasant minutes each day reading to, explaining to, joking with, or questioning their children. These brain changes become permanent.

Teachers' knowledge about the brain and how it responds to learning is extremely important. A great deal of what some teachers do in their classes does not enhance learning. For instance, most teachers lecture at some point during the day. Long ago, studies found that among college students, students paid attention to only 50 percent of the average lecture. They recalled only 45 percent of the information immediately after a lecture. A week later, however, students recalled only 17 percent of the information that their teacher had presented using the lecture format.

Emotions Are Critical to Learning

The human brain mediates our movements, senses, thinking, feeling, and behavior. Learning has to do more with emotions than with IQ. In *Molecules of Emotion: The Science Behind Mind-Body,* neuroscientist

Candace Pert[31] maintains that emotions are not found in the brain alone but rather throughout the entire body. We do not think with just our brains; we think with our bodies also. Similarly, in *Smart Moves: Why Learning Is Not All in Your Head*, neuropsychologist Carla Hannaford[32] maintains that our emotions mediate the context of our learning and that in order to learn, learners must form an emotional commitment. "Our mind/body system learns through experiencing life in context, in relationship to everything else, and it is our emotions, our feelings that mediate that context. In order to learn, think or create, learners must have an emotional commitment."

How young people feel is extremely important to their learning process. When they are enthusiastic and do not feel stress, learning will take place. If the conditions are negative and young people do not feel safe, learning will not take place. According to David Sousa,[33] how students feel in the classroom determines the amount of attention they devote to the lesson. When students feel threatened, they shut down the learning process and, Daniel Goleman[34] claims, "hijack" the rest of the brain.

What Brain-Based Learning Suggests for Teachers

How the brain works has an important impact on what kinds of instructional techniques and learning activities are most effective with children and adolescents. A brain-compatible teacher is one who understand the principle of brain-based education and who uses strategies in a purposeful way. If you are a teacher working with students of any age, it is important to become aware of instructional techniques that promote brain-based learning. Three instructional techniques associated with brain-based learning are:

1. *Orchestrated immersions*: Teachers create learning environments that fully immerse students in an educational experience.
2. *Relaxed alertness*: Teachers work to eliminate fear in learning, while at the same time maintaining a highly challenging learning environment;
3. *Active processing*: Teachers allow the learner to consolidate and internalize by actively processing information.

Brain-based theory suggests that teachers must design curriculum around student interests and make learning contextual. Teachers place students to learn in teams and to use peripheral learning. To engage students, teachers structure learning around real-life problems, encouraging them to also learn in settings outside the classroom and the school building. Assessment of students should help young people to understand their own learning styles and preferences. Such knowledge equips students to monitor and enhance their own learning process. As Renate Caine and her colleagues[35] state in their book *12 Brain/Mind Learning Principles in Action*, three interactive elements are critical to this process:

- Teachers must immerse learners in complex, interactive experiences that are both rich and real. One excellent example is immersing students in a foreign culture to teach them a second language. Educators must take advantage of the brain's ability to parallel process.
- Students must have a personally meaningful challenge. Such challenges stimulate a student's mind to the desired state of alertness.
- In order for a student to gain insight about a problem, there must be intensive analysis of the different ways to approach it, and about learning in general. This is what is known as the "active processing of experience."

Given that brain research indicates that emotions assume a critical role in teaching, one of the most important things teachers can do is to bond with their students. I recommend that each student in a school should have one person in the school who will act as a mentor and help him or her to make an emotional connection. Even small actions, such as having a teacher stand in the doorway and greet students as they come in helps students to be more receptive to learning.

Brain-based learning also suggests that feedback is best when it comes from reality rather than from an authority figure. Young people learn best when solving realistic problems. The best problem solvers are those who laugh. The best way to teach students is not through lecture, but by participation in realistic environments that let learners try new things safely.

Moreover, movement should be an important part of teaching. The brain is a pattern recognition organ; therefore engaging students in a movement exercise every 30–60 minutes can prevent it from sleeping and help it to increase attention span. Finally, because the brain is better at some activities than others and has more neuron paths for those activities, the best way to improve student weaknesses is to teach them to use their strengths to deal with difficulties. Put simply, there is more real estate in the brain devoted to the student's strengths. Teachers must learn how to help students use their strengths as the foundation for other kinds of learning instead of trying to get them to build upon something where the brain is already cortically disinvested or underinvested.

The next section of this chapter provides a detailed analysis of how we develop strengths. An overall theory of strengths development is presented in which I include the relationship of strengths not just to learning but also to mental health and mental disorder.

THE SMITH THEORY OF BRAIN DEVELOPMENT AND STRENGTHS

Currently, there is no existing theory of strengths development. This section contains my modest proposal for such a possible theory. Strengths-based development is an emerging area that traces its roots to research in a number of areas including brain development theory, multiple intelligences, positive psychology,[36] neuroscience,[37] and the recent studies on strengths leadership and management.[38]

Children learn and develop strengths in the areas that produce the most synaptic connections in the brain. This situation occurs because *the brain is the biological organ of learning.* It contains the basis of mental processes that underlie mental functioning, often referred to as thought or mind. Learning is a function of the effectiveness of synapses to produce signals and initiate new signals along connecting neurons.[39] The thinking patterns formed in the brain consist of analysis, which are interrelated processes of remembering and comparing mental data, and synthesis, which entails organizing, integrating, evaluating, detecting relationships, and making connections. A person engages in analysis and synthesis based on the structural patterns of interconnections of nerve cells or neurons.

As the brain learns and masters new skills or content, it needs less energy. David Halstead, president of Brain Power Learning Group, maintains that when a child or youth is presented with a new idea, it takes 75 millivolts to get the brain's neurons to fire. When a young person uses a neuron connection for a skill or content a number of times, the brain requires less energy to process the information, usually about 50 minivolts. Gradually, for knowledge or skill that is used repeatedly, such as $3 + 3 = 6$, the brain will develop a well-formed synapsis in which the neurons are wired together.

Individuals develop talents and strengths as a result of the repeated formation of synaptic connections in neural networks. As children age, they develop stronger synapses within the network of brain connections, and weaker connections tend to wither. After a young person reaches about age 15, his or her unique network of synaptic brain connections remain fairly stable and do not change. Brain research provides scientific evidence for the belief that talents, recurring patterns of thoughts, feelings, or behavior do not change significantly over time.

The Brain and Stages of Strengths Development

Human strengths development is a process that involves several states or stages. *Stage 1* involves the brain, and it has several phases. During *Phase 1* of the brain development stage of strengths, critical synaptic connections are formed within the brain. These connections are influenced highly by one's genetics. *Phase 2* of the brain development stage signals the significant influence of one's environment outside the womb. It consists of sensory inputs and interactions with one's parents, siblings, and family members. The infant makes repeated use of some synaptic connections. Some strengths grow stronger as we age (wisdom) while other strengths grow weaker, such as our physical strengths. *Phase 3* of the brain development stage of strengths entails repeated use of these synaptic connections, which creates neural pathways and networks that provide hints or evidence of the child's strengths. Children who use certain neural networks or synaptic connections repeatedly develop knowledge and skills in those areas. Such knowledge and skills may later mature into talents and strengths.

Stage 2 of strengths development involves the identification of one's talent(s) or things that one does with excellence; *Stage 3* is the naming and claiming one's talents as points of strength; *Stage 4* is the incorporation of talent and strengths into one's concept; *Stage 5* is the acquiring of the necessary knowledge and skills to perfect one's strengths; *Stage 6* entails the practice and repetition of already strong neurological synapses; and *Stage 7* is application of strengths in several different settings.

Differences in People's Strengths

People differ in five dimensions of strengths: (1) their specific strengths or combinations of strengths, (2) the relative intensity of their strengths, (3) their unique combinations of strength, (4) the degree to which they have developed their strengths, and (5) the extent to which they apply their strengths to achieve their goals or to find life satisfaction.[40]

Relational Component of Strengths Development

Although strengths development is a process that is first begun in the brain, it is later continued as one interacts with caregivers and the environment. Strengths development takes place most easily within the context of a trusted relationship where we express our intentions to grow in a particular area. For instance, a young girl tells her father that she wants to become an artist. The father buys his daughter numerous art supplies, comments positively on her paintings, and takes her to art shows. He arranges for art lessons and a mentor in the type of paintings that she likes making the most. The girl's artwork becomes important to and a source of pride for both her and her father. Strengths development is almost inevitably located in a relationship that nurtures an individual. Somewhere along the line, someone encourages the development of the strength, expresses support for it, and assists the person while he or she is in the process of improving and perfecting the strength.

More often than not, our ability to develop our strengths lies in our perceived social support or relational support for our strengths. Parents can provide emotional and instrumental support for the development of their children's strengths. A young boy living in the inner city tested very high on a musical ability test. He was offered free piano lessons for a year, but his parents could not afford to buy a piano. After a year or so practicing on the school's piano, he gave up his goal to learn how to play the piano. Relational support provides positive reinforcement for development of our strengths.

Strengths development affects our relationships with others because it increases both our self-awareness as well as our awareness of others. As we become aware of our strengths, we also begin to notice the strengths that others have. We all go through a strengths progression that entails self-awareness of strengths, awareness of others' strengths, and self-management of our strengths.

Children's Brains without Dad

The relational connection with brain development and hence strengths development is revealed in recent research by German biologist Anna Katharina Braun. Most people say that two parents are better than one. A research team led by Professor Braun[41] of the Department of Zoology and Developmental Neurobiology at the University of Magdeburg in Eastern Germany conducted research on animals that are typically raised by two parents, in the hopes that they might better understand the influence of children being raised by a single parent. Dr. Braun used laboratory rats called degus or brush-tail rats (*Octodon degus*), a species of rodent closely related to guinea pigs. When degus are babies, they are developmentally similar to human babies. Degus grow up under family conditions that resemble closely those of human infants. According to Dr. Braun, when these animals are born they are at roughly the same stage of development as a human infant. In their natural environment, degu infants are raised jointly by their father and mother and are extremely communicative, using whistling tones to carry on intensive "conversations."

When degus were deprived of their father, the degu infants exhibited both short- and long-term changes in nerve cell growth in different regions of the brain. These researchers also examined how these physical changes affect offspring behavior. Their preliminary analysis revealed that fatherless degus exhibit more aggressive and impulsive behavior than those raised by two parents.

In a study recently published in the journal *Neuroscience*,[42] half the degus were raised with two parents, while the other half were raised by a single mother because the father was removed from the cage one day after the birth of his offspring. Braun and her colleagues reported that in the two-parent families, the degu mothers and fathers cared for their offspring in similar ways, which involved sleeping next to or crouching over them, licking and grooming them, and playing with them. Surprisingly, the fathers even showed a "nursing type" position with the offspring.

Single-parent degu mothers did not change the frequency of their interactions with their offspring very much. Despite this observation, the degu infants experienced significantly less touching and interaction than those with two parents—primarily because of the absence of the father degu.

After Braun and her colleagues found that the degu within the mother-only family received significantly less touching and interactions than those in a family with both father and mother, they looked at the neuron cells that send and receive messages between the brain and the body of some degu at the day 21, the approximate time they were weaned from their mothers, and others at day 90, which is considered adulthood for the species. Neurons have branches known as dendrites that conduct electrical signals received from other nerve cells to the body of the neuron. The leaves of the dendrites form dendritic spines that receive messages and serve as the primary contact between neurons.

Dr. Braun and her associates found that at 21 days, the fatherless animals had less dense dendritic spines, compared to animals raised by both parents, even though they "caught up" by day 90. Despite this catching up, the length of some types of dendrites was significantly shorter in some parts of the brain, even in adulthood, in fatherless degu. Dr. Braun concluded that through their interactions with their children, parents leave their footprints on the brain of their children.

Dr. Braun's work has researchers looking more intently at the prevalence of single-parent households in the United States. Dr. Braun's future research will focus on investigating whether degu pups' brains can be rewired by introducing a substitute caregiver, such as a grandmother, or whether other social and emotional enrichment can help "repair" the fatherless degu. The bottom line, according to Dr. Braun, is that parents help to sculpt their children's brains.

It is my hypothesis that children in two-parent homes are better able to identify and develop their strengths than those raised in single-parent homes. It is the interaction with both parents that helps a young person to identify his or her strengths. Moreover, the presence of both parents typically provides more opportunities for children to develop their strengths.

Strengths Awareness and Attention

Strengths development is an attentional and noticing process. We have to choose to focus on our strengths in order to develop them. As we make decisions about what we will concentrate our attention on, we get feedback regarding our strengths. We come to recognize our talents and the value that accrues to them as we engage in activities involving our strengths. When we gain awareness of our strengths, we may make a conscious effort to seek out opportunities to use them. Awareness of strengths usually is based on our own performance evaluation of certain activities or on the feedback that we gain from those in our inner and outer circles—parents, friends, and teachers. As Mark Katz stated in his book *On Playing a Poor Hand Well*, "Being able to showcase our talents and to have them valued by Important people in our lives, helps us define our identities around that which we do best. This is how people develop a sense of mastery. The reverse is true as well. If you spend a disproportionate amount of your life doing things that you do poorly, and do these things around important people who see you only in this light, you're apt to define yourself in harsh and devaluing ways."[43]

As young people engage in strength awareness, their feelings about themselves become more positive. They may feel proud of themselves and come to value themselves as worthwhile. Positive strength awareness promotes a positive self-concept and facilitates feelings of self-efficacy in the strength area.[44]

Cognitive Component of Strengths Development

Strengths development also has a cognitive component, in that we develop cognitive strength schemata about that which we do well. Cognitive schemata function as organizers of meaning regarding all aspects of our worldview, including our relational views toward self, our strengths, others, and the world in general. All of us develop strength and weakness cognitive schemas that guide our actions. Cognitive schemata, when triggered, can generate automatic thoughts, strong affect, and behavioral tendencies. Some people fear that they have no real strengths, and therefore they become defensive when others try to help them discover their strengths. Teachers need to understand the cognitive schemata that students have developed about their strengths and their weaknesses. What automatic thoughts come to the forefront when a student thinks about his or her strengths and weaknesses? Is there pain or pleasure in a student's cognitive strength schemata?

Capitalizing on Our Strengths

Our strengths usually lead to a flood of positive emotions. Research by Fredrickson[45] has reported that positive emotions are worth cultivating because they help individuals to achieve psychological growth and improved well-being over time. Positive emotions function as internal signals for a person to approach or continue an activity. Based on a large body of research on positive emotions, Fredrickson has offered the broaden-and-build theory, which states that "certain discrete positive emotions-including joy, interest, contentment, pride and love—although phenomenologically distinct, all share the ability to broaden people's momentary thought-action repertoires and build their enduring personal resources, ranging from physical and intellectual resources to social and psychological resources. Frederickson found that positive emotions can undo lingering negative emotions (for instance, depression). Positive emotions can also fuel individuals' psychological resiliency. "Individuals who experienced more positive emotions than others became more resilient to adversity over time, as indicated by increases in broad-minded coping. In turn, these enhanced coping skills predicted increased positive emotions over time."[46] Frederickson also found that although positive emotions are fleeting, they are the vehicle for individual growth and social connection: "By building people's personal and social resources, position emotions transform people for the better, giving them better lives in the future."[47]

The point of citing Frederickson's research on positive emotions and her broaden-and-build theory is that strengths produce positive emotions in youth. Watch the face of your child, partner, or friend when you talk about their strengths as opposed to their weaknesses. Focusing on youths' strengths produces a flood of positive emotions that will lead to their overall better academic and psychological functioning. This situation occurs even when the teacher's focus on students' strengths is fleeting.

Strengths Development: A Lifelong and Intentional Process

Strengths development is a lifelong process that involves a dynamic interplay of a number of forces, including neural pathway development, instruction, observational learning, and culture. Strengths reflect individuals' dominant pattern of thought and feeling that they use in a productive manner to achieve their goals. Strengths development involves applying one's strengths rather than fixing one's weaknesses.

Strengths development involves a process of self-examination, reflection, and self-discovery. To this extent, it is almost invariably focused and intentional in nature. To really know your strengths, you have to look inward, become introspective, and be deeply honest with yourself about who you are.

Strengths development is an *intentional process*. It involves putting intentional energy into one of your strongest areas. To achieve the best results, choose one strength that you want to develop and then create a strategy to enhance it. For instance, a young boy who loves playing the drums chooses to practice two hours a day in order to get better. Larry Bird once said that in order to make a clutch basketball shot that won the game in the last few seconds, he had to practice shooting that shot a thousand times during that week. For strengths to truly exist, you must apply them in action; otherwise, you are talking about potential rather than strengths. Strengths involve practice, repetition, and more practice.

Theoretical Foundation for Strengths-Based Theory

Strengths-based theory also builds its foundation on the growing body of resilience literature and research. *Resilience* is defined as the process of struggling with hardship, characterized by the individual's accumulation of small successes that occur with intermittent failures, setbacks, and disappointments.[48] Resiliency research establishes that individuals possess an innate capacity for bouncing back. Resiliency provides the process by which strength is developed. Moreover, a resiliency perspective maintains that an adaptational quality of resilience strengths exists. Resilience is not a fixed trait; it is instead a dynamic, contextual process developed as a result of the interactions between individuals and their environments.

The strengths-based model also draws on need theories. Maslow's[49] needs hierarchy provides part of the theoretical explanation for human motivation to build and express strengths. Maslow posited a hierarchy of needs based on two groupings: deficiency needs and growth needs.

Updating Maslow's theory, Deci and Ryan[50] suggested three needs that are not necessarily ordered: the need for autonomy, the need for competence, and the need for relatedness. By way of comparison, strengths-based theory proposes that individuals have an innate need to recognize their strengths. Their need to recognize strengths, however, is not necessarily premised on complete satisfaction of their lower order safety needs. Young people who are given opportunities for positive ways to develop their strengths have different life experiences than those who are not given such opportunities. The needs for competence and relatedness described by Deci and Ryan are partly addressed in the competency stage of strengths-based therapy.

People develop strengths as part of their driving force to meet basic psychological needs, such as belonging and affiliation, competency, feeling safe, autonomy, and/or finding meaning and purpose in life. Our psychological need to feel competent motivates us to develop our cognitive, problem-solving strengths. Our need to find meaning in our lives motivates us to seek other people, places, and transformational experiences that give a sense of purpose. Our nurturing and relational strengths are developed out of our psychological need for belonging and out of our need to relate to and to connect with others.[51]

In addition, Frankl's[52] logotherapy forms a cornerstone for strength-based therapy, with its emphasis on the search to find meaning out of adversity. Greenstein and Breitbart described Frankl's belief in the importance of life meaning by noting, "Having a feeling of purpose and meaning can also help alleviate the distress caused by these painful facts of life [for example, terminal illness] in the first place" (p. 487).[53] Similarly, the strengths perspective focuses on helping youths to find meaning out of their adverse life circumstances.

Furthermore, the strengths-based model is founded on concepts within the multicultural literature.[54] All cultures have strengths, and some cultures value certain strengths more than others. In cultures described as individualistic, such as that of the mainstream United States, autonomy is a highly valued personal strength, whereas in collectivist cultures, such as parts of Asia, social competence and connectedness skills are valued. Cultural socialization may provide protective factors, which insulate or buffer individuals from the harmful effects of a racially discriminatory environment.

10 Propositions for Strengths-Based Theory

Ten propositions outline the basic principles of strengths-based theory. The 10 propositions for strengths-based counseling provide the theoretical framework for strengths-based teaching and counseling.

Proposition 1

Humans are self-righting organisms who engage perpetually in an ongoing pattern of adaptation to their environment, a pattern that may be healthy or unhealthy.[55] Strengths develop as people try to right themselves as they adapt to their environment.[56] All people engage in the self-righting mechanism, although some are more effective at it than others. The self-righting mechanism allows people to develop strengths for survival, which may be archetypal and encoded in their genetic makeup.

Proposition 2

People develop strengths as a result of internal and external forces and as part of their human driving force to meet basic psychological needs (e.g., safety, belonging and affiliation, autonomy, meaning and purpose in life).[57] For instance, our social competence strengths, including nurturing and relational strengths, are human efforts to satisfy the psychological need for belonging and our need to connect with others. Our need to experience power and accomplishment is a function of our mastery motivational system.[58]

Proposition 3

Each individual has the capacity for strengths development and for growth and change.[59] Strengths development is a lifelong process that is influenced by the interaction of individuals' heredity and the cultural, social, economic, and political environments in which they find themselves. People develop strengths through resiliency. Resilience strengths are critical survival skills that typically may be intrinsically motivated or biologically driven but culturally expressed. In part, survival needs drive healthy strengths development. All people also have a natural drive for positive growth and a natural tendency to seek the realization and/or expression of their strengths and competencies. Strengths-based teachers and counselors engage and support this natural drive when they help youth to identify their strengths.

Proposition 4

Strength levels vary, ranging on a continuum from low to high.[60] People's level of strength is influenced by several contextual factors, including the environment in which they are raised, the people to whom they have been exposed, and the available role models in their lives. Individuals raised in resource-deprived environments may evidence different strengths than do those raised in environments that are rich in community, family, and individual resources. Strengths will vary even within families, because each person's contact with resources and others differs.

Proposition 5

Strength is the end product of a dialectical process involving a person's struggle with adversity. Riegel[61] asserted that human existence appears to be influenced by basic dialectics (e.g., happiness and sorrow, autonomy and dependency). Growth may depend on the losses we experience during our lifetimes.[62] Thus one goal of counseling is to intervene in such a manner that the counselor helps a youth to achieve an optimal balance between dialectical pairs (e.g., happiness and sorrow) with regard to any given circumstance.

Proposition 6

Human strengths act as buffers against mental illness.[63] Through the process of resilience development, individuals become aware that they have internal resources permitting them to overcome or to mitigate obstacles. Individuals gain what might be labeled "strength awareness," which has the net effect of giving a sense of self-efficacy or authentic self-esteem derived from observing their strength in action.[64] Individuals' strength awareness and authentic self-esteem serve as mediating forces or buffers when signs of mental disorder occur. For instance, individuals sense that something is wrong with them, and they seek remedy. Their strengths alert them that their mental health or survival is somehow threatened. Schools need to be concerned with the emotional intelligence and emotional health of students, because long after the facts of a particular subject are forgotten, issues dealing with emotional intelligence remain.

Proposition 7

Young people are motivated to change when parents and teachers focus on their strengths rather than on their deficits, weaknesses, or problems.[65] When school personnel focus on young people's strengths, they provide an external verbal and relational reward. Strengths-based classrooms build the following strengths: courage, optimism, personal responsibility, interpersonal skills, perseverance, and purpose.

Proposition 8

Encouragement is a key source and form of positive regard that the teacher, parent, and counselor intentionally provide to effect behavioral change in a youth. In both teaching and psychotherapy, encouragement functions as the fulcrum for change. It provides the basis for individuals to be willing to consider change in behavior and self. The strengths-based teacher builds an arsenal of encouragement techniques, including the compliment.

Proposition 9

In strengths-based education, the teacher consciously and intentionally honors the student's efforts and struggles to deal with his or her academic challenges and classroom behavior issues. The teacher's strengths perspective philosophy creates a classroom atmosphere that dignifies and respects young people.[66]

Proposition 10

The strengths-based teacher understands that people are motivated to change dysfunctional or self-defeating behavior because they hope that doing so will bring about the desired life changes and anticipated rewards. Hope mobilizes us.[67] It functions to create within us a sense of anticipated or expected positive reinforcement for behavioral or attitudinal changes. Hope for a better future sustains students' positive participation or involvement in education. Students who evidence a higher sense of hope are hypothesized to achieve their educational goals at a higher rate than those who are pessimistic.

Adaptive Mental Health

Healthy psychological development takes place when we are not only aware of our strengths but also able to capitalize on and use our strengths in a positive manner to achieve our goals. We do not focus on our weaknesses. Instead, we learn how to manage our weaknesses. People who work in areas of their strengths express the greatest life satisfaction.

Summary of Principles of Strengths Development

Training and education can help you develop your strengths, if you are lucky enough to have a teacher or a parent who knows how to do so. Most parents and teachers focus on what needs to be fixed in children, what needs to be improved, rather than on their naturally occurring talents. Strengths are developed as young people engage in the learning process. All learning is emotionally based. Positive emotional attachments to caregivers produce greater neural networks and facilitate a child's learning. Therefore, the process of learning about your strengths is emotionally based. Some principles of strengths development are:

- Strengths development takes place most easily within the context of a trusted relationship where you express your talents and desires. Our relationships influence our strengths and talents. Parents and teachers with whom children have bonded are the most natural developers of youths' strengths. Students are taught to identify the most important people in their lives. They learn how to assess whether or not their friends are influencing them in the right direction. If their friends are holding them back, then they need to make new ones. Students are taught to place their personal relationships into several categories: (1) *inspirational people*—people who inspire them when it comes to their strengths and their dreams; (2) *refiners*, people who sharpen their ideas; (3) *supporters*, people who support their dreams and strengths with words, financial support, time, and commitment—people you can count on in time of need; (4) *detractors*, people who detract you from your dreams with their issues, goals, and problems; and (5) *haters*, people who deny your talent, strengths, hinder your efforts, and impede your dreams—they "hate you and your strengths." Students learn how to look for relationships that reinforce their strengths and talents.

- Strengths development involves a process of self-examination, reflection, and self-discovery. To this extent, it is almost invariably focused and intentional in nature. To really know your strengths, you have to look inward, become introspective, and be deeply honest with yourself about who you are. When you spend focused time thinking about your experiences, you promote strengths development.
- Strengths develop best when you use the talents that underlie them in a variety of different settings. For instance, a young child who evidences writing skills might begin to write stories for the school newspaper or letters to grandparents.
- For strengths to truly exist, you must apply them in action; otherwise, you are talking about potential rather than strengths. We have all heard about the strengths that some people say they have but who rarely show them. Strengths involve practice, repetition, and more practice.

Strength Zones

I propose that *every student has strength zones*. They are broad areas or categories of strength. They are pockets of potential excellence for each person. You have a competitive advantage in your strength area. People usually praise you for your competence in your strength zones. Therefore, when you are trying to find out what your strength zones are, think about what people have praised you for doing. You are already doing well in your strength area. You have developed a level of competence in your strength zone with relative ease. You know you are in your strength zone if something is working for you.

Strength zones suggest several attributes that contribute to positive or negative social and emotional functioning.[68] Strength zones are

---

STRENGTHS ZONES

Everyone has strengths zones, areas in which he or she has some natural talent to perform well.

Your strengths zones emit strength signals that let you know how strong your strengths are in given areas.

Other people may pick up your strengths signals before you do.

Listen for what people praise you for and you will get some idea of your strengths signals.

Your belief in your strengths zones increases the strengths signals that you emit.

Focus directs your strengths. If you want to be successful, you must focus on what you can do rather than on what you cannot do.

---

needed because they help a teacher identify a youth's positive attributes, focus on what is going right in his or her life, and place such strengths within an overall framework of the youth's psychological and social functioning.

Within every strength zone, there is a signal strength. A signal strength can be compared to the kind of strength that is evident in radio frequencies. In telecommunications, especially in radio, signal strength refers to the magnitude of the electric field at a reference point that is a significant distance from the transmitting antenna. Sometimes it is also referred to as field strength. Usually, it is expressed in voltage per length or signal power. There are high-powered transmissions, such as those used in broadcasting, and low-power systems, such as those used in mobile phones. Weak signals can be caused by destructive interference. The cost of transmitting some signals—in rural areas for instance—may be quite high. It is unlikely that some rural areas will ever be covered effectively by cell phones, for example, because the cost of erecting a cell tower is too high for only a few customers.

To continue the signal metaphor, each person has a strength zone that has a signal strength. For instance, Johnny might have a strength zone that involves the creative arts. Within that strength zone, he has a strong strength signal for playing the piano or for playing the drums. A person's signal strength represents how strong a specific area is within the strength zone. Strength signals are usually graded on a high, medium, low, or deficit/weakness basis. Despite his musical strengths, Johnny cannot sing very well. His strength signal for singing is very low. Of course if he insists, Johnny might work on his singing until it gets to a point where people will listen to him, but his signal strength is still not very strong. It simply costs too much in terms of human effort and time to increase the signal strength of Johnny's singing.

Scholars are in the initial stage of defining, isolating, and categorizing the human strengths that cut across cultures. I have identified 11 strength zones that have emerged from the literature. These strength zones are presented to assist teachers, parents, and counselors in assessing young people's strengths. The 11 strength zones are (1) wisdom, (2) emotional strengths, (3) character strengths (such as honesty, discipline, courage), (4) creative strengths, (5) relational and nurturing strength, (6) educational strengths, (7) problem-solving, decision-making, and leadership strengths, (8) economic and financial strengths, (9) social support strengths, (10) survival strengths, and (11) physical and kinesthetic strengths. People may possess strengths in several categories simultaneously. Few of us possess strengths in all zones, simply because each individual has limitations and weaknesses.

Wisdom

Throughout the centuries, most cultures have valued wisdom and spiritual strength, and therefore wisdom is presented as the first universally recognized human strength.[69] Wisdom is usually age related, in that older people are considered wise and young people foolish. People become wise as they mature in a given culture. Another dimension of wisdom is that it involves a changing balance between a person's acting and reflecting. In general, young people are not inclined to display wisdom because they tend to act rather than to reflect upon the consequences of their actions. Hence youth may have the capacity to be wise, but often they are too impulsive to reflect this strength. Moreover, the ability to be wise is also related to one's capacity to be detached from a situation.

Most people recognize, however, that there are some children who are wise beyond what their years might suggest. Americans use the phrase "out of the mouths of babes" to characterize children's wisdom. The wisdom of youth is that they tend to see what is really there. Some young people are excellent at discerning the intentions of adults. Consider the case of Alexandra Scott, who was only four years old when she started a national crusade for funding cancer research. In July of 2004 Alex and her brother Patrick held their first lemonade stand to raise money for doctors to find a cure for cancer.

A STRENGTH ZONE IS NEVER ENOUGH

"Life is a 10-speed bike. Most of us have gears we never use."
—Charles Schultz

Identify your strengths and believe in your potential.
Self-belief increases your strengths.
Initiative activates your strengths.
Focus directs your strengths.
Practice refines your strengths.
Relationships nurture your strengths.
Character and integrity protect your strengths from falling into misuse.

Alex had cancer herself, and even at the age of four she was determined to do something about it. She held a lemonade stand each year until she died at the age of eight. Her idea took hold and soon there were Alex's Lemonade Stands all over the country. During her four years of selling lemonade, Alex raised $1 million.

Emotional Strengths

A second strength category consists of emotional strengths and its close ally, emotional intelligence. Emotional intelligence deals with one's ability to discern and understand emotional information about oneself, others, and one's environment. It is the ability of people (no matter their age) to use their awareness of emotions to manage behavior and relationships with others.[70] Emotional intelligence is related to temperament styles, which are believed to be present at birth. Emotional self-regulation refers to the strategies we use to accomplish our goals. Emotional self-regulation requires a person's voluntary or effortful management of emotions.

Although some individuals maintain that children do not have emotional strength, case studies have pointed out that children do have such strength, sometimes beyond that of adults. For instance, television interviews with children suffering from cancer at St. Jude's Hospital reveal young people who are sometimes better able to deal with their illness emotionally than are their parents. Consider the life story of Kyle Maynard. Kyle's parents had to deal with the shock of his being born with a rare disorder called congenital amputation (he has no forearms, shortened legs, and stands only four feet tall). Yet his parents allowed him "no excuses," and despite no forearms and shortened legs, Kyle became a champion wrestler in Georgia. It was simply amazing to view on the television old pictures of Kyle as a toddler scurrying on the floor with no forearms or legs, laughing as he moved around family members who had the use of their legs and forearms. Kyle focused on what he could do well. His emotional strength allowed him not only to endure but also to flourish.

Emotional strength has to do with perspective taking, good regulatory behavior, and resiliency. Emotional strengths pertain to what we focus on in others, our ability to take another's perspective (empathy), and our degree of "other awareness." *Emotional strengths are also influenced by individuals' temperament.* For instance, children's temperament styles may influence their ability to relate to others. Children whose temperament style conflicts with their teachers' may experience problems in school. Emotional strengths also involve self-management, which the strengths perspective considers central to positive human development.

Character Strengths

A third strength category is labeled character strengths, and includes such behaviors as integrity, honesty, discipline, courage, and perseverance. I had the pleasure of seeing four-year-olds running from a parent who was playing the role of a scary monster. The kids were screaming with glee, with the exception of one little girl, who was totally frightened by the parent and started to cry. Despite being way ahead of the parent playing monster, one boy heard his friend's cries and returned to console her and to explain that it was just "play." It took a lot of courage and empathy for him to give up his lead and come back to comfort his friend.

Creative Strengths

These strengths include children's, adolescents', or adults' ability to appreciate the arts and to express themselves in writing, voice, and other art forms. Creative strengths also involve novel ways of thinking and viewing the world. There are numerous child prodigies in various creative areas. There are children younger than four who play the violin quite well. Others are beautiful painters and artists at the tender age of six. Still others have voices that are excellent, well beyond what one might consider normal for their age. Recently, a nine-year-old boy wrote a book about how to get a date with girls.

Nurturing Strengths

A fifth strength category encompasses nurturing strengths, including a child's, an adolescent's, or an adult's ability to nurture others.[71] Children develop their relational and nurturing strengths from a psychological need for belonging. They may display their relational strengths very early in life, in terms of how they respond to their parent's overtures for love and affection. One sees young children using their nurturing strengths most often during play with other children.

Educational Strengths

A sixth category consists of educational strengths, which include such factors as academic degrees, level of educational attainment, informal education, grades in school, and so on. This category becomes important for children as soon as they enter school, and for many children this is at the age of three or four in early childhood programs. Children who are labeled learning disabled may face ridicule from their friends and other family members. Learning disabled children also have strengths that should be recognized.

Problem-Solving/Decision-Making Strengths

This category contains individuals' problem-solving and decision-making strengths, and their ability to think and reason. Children's abilities in this area grow as they develop a greater cognitive capacity. Schools should actively teach problem-solving and decision-making strengths to help young people make wise choices about the friends they choose and the activities in which they participate. Young people require assistance with decision making and problem solving. Leadership is another important strength. To what extent does the child or individual evidence leadership abilities? Effective leaders know how to problem solve and to make good decisions.

Economic or Financial Strengths

Typically, adults do not view children as having economic or financial strengths. Yet these strengths can be seen very early in life, with children's construction of lemonade stands and exploring other ways to earn money. Many of the wealthiest people in the world have said that their efforts toward accumulating wealth began very early in

---

STAY IN YOUR STRENGTHS ZONES

True learning comes from staying in your strengths zones.

It stems from a process of strength refinement in which you increase your strengths signals by practice and persistence.

Understand your strengths signals.

Become knowledgeable about your learning process and your teachable moments.

Teach yourself to be teachable in your strengths zones.

---

life—with paper routes, garage sales, lawn cutting, and various other schemes in the neighborhood to make wealth. For adults, economic and financial strengths entail a person's ability to secure a job and to provide for his or her family.

Social Support Strengths

This category refers to individuals' ability to secure or to make good use of social support and community strengths. Although at first glance social support skills appear to be restricted to adolescents and adults, they are not. When in distress, some toddlers are able to seek and secure the support of their caregivers, while others become frightened and withdraw into themselves. Even before age two, some infants know what to do to bring a parent to his or her rescue. Social support-seeking skills grow as the child matures. Young people who are often labeled as "popular with the kids" usually have great social support skills.

Survival Strengths

These strengths help people to avoid pain and to provide for their basic physiological and safety needs. Survival needs often refer to a person's health status or his or her encounter with life-threatening events.[72] The brain is like a resilience library. It stores data and information on our survival and well-being but discards other data.[73] Children have survival strengths, just as adults do. Not long ago, there was a television news story about a two-year-old who survived by eating various food in the cupboards he could reach, while his mother lay dead on the floor. There have been numerous stories about four-year-olds calling the 911 emergency number when their parents went into insulin shock or suffered a heart attack. There are reports of "street children" who have been abandoned by their families, but who nevertheless set up their own survival communities with other children. Such behavior indicates survival skills.

Body, Kinesthetic, or Physical Strengths

Some children demonstrate fantastic strength at an early age. Consider Tiger Woods, who played golf at ages two through four years. Then there is Michael Phelps, the great swimmer who won eight Olympic gold medals. The ability to move one's body in a sport is an important strength that is valued throughout the world.

SUMMARY

This chapter has examined brain theory and learning. The brain is a wonderful garden that bears fruit throughout our lives. A great deals depends upon what is put into this garden, the paths that are created or left relatively bare. Core principles of brain-based learning were presented and teaching suggestions were made regarding how to incorporate brain-based concepts into instruction. The second half of this chapter presented strengths-based theory. Eleven categories of strengths were discussed with examples demonstrating how children may demonstrate such strengths. This chapter provides the foundation for how educators and counselors can institute strengths-based practices in their schools.

4

The Strengths-Based School's Component 1: A Strengths-Building Pyramid

The job of the educator is to find the germ of virtue concealed in the kernel of every fault.

—Goethe

BEHAVIOR: THE GARDEN OF OUR EMOTIONS

Each of us has metaphors to describe how we see life. I conceptualize behavior as a garden of a child's or young person's emotions. We all build different types of gardens from our life experiences. In each garden, there are a myriad of emotions—happiness, sadness, anger, rejection, acceptance, belonging, and loss. Each one of us has to build a garden inside of us. We have to decide what the landscape will be. Will it have rocks and stones? What kinds of flowers will be permitted to live in our gardens? What colors will be allowed to say hello to us each morning? Yellow and reds dominate my garden, yellow perhaps symbolizing my sense of hopefulness about myself and the world, and red roses, my passion for life.

Children's behavior reflects the garden of their emotions. They need help in designing and cultivating their gardens, and for that matter, so do adults. Children come to school eager to learn about building their own gardens. Far too many leave school with the feeling that somehow weeds were placed in their gardens during their tenure in school. There is probably enough blame to go around trying to figure out who is responsible for the weeds. Dropouts, for instance, have decided that they will take their gardens someplace else to be

---

YOUR MIND

"Your mind is a garden
Your thoughts are the seeds.
You can grow flowers or
You can grow weeds."

—Author Unknown

---

cultivated. In contrast, students who have learned about their strengths in school feel a connection to school and education; and so they stay, graduate, and continue their education, having witnessed for themselves what sunshine can do for plants.

Gardens can be changed. Throughout our lives, we modify our gardens based on what we have experienced and learned. The gardens that we plant and design for ourselves are with us to the very end. Although our gardens vary in their designs and colors, most of them have similar elements. For instance, most gardens contain flowers that mirror our feelings about ourselves and others. Another group of flowers are those that hug the garden's border and help individuals self-regulate their behavior. Still another patch of flowers reflect our dominant thoughts about the world—our worldview.

Part of the job of an educator is to help young people build their gardens. Teachers help young people to identify their dominant strengths and talents—the focal points of their garden. They also help youth to cultivate and weed their gardens. This chapter, then, deals with the inward garden, young people's garden of behavior. The chapter begins by defining what constitutes a strengths-based school. Next, I outline five components of a strengths-based school. The focus of this chapter is on Component 1 of the strengths-based school, namely, the importance of developing youths' emotional intelligence as a cornerstone of any viable garden. I emphasize the emotional side of kids' development because research on the brain suggests that all learning is mediated by our emotions. A strength-building pyramid is introduced as a way of having teachers and parents conceptualize what a strength-based school looks like.

Definition of Strengths-Based Schools

A strengths-based school is one that places its emphasis on developing young people's strengths. Such schools teach young people how to manage their weaknesses. They maintain that focusing on children's strengths is the way to motivate them and to get them to achieve. In strengths-based schools, teachers use students' strengths as a way to help them improve upon their weaknesses.

Strengths-based education uses concepts derived from brain-based education, self-theory, and multiple intelligences theory. Young people develop strengths when there is a strong, positive emotion associated with a learning activity. Such an emotional bond promotes learning. Teachers and parents facilitate the academic and social development of young people when they promote student trust, provide encouragement and support, and teach directly mental health and life skills. Strength-based schools involve:

- Taking a different path for educating and teaching youth
- Choosing a paradigmatic shift in thinking about what really helps youth to become positive contributing human beings
- Learning how to recognize the good in our children and youth
- Encouraging youth and instilling them with hope
- Focusing on what youth want like for themselves—their hopes and dreams
- Emphasizing what youth are doing right and teaching them how to modify what they are doing wrong

Core Strengths-Based Beliefs about Children and Families

Dennis Saleebey[1] has been instrumental in describing the strengths perspective. According to him, the strengths perspective means that, "To me, the essence of the strengths perspective is that you actually believe that everybody—every community, every family, every individual—has a fund of knowledge, of capacities and skills, of personal traits and resources that exist within them." Similar to Saleebey, I maintain that:

1. All children and families have strengths.
2. Children's and their family's motivation to work cooperatively with a school is increased when school and mental health officials focus on describing children's strengths instead of their deficits.
3. School plans and treatment plans must be based on the strengths of children.
4. Youth change comes when they use their inherent strengths and resources to deal successfully and prosocially with a situation and when they are supported by caring, prosocial relationships.

5. Positive change takes place in a youth's life when he or she is helped to create a life plan that is based on his or her strengths and talents and when he or she has the hope to carry out such a plan.

6. Educators and counselors are more likely to help young people change their behavior when they focus on what is positive and strong in them ("what is right" and "what is working" with them) rather than on what is wrong with them.

7. A youth's negative experiences may not necessarily be predictive of his or her later life of pathology, as negative experiences may strengthen or weaken him or her.

8. A youth is viewed as more than his or her problem.

9. Youth excel *primarily by maximizing their strengths,* rarely by fixing their weaknesses.

The Strengths-Based School

The strengths-based school has five components:

1. The *social-emotional learning curriculum,* which involves: (a) the 10 skills of life and educational success, (b) building blocks of resiliency development, and (c) learning circles and class meetings

2. The *academic curriculum,* which involves the core curriculum, students' learning styles, strengths-based assessment, and competency and mastery of subject matter

3. A *caring school and a positive school culture and school climate* (which involves hiring and/or developing caring teachers, and training teachers in techniques of student encouragement and in the use of positive expectations for achievement)

4. A *prevention emphasis,* which attempts to tackle problems before they start

5. A *union of schools officials, parents, and communities* working collaboratively

Component 1: The Social-Emotional Curriculum

This chapter focuses on the first component of the strengths-based school, and that is the social-emotional curriculum. The push to have schools institute a social-emotional curriculum can be traced directly to the research on the brain. As researchers learned more about the brain, they began to understand the role of emotions—what parts of the brain generate and control a young child's emotions. Youth cannot learn academic subject matter if their brains are being hijacked by strong flight-or fight emotions.[2] Educators have it backwards when they emphasize the importance of academics over emotional intelligence. Without a calm mind, students cannot learn. Learning takes place in an emotionally safe classroom environment. Deal first with young people's emotions, and then you might have a chance to teach them the content of academic subjects.

Moreover, understanding young people's emotions is critical because we know that disciplinary problems in school are major factors that impede the learning process and that cause new teachers to leave the teaching profession. In 2003–4, Heartland Institute surveyed 725 middle and high school teachers and 600 parents of teens. A major finding was that student discipline problems seriously obstruct teaching and learning in American schools.[3] The survey findings indicated that there is an increasing number of distracting and disrespectful student behavior that interferes with the classroom environment and forces many teachers to leave the teaching profession. The report stated:

> Rowdiness, disrespect, bullying, talking out, lateness, and loutishness—these misbehaviors are poisoning the learning atmosphere of our public schools, said Public Agenda President Ruth A. Wooden. "At a time when the achievement stakes for have never been higher, the fact is that in school after school, a minority of students who routinely challenge legitimate school rules and authority are preventing the majority of students from learning and teachers from teaching.

The survey revealed that teachers perceive parents as being part of the problem. Nearly 82 percent of teachers and 74 percent of parents stated that they believe that the failure of parents to discipline their children is a major cause of the problem. Nearly half of the teachers surveyed stated that today's teachers are softer on discipline because they cannot rely on parents or the school administration to back them up.

A third of the teachers (34 percent) responded that they know colleagues who have left the teaching profession because of student misbehavior and difficulties in maintaining discipline. A third (34 percent) had also thought about leaving teaching themselves. Three-quarters of teachers (78 percent) said that persistent student offenders who should be removed from school are permitted to stay.

My point in raising these statistics is to indicate the reasons that teaching emotional intelligence in schools is imperative. If parents are not teaching self-regulation and emotional intelligence at home, schools have a responsibility to make sure that their students are given the necessary tools to earn a living, get along with others, and succeed in life.

Emotional Intelligence and the Role of Schools

Daniel Goleman's[4] best-selling book, *Emotional Intelligence (EI)*, popularized the term *emotional intelligence*. For decades, the American public had placed a great deal of emphasis on intelligence associated primarily with a limited number of skills such as logical reasoning, math skills, spatial skills, analogies, and verbal ability. These skills, which are largely academic in nature, were considered genetic, inherited, and thus immutable. It was assumed in many circles that a person's future is largely controlled by skills and aptitudes. Gradually, questions arose about what could be changed in young people's lives if one could not change their so-called inherited intelligence. What can we do that will help our children to succeed in life and turn out to be decent people? What causes people of high IQ to fail in life, while those of modest IQ succeed?

Researchers believed that something was missing in the equation—that although they could predict academic performance based on IQ, something was missing when it came to overall life success. The A students were not running Wall Street and the top corporations in the world. No, it was the C students who held such positions. Former President George W. Bush, for example, has made no secret of the fact that he was a C student at Yale who became president of the most powerful nation in the world. The richest man in the world, Bill Gates, dropped out of Harvard University. Where are the A students? Someone once said that the A students are teaching in universities, making less than $125,000 a year, while the C students are on Wall Street making millions in bonuses. There is hope for all those mothers and fathers who cannot put on their bumper sticker "My son/daughter is an honor student at . . . "

What is it, then, that helps the former C students succeed in life, whereas the A students trip up, fall flat on their faces, and sometimes make a mess of their lives? The major factor missing in the success equation has come to be known as emotional intelligence. For the most part, schools did not acknowledge this type of intelligence, and they spent little time either nurturing or rewarding it as a strength in students. An emotional intelligence grade was simply missing from students' report cards. Who really cared about their emotional intelligence? What really mattered was students' academic intelligence—what scores they achieved on their SAT and PSAT tests rather than whether they know how to motivate others.

In his book *Working with Emotional Intelligence*, Goleman[5] points out that the rules in the workplace have changed. They have little to do with what we were taught in school. For instance, in schools, academic abilities were viewed as all significant. Now, academic abilities are largely irrelevant to the new standard. Most organizations assume that you already have the intellectual ability and technical knowledge needed to do your job. The new standard in the work world focuses on personal qualities, such as initiative and empathy, adaptability and persuasiveness. Schools need to match what they are teaching in schools with what is valued in the American workplace. They must begin to educate young people in the skills of emotional intelligence and in presenting and managing themselves in the workplace.

The Connection between Brain Research and Emotional Intelligence

Developments in neuropsychology provided a major influence on the school of emotional intelligence. More than 50 years ago (1952), neurologist Paul Maclean[6] introduced the idea of the limbic system as the brain's emotional center. MacLean proposed that our skull contains not one brain but three, and that each one represents a distinct evolutionary stratum that had formed upon the older layer before it. He called it the triune brain. As the director of the Laboratory of Brain Evolution and Behavior in Poolesville, Maryland, MacLean maintained that the three brains functioned like three interconnected biological computers, with each having its own special intelligence, its own subjectivity, its own sense of time and space, and its own memory. He called these three brains the neocortex or neo-mammalian brain, the limbic or paleo-mammalian system, and the reptilian brain, which is the brain stem and cerebellum. Although each of the three brains is connected by nerves to the other two, each appears to operate as its own brain system with distinct capacities.

MacLean's work forced neuropsychologists to rethink how the brain functions. Previously, the prevailing belief was that the highest level of the brain, the neocortex, dominated the other, lower levels. MacLean demonstrated that the physically lower limbic system, which rules emotions, can hijack the higher mental functions when it desires to do so.

It was Joseph LeDoux, a neuroscientist at New York University, who was the first to discover the central role of the amygdala in the emotional brain. His research was contained in two critically acclaimed books, *Sensory Systems and Emotion*[7] and *Emotion and the Limbic System Concepts in Neuroscience*.[8] LeDoux's research helped us to understand emotion life because he was the first to work out neural pathways for feelings that bypass the neocortex. Feelings that take the direct route through the amygdala contain our most primitive and potent emotions; therefore this pathway explains how the power of our emotion can overwhelm our rational (neocortex) mind.

LeDoux's work demonstrated how the architecture of the brain gives the amygdala a privileged position as an emotional watchdog, able to take over the brain's functioning. According to him, sensory signals from the eyes or ears travel first in the brain to the thalamus, and then cross a single synapse to the amygdala; a second signal from the thalamus is routed to the neocortex—the thinking brain.

Based partly on LeDoux's research, Goleman contributed the concept that our emotions matter for our rationality. Our emotional faculty guides our day-to-day decisions. Either it can either work hand in hand with the emotional mind or it can disable or hijack the rational mind. In some respects, we have two brains, two minds, and two different kinds of intelligence: rational and emotional. How well we do in life is determined by both our emotional and rational mind. It is not just IQ that matters, but our emotional intelligence as well. Our intellect functions best when combined with emotional intelligence.

According to Coleman,[9] emotional intelligence (EI) consists of a person's self-awareness and his or her ability to control emotions. He maintained that a person's emotional intelligence has a profound influence on where the person ends up in life. Goleman outlined two components of emotional intelligence: (1) personal competence and (2) social competence.

Personal competence refers to competencies that determine how we manage ourselves. A partial list of personal competence areas are:

- Self-awareness
- Knowing one's internal state, preference, resource, and intuition
- Emotional awareness: recognizing one's emotions and their effects
- Accurate self-assessment: knowing one's strengths and limits
- Self-confidence: a strong sense of one's self-worth and capabilities
- Self-regulation: managing one's internal state, impulses, and resources
- Self-control: keeping disruptive emotions and impulses in check
- Conscientiousness: taking responsibility for personal performance
- Achievement drive: striving to improve or to meet a standard of excellence
- Optimism: persistence in pursuing goal despite obstacles and setbacks

Social competencies determine how we handle relationships. This category includes:

- Empathy—the ability to yourself in another's shoes on an as-if basis
- Awareness of others' feelings, needs, and concerns
- Understanding others: sensing others' feelings and perspectives and taking an active interest in their concerns
- Developing others: sensing others' developmental needs
- Adeptness at bringing about desirable responses in others
- Influence: using effective tactics for persuasion
- Building bonds: nurturing instrumental relationships
- Conflict management: negotiating and resolving disagreements
- Collaboration and cooperation: working with others toward shared goals

Pain-Based Behavior: Another Reason for Social-Emotional Training

Every garden has some flowers that do not fare well. In the past, American public schools have tended to yank the poorly performing flowers out of their classrooms and place them into special locations—places where they are supposed to get help that will help them to grow and blossom. But my experience has been that students yanked out of one class and placed in another special class seldom do well. On the contrary, the pain that brought about their disruptive behavior becomes intensified rather than reduced.

Recently, researchers have begun to examine youth's acting-out behavior in terms of the *framework of pain-based behavior*. In his book *Pain, Lots of Pain*, Brian Raychaba[10] described the inner world of troubled Canadian youth who had been removed from their families and sent to alternative settings. Raychaba observed that these youth felt powerless at being at the mercy of life events that they could not control. The most consistent theme was that the youth believed that the trained professionals who worked with them seldom understood their pain.

James Anglin[11] has provided some support for the theory of pain-based behavior. After studying the cultures of 10 residential treatment programs for youth in Canada, he concluded that every young person was feeling deep emotional pain. Anglin proposed that the emotional and behavioral problems of youth should be called "pain-based behavior," and concluded that educators and counselors who deal with troubled youth must receive training in responding to the pain and needs of youth.

Strengths-based schools seek to integrate the latest findings on youth's pain-based behavior into its discipline policies. Such schools maintain that discipline must be founded on something larger than adult coercion and punishment. Coercive discipline, while necessary in some instances, actually triggers and intensifies pain-based emotions. The word *punishment* comes from the Latin word *poèna*, which means pain. Few medical doctors would administer more pain to a patient already in pain. Yet this is what educators do when they use coercive discipline.[12] Coercive discipline results in fighting pain with more pain. Instead, discipline policies should serve to teach youth prosocial behavior and values. In strengths-based schools, teachers are trained: (1) how to assess the private logic behind students' self-defeating behaviors, and (2) how to respond to youths' needs rather than react to their pain-based behavior. The social pain that young people experience in schools is very real.[13]

A study by researchers at UCLA found that physical and social pain is recorded in similar ways in the human brain.[14] Psychologists used brain scans to examine the reactions of youth excluded by peers from a computer-simulated game. They found that this contrived social rejection aroused the same pain centers of the brain that are activated by Physical pain.

Strengths-based schools use principles from restorative justice in its discipline policies. *Restorative discipline* focuses on repairing the harm that a youth's behavior has caused to relationships. Students are taught how to express their feelings, to respect the feelings of others, to recognize the hurt that they have caused to others, and to develop strategies to repair the harm caused.

Research Findings on the Social-Emotional Learning Curriculum

Teachers are the head landscapers and social-emotional leaders in their classrooms. Their knowledge regarding how to tend children's behavior gardens is extremely important. A number of researchers have translated information about the brain and about emotional intelligence into what has become known as the social-emotional learning (SEL) curriculum.[15] An SEL curriculum teaches kids how to recognize and regulate their emotions, thereby increasing their emotional intelligence quotient. Effective social and emotional education can modify a classroom or even an entire school's culture. School programs address such behavior as bullying, acting out, interrupting, violence, and choices. The most effective SEL programs are integrated into the school's academic curriculum.

Research indicates that social and emotional learning programs result in higher student academic achievement, increase "on task" student behavior, increases students' focus, and promote learning collaboration. The social decision-making/problem-solving program has reported the following findings:[16]

- After training, teachers improved in their ability to promote children's social decision making and problem solving.
- Children receiving the program improved their social decision-making and problem-solving skills relative to control groups. More specifically those receiving the program were more sensitive to others' feelings, had a better understanding of consequences, showed an increased ability to size up interpersonal situations and plan appropriate actions, were more socially appropriate in the way they coped with problems and obstacles, and used what they learned in situations occurring both inside and outside the classroom.
- Young people who were followed up in high school evidenced greater positive, responsible, and prosocial behavior and decreased antisocial, self-destructive, and socially disordered behavior in comparison with control young people who did not receive the program.

THE GARDEN OF OUR MINDS: TEACHING CHILDREN TO CHANGE THEIR THOUGHTS AND EMOTIONS

A Strengths Framework for Schools

Most young people know more about what they cannot do well and very little about what they do well. In all fairness, parents and teachers do not intentionally set out to produce deficit thinking in young children. Most parents and teachers simply want the very best life for children, and to achieve that, they want them to improve or be outstanding in as many areas as possible. A major problem is that most of us have been exposed to deficit language, and few of us have adopted a language of strengths. We talk in the language that we know to children.

This section presents a strengths-based framework for helping students to deal with social-emotional issues at school, at home, and during their leisure with peers. The teacher begins the school year with the idea that every student has strengths and that these can be incorporated into the day-to-day classroom activities. During the first week of class, each student is helped to identify at least one strength that he or she has. Parents are also enlisted to help their children identify their strengths. To assist both students and their parents in identifying strengths, the teacher distributes and sends home a strengths checklist. Students and parents are told to not limit their mentioning of strengths to those presented in the checklist.

In working with schools to establish a strengths-based approach for creating a social-emotional curriculum, I have constructed a Strengths-Based Assessment Toolkit©, which is sold separately from this book. The toolkit contains five instruments, two of which are described herein.

Depending upon the age of the young person, *The Strengths Checklist* either can be self-administered by students or can be administered by teachers, parents, or counselors. The instrument was constructed for late elementary, middle school, and high school students (Table 4.1).

Another instrument in the Strengths-Based Toolkit is the Strengths-Based Inventory©, which I developed for helping schools to uncover students strengths by having them take a simple self-report inventory. This inventory is intended primarily for kids in Grades 7–12. The Strengths-Based Inventory measures strengths in nine different areas: (1) peers and friends; (I have at least one close friend); (2) self-esteem and emotional understanding of self and others (I know my own strengths); (3) family strengths (I feel loved by my parents and family members); (4) educational strengths (My school is a safe place to be); (5) community strengths (I have found ways to contribute positively or to volunteer in my community); (6) coping skills, problem solving, and resiliency strengths (I can identify behaviors that are causing me problems in life); (7) purposeful life (I feel that my life has meaning and purpose); (8) skills and competencies (I have good communication skills); (9) quality of life (includes economic and health issues—I have enough food and clothing).

Once students and parents provide an initial strengths report to the classroom teacher, the teacher can gain insight into a child's or youth's behavior. Gradually, teachers build a strengths profile for each student in their classes. The teacher takes a number of opportunities to help students identify their strengths, and they also might point out strengths to them.

The strengths-based approach that I advocate uses the strengths pyramid throughout the school. The strengths pyramid occupies three parts of the pyramid. The first part emphasizes helping

Table 4.1   The Strengths Checklist

DIRECTIONS: The table that appears below consists of a number of words that can be used to describe yourself, or to identify qualities that you have. You will notice that the words are all positive. This is not an accident. We want to know more about your personal strengths and abilities, and this is one way of quickly getting some information.

We would like you to go through the list and rate each word for how well it describes you. There are no right or wrong answers.

You can use this scale to rate each word:

1. This is really like me.
2. This is somewhat like me.
3. This is a little like me.
4. This is not really like me.
5. This is definitely not like me.

If you are not sure about the meaning of a word, your teacher or counselor will help you.

Word	#	Word	#	Word	#	Word	#
Spiritual		Tactful		Compassionate		Self-assured	
Reflective		Nonjudgmental		Conscientious		Friendly	
Persuasive		Trustworthy		Perceptive		Persistent	
Self-controlled		Energetic		Optimistic		Intelligent	
Artistic		Insightful		Calm		Broad-minded	
Decisive		Flexible		Intuitive		Honest	
Good-natured		Organized		Detail oriented		Decisive	
Sociable		Perceptive		Discreet		Good learner	
Reasonable		Self-controlled		Tenacious		Sociable	
Enthusiastic		Hopeful		Responsible		Resourceful	
Punctual		Empathetic		Determined		Courageous	
Industrious		Sensible		Humble		Fair-minded	

Note: Copyright © Elsie J. Smith.

students to develop their strengths. Students learn that strengths can develop from everyday life experiences (Figure 4.1). For instance, if a struggling student identified playing basketball as one of his strengths, the teacher might encourage him to view the classroom as a basketball court and the teacher as his coach. He might be encouraged to exhibit good sportsmanship in the classroom and to demonstrate respect for the other team—other people and groups within the classroom. Because the teacher has helped the youth to identify positive strengths, he is now in a position to encourage him to use his natural talents/strengths to make good decisions throughout the school year.

Sometimes young people, teachers, and parents find it difficult to identify strengths. These are strengths indicators that help us to determine our strengths (most of these were mentioned in the chapters 1 and 2):

- Your yearnings: What are the things you long to do, the things you have always wanted to do?
- Things you learn rapidly; things that make "intuitive sense" to you
- Things that seem to come naturally to you
- Glimpses of excellence: When have you have had moments of thinking "Wow, how did I do that?"
- Your sense of satisfaction; times when you think "When can I do this again?"

Another approach is to ask students to identify their top five strengths in any area that they believe is important to them. Next, students are asked to describe how each one of their strengths work together. Students also learn how to appreciate the strengths in others. They are asked to complete a scavenger hunt in class. They are also asked to work in groups of two or three to discuss each other's strengths. After 10–15 minutes of discussing strengths, students introduce or acknowledge a classmate and share with the class the strength he or she has learned about. A scrapbook of strengths can be used with individual students, entire classes, families, community groups, and support groups. In working with groups, members would create *Our Scrapbook of Strengths*.

Our Scrapbook of Strengths gives a teacher an opportunity to acknowledge and recognize the existing strengths of the class and to identify ways in which the class can make use of such strengths.

Another approach is to have students complete a form titled "Where My Strengths Might Take Me." Students reflect on their strengths and how they might have an impact on their lives. What do you feel a sense of mission or destiny about? In addition, students might be asked to complete their own individual *scrapbook of strengths*.

The Strengths-Building Pyramid

© **Elsie J. Smith**

<u>Using the Strengths-Building Pyramid, students learn how to:</u>

✓ Identify and develop their strengths;

✓ Observe and value the strengths of others; and

✓ Build respectful, cooperative and productive relationships.

Figure 4.1 Strength Pyramid

Other strengths-based class activities include having students construct a strengths journal or a strengths portfolio. The strengths portfolio could be used to record strengths that the youth has recently discovered, or it may contain examples of how he or she applied certain strengths. Teachers can incorporate strengths into English or writing classes. For instance, students might be required to read a story that deals with a main character's lack or presence of strengths. Writing assignments might be: "How I Used My Strengths in My

Community" or "Strengths I Use with My Family (or Friends)." Students can keep a record of their strengths in relationship to the academic subjects (math, English, reading, science, etc.). They might be asked to consider their relationship and emotional strengths and to write a brief essay on how they applied them in everyday life.

Another technique teachers might use is a *strengths-sharing circle.* Sharing circles have been used for a number of classroom activities. Strengths-sharing circles require youth to become aware of other students' strengths. Another purpose of such sharing is to improve communication among students and to enhance their interpersonal skills. As students listen to their classmates' perspectives on their strengths, students become more self-aware and their empathy for others increases. Teachers assist students in helping to apply their strengths in the following situations:

- Learning concepts, principles, theories, facts, and information
- Achieving levels of excellence in academic tasks
- Overcoming disappointments and remaining motivated
- Building and sustaining healthy relationships
- Assuming and fulfilling leadership functions and roles
- Being of service to others
- Identifying and pursuing a sense of meaning, destiny, and purpose in life.
- Identifying and pursuing a career or a profession

Teachers can use students' strengths to increase their learning engagement. The extreme form of student disengagement is reflected in the high dropout rate from schools. Engaged students believe that they are competent, that they have the capacity to succeed, that they matter to their teachers, and that they have a sense of school belonging.

Jessica Tyler completed a dissertation on the impact of strengths-based development on student engagement at Texas Christian University.[17] The study included over 1,600 students and 90 teachers from three traditional high schools, one traditional middle school, and two alternative educational settings within a Midwestern school district that had a total enrollment of approximately 20,000 students. Almost 50 percent of the teachers in the study received a strengths-based intervention, a Gallup Seminar called Strengths Spotlight™. The seminar emphasized helping students understand, apply, and grow in their areas of their strengths. Student and teacher strengths were measured by the Clifton StrengthsFinder™ , an online assessment based on over 30 years of research on what makes people successful. Students in the two alternative educational settings, who had the opportunity to learn about their own strengths and the strengths of others, evidenced more positive perceptions about the school environment. Students improved in their overall engagement. Tyler discussed teacher engagement as a precursor to student engagement.

Student engagement is necessary for learning and academic achievement. Identifying and using students' strengths can be used to engage the class by appealing to their interests and by capturing their attention. When teachers are aware of students' strengths, they gain a more balanced understanding of each student. Teachers can use such information for deciding how to place students into collaborative class groups.

Designing a Strengths-Based Classroom

In designing a strengths-based classroom, the teacher keeps a record of student-identified strengths as well as her or his own log book of strength observations made during class. Teachers note student strengths when students participate in various activities. Strengths inventories and observations can be used to inform Individual Education Plans, for interdisciplinary teams, and for report cards. Students learn that teachers take notice of their strengths. Strengths files can be passed from one teacher to the next.

To engage students on a continual basis, teachers create a wall of strengths on a bulletin board containing the student's picture, a brief profile, or a self-portrait on a single sheet of paper. The strengths wall can be used as a bonding point for the entire class. The teacher works with students to develop a wall of their class strengths. For example, a class might list their multicultural diversity as a strength or their ability to get along with each other as a strength. Other classwide strengths include a class's ability to work quietly on task or to help others.

The strengths-based classroom is student centered rather than teacher centered. It is designed to involve students of multiple learning styles, and it contains interactive learning experiences. A strengths-based classroom is governed by the following 12 student/class/teacher principles:

1. I know what is expected of me in class.
2. I have the materials and equipment I need to do my class work and homework right.
3. In class, I have the opportunity to do what I do best every day.

4. In the last seven days, I have received recognition or praise for doing good work in class.
5. My teacher(s) seems to care about me as a person.
6. There is someone at school who encourages my development.
7. In my class, my opinions seem to count.
8. I feel important in my class; I matter to my classmates and teacher(s).
9. My classmates are committed to doing quality work.
10. I have a best friend at school.
11. In the last six months, someone at school has talked to me about my progress.
12. This last year, I have had opportunities at school to learn and grow.

Managing Student Weaknesses

Students learn how to manage their weaknesses so that they do not sabotage their strengths. They learn that weakness fixing prevents failure, but that strengths building leads to excellence. They come to understand that developing and applying strengths results in reaching levels of personal excellence and their fullest potential. Managing weaknesses make take the form of getting assistance, delegating, or working to achieve a designated level of competence, what I label as functional competency. Teachers can encourage students to use their strengths to deal with their academic and personal struggles. For instance, a student might have a musical strength, and the teacher might encourage her to use this strength to help with her math weakness.

Student Misbehavior and Strengths

Emphasizing students' strengths is a good way to reduce disciplinary problems within the classroom. In disciplining students, teachers point out what is working, and they work with students on ways to manage their weak points and misbehavior. Teachers arm students with mind-calming techniques, such as breathing. A most powerful technique to control our emotions is our capacity for conscious breathing. When we notice our breathing (pay attention to it), we can shift our physiological reaction and start to calm down. As we focus on our breathing, our ability to project to the future (as we do in fear) or to live in the past (as we do with anger) is reduced. Breathing deeply into our diaphragm and making our exhalation longer than our inhalation, shifts us to a more relaxed state. Deep breathing also increases the amount of oxygen we inhale. The brain functions better when the brain is oxygenated. Moreover, longer and slower brain waves are similar to the ones our brains make when we are relaxed and calm.[18]

Teachers can instruct students on how to use mental visualization to achieve their goals and to eliminate disruptive misbehavior. Students learn to change the focus of their attention of their minds—on something that is positive and calming. If students become aware that someone or something has triggered negative emotions within them, they can imagine a scene in which they feel comfortable, content, and at peace. As they become involved in the imagined relaxing scene, their heart rate will drop and they will relax. Their bodies are responding to the imagined scenes as if they were real instead of the situation that just triggered them. Examples of imagined scenes include a sandy beach, a favorite childhood spot, or a quiet garden. We are all triggered at one time or another. There are a range of techniques, including progressive muscle relaxation, distraction, and meditation, that teachers can instruct students how to use to deal with events that have triggered their emotional brain.

Strengths-Based Classroom Management and Rules

The teacher functions as the role model for making appropriate strengths-based statements and routines in the classroom. Teachers can use strength compliments to get a straying student back on track. A teacher might say: "You worked hard today in math and English class. You should be proud of your effort." Students and teachers agree on a mutual contract of behavior to be displayed within the classroom. Students sign the contract to show that they agree to obey the rules that they have helped to develop. One item in the classroom contract might be: "I agree to use my strengths to tackle my weaknesses in this class." Another item of agreement could be: "I agree to respect and to honor the strengths of other students in my class." "One of our strengths as a class is our ability to get along with each other. If we should disagree with another person, we use calming techniques to quiet our feelings so that we can respond appropriately to the situation at hand."

Framework 1: The Ten Life Skills and Mind Gardens

A major theme that pervade this book is that we all have *mind gardens*. Our thoughts have real power because they can serve to propel us forward or cause us to cower in fear. In strengths-based schools, students are taught to design, monitor, and protect their own mind gardens. They are to pay attention when thoughts flash repeatedly across their minds. Negative thought seeds grow patches of thorny thistles into their daily lives. They learn that many of the problems and difficulties they are facing in school and at home had their beginnings in the seeds of self-doubt, fear, and anxiety that they were continually planting in their minds. Teachers ask students: "What are you going to grow in your mind garden—seeds or weeds?" Teachers instruct students that they are the landscapers and that they can cultivate their own mind garden. They learn how to reject negative thoughts by saying to themselves: "I will not plant this weed in the garden of my mind." "I will consciously choose to plant a positive thought about my strengths and about other people." As students consciously cultivate their own mind gardens, they begin to see the changes in their lives. Not only do obstacles and barriers seem far less menacing, but also the things which they thought impossible to achieve are not so impossible after all.

Strengths-based schools use two overarching frameworks to teach social-emotional skills. The first framework is labeled the 10 life skills. Students can decide to cultivate the 10 life skills or to let them wither on the vines of their mind. I maintain that long after the facts are forgotten for academic courses, young people will need certain life skills to guide them on their life's journey. The ten skills of life provide a shared vision that serves to unite teachers, administrators, students, and parents to work toward achieving these skills.

A detailed list of the class exercises and lesson plans that correlate with these skills is available in a separate publication. Only a brief mention of activities is provided herein. Teachers are trained in instruction for the 10 life skills, which are as follows:

- **Life Skill 1: The Power of Positive Belief in Self (Self-Esteem).** Exercises are developed to reinforce young people's strengths. Have students make a list of personal strengths and build positive self-statements about each one. Another lesson introduces students to Albert Ellis's ABC model.[19]
- **Life Skill 2: The Power of Attitude.** A child's attitude is a powerful tool for both positive and negative action. Develop a class discussion on perspective taking.
- **Life Skill 3: The Power of Understanding One's Own Strengths and Weaknesses.** List three strengths that you have. List ways that you allow your weaknesses to trip you up.

- **Life Skill 4: The Power of Learning How to Communicate Effectively.** Students learn how to use I statements to communicate their feelings. They are also trained how to listen respectfully to others.
- **Life Skill 5: The Power of Being a Problem Solver and a Person Who Can Cope.** Students are taught a five-step approach to problem solving. They learn a four-cell technique for decision making from which they generate the pros and cons for different actions.

Lessons are also developed to teach students behavior-oriented techniques to help them cope with difficult emotions or stressful situations, such as when a student is arguing and threatening to fight. The teacher instructs students in a variety of skills and strategies, including controlled breathing and muscle relaxation, and guides them as they practice each technique. The teacher helps students to construct and recall a positive visual image which they can call to mind when they feel angry or anxious.

- **Life Skill 6: The Power of Building Supportive Relationships with Others.** Lessons are developed on empathy so that students learn how to place themselves in someone else's shoes. They learn the skills of conflict resolution.
- **Life Skill 7: The Power of Finding Your Purpose in Life.** Students undergo an in-depth analysis of their own strengths, partly for the purpose of determining their purpose in life.
- **Life Skill 8: The Power of Establishing Goals and a Life Plan of Action.** Students learn the skill of establishing goals and a life plan of action.

One requirement of all students in strengths-based schools is that they must develop a life plan. Teachers focus on helping students to learn what motivates them to achieve and to accomplish their goals. Most of us find that we need to motivate and remotivate ourselves again and again. Therefore, we have to learn what motivates us and what keeps us from accomplishing our goals. Strengths-based schools maintain that student motivation begins with:

- Clearly defined goals in all areas of a student's life
- A positive attitude about self
- Skills necessary to achieve desired goals

It is difficult for students to be motivated if their goals are unclear, if they have a negative attitude about themselves, and if they do not have the necessary skills to achieve their goals. Students are taught how to push aside their resistance to accomplishing their goals. For instance, a student might say: "I will worry about whether or not I am going to succeed with this goal for 10 minutes—after I complete step 1 of my goal."

Life career plans are designed to give young people a sense of purpose in life. Research has shown that young people who have a sense of purpose achieve at a higher level in life than those who lack purposefulness. For too many American youth, career development and life planning begins in their junior and senior years when they make choices for college. Life planning is more than choosing a college to attend. Young people who attend strengths-based schools do not fall into the trap of spending their first two years at college floundering and wondering what their major will be. They already have a sense of purpose in life because they know a great deal about themselves, and they understand how to use their strengths to achieve their goals.

- **Life Skill 9: The Power of Persistence: Adopting a "Whatever It Takes" Attitude.** Students are asked to participate in several exercises in which they are asked to persist without any tangible reward other than their own internal self-satisfaction that they have performed a task quite well.
- **Life Skill 10: The Power of Establishing a Life of Integrity and Moral Behavior.** Students are introduced to the concepts of moral behavior and integrity. They are engaged in exercises based on Kohlberg's theory of moral development.

The strengths-based school helps young people reflect on the kinds of people they are becoming by examining their actions. During the last five minutes of class, ask students to reflect on the lesson and write down what they have learned. Then ask them to consider how they would apply this approach or skill to their own lives. On a weekly basis, students reflect on what they have planted in their gardens for the past week and what changes they would like to make.

Framework 2: Strengths Domain

The second framework used in strengths-based schools is based on the concept of strengths domains. Teachers assess, record, and nurture seven domains, including: (1) Domain 1: strengths within the individual (creative strengths, resilience, etc.), (2) Domain 2: strengths within the family (communication, protection of family members, two-parent family, etc.), (3) Domain 3: strengths at school (school bonding, sense of belonging, academic achievement), (4) Domain 4: strengths with peers (prosocial peers); (5) Domain 5: strengths within neighborhoods and communities (safe neighborhood, opportunity to participate in community activities); (6) Domain 6: strengths from faith, spirituality, and culture (spiritual identification, church, synagogue, or mosque social support), and (7) Domain 7: strengths from mastering the 10 skills of life. The second framework taps into more students' strengths than does the one that focuses only on life skills. This framework is responsive to the various domains with which youth come into contact. A separate publication contains assessment inventories for these domains.

Resiliency

Another part of the social-emotional curriculum involves teaching children to become resilient in the face of adversity. The term *resiliency* is derived from a Latin word meaning to jump or bounce back. Resilience takes place when a child shows competence after exposure to significant risk factors.[20] Resilience refers to children's ability to adapt in the face of significant adversity and to develop social, academic, and career competence, despite negative risk factors in their environment. The resilient child achieves positive life outcomes despite growing up with a mentally ill parent or having been raised in poverty. Children can be taught to become resilient, and the proposed strengths-based program focuses on helping them to become resilient in dealing with everyday life's difficulties.

Protective Factors That Promote Young People's Resiliency

Protective factors can be defined as those internal and external factors that buffer a young person from experiencing the full impact of risk factors in hi or/her environment. Three key factors have a profound and significant influence on healthy youth development. These are:

1. The child or youth has developed *meaningful relationships with family and friends.*
2. The child or youth has developed the *life skills necessary to succeed academically and personally.*
3. The child or youth has opportunities for *meaningful participation in his/ her family, school, and community.*

Henderson and Milstein[21] list the following *environmental protective* factors:

1. The family promotes close bonds.
2. The family values and encourages education.
3. The family sets and enforces clear boundaries (rules, norms, and laws).
4. Parents express high and realistic expectations for their children's success.
5. Parents encourage goal setting and mastery.
6. Parents provide leadership, good decision making, and opportunities for the youth to participate in family affairs.

Resiliency Training for Young People

Strengths-based schools provide resiliency training for students to help them deal with powerful emotions, such as anger. As pointed out in the section that dealt with deep breathing, most people benefit from learning self-quieting and calming techniques. The benefits of such self-quieting techniques can include: increased self-awareness and self-understanding; increased ability to relax the body and release physical tension; improved concentration and ability to pay attention; the ability to deal with stress better; and positive thinking and reduced intrusion of negative thoughts. In a study involving adults, Davidson et al.[22] found that meditation reduced stress, promoted well-being, strengthened the immune system, and increased the gray matter in the brain. Just recently, Suttie[23] has examined mindfulness as an approach to working with children.

Lantieri,[24] cofounder of the Resolving Conflict Creatively Program (RCCPP) and now director of the Inner Resilience Program in New York City, is presently helping New York City kids to develop inner resilience by introducing them to calming techniques. One of the strategies for helping kids to develop inner resilience is to have teachers create *"peace corners"* for students. A peace corner is a special place set aside in the home or classroom where young people can go whenever they need to regain their inner balance. Within limits, children can go to peace corners when they feel overwhelmed, stressed, angry, or out of control emotionally.

Peace Corners for Children in Classrooms

We all need save havens and places that we can visit to regain our composure. Sometimes instead of sending a youngster to the principal's office, it might be better to offer her the opportunity to regain her composure on her own so that she can reflect on what happened. In her book, *The Power of Relaxation*, Thomas[25] describes a designated quiet time with children as "heart and soul time." Strengths-based schools encourage teachers to have "peace corners" and "heart and soul time" for their students on a regular basis because such techniques increase the inner resilience and coping skills of children.

Morning Meetings and the Strengths-Based School

A significant focus of the strengths-based school is on morning meetings and classroom meetings. Morning meeting is part of the practices of the responsive classroom developed by the Northeast Foundation for Children.[26] Morning meetings are designed to serve as a transition from home to school, to help young people feel welcome and known, to set the tone for the day, to create a climate of trust, and to encourage inclusion and cooperation among youth.

During the beginning of the academic year, a morning meeting should be used every day at the beginning of the day for 20–30 minutes. As the classroom climate becomes one of cooperation and trust, the morning meeting may be reduced to two to three times per week. The morning meeting consists of four components:

1. *Greeting*: Children greet each other by name, and they may engage in handshaking, clapping, singing, and other activities.
2. *Sharing*: Students share some news of interest to the class and respond to each other, and they practice communication skills and learning about each other.
3. *Group Activity*: The entire class participates in a short activity together, thereby building class cohesion.
4. *News and Announcements*: Students develop language skills and learn about the events of the day by reading and discussing a daily message posted on a chart by the teacher.

Learning Circles and the Strengths-Based School

Learning circles are small and diverse groups of people (usually 6–12) who meet regularly to focus their different viewpoints into a common understanding of an issue or problem. The history of learning circles can be traced to early native councils of elders in indigenous cultures. Such cultures constructed wisdom circles to understand problems in a shared community. Quality circles used in corporate settings to encourage participatory management and team leadership constitute another forerunner of learning circles. Finally, learning circles can be traced to study circles, which were used in the United States as a form of adult education to help individuals and communities come together.

The physical shape of the learning circle symbolizes the equality of students and teacher. Everyone can see everyone else when he or she is speaking. The structure of learning circles in the classroom helps to promote a nonthreatening environment. Learning circles facilitate the development of higher student emotional intelligence because students learn to examine their own values and to empathize and show respect for others.

SUMMARY

The gardens we make in life reflect our emotions and feelings. This chapter examined the first component of a strengths-based school—the social-emotional curriculum. A definition of the strengths-based school was given, along with its characteristics. Core beliefs about students and their families were discussed. The strengths-building pyramid was offered. It was recommended that schools adopt programs that promote emotional intelligence. Two frameworks (10 Life Skills) and strength domains (7) were presented. Techniques were presented for developing a school's social emotional curriculum (peace corners, morning circles, and learning circles).

Component 2: Improving Instruction—The Academic Curriculum

EDUCATIONAL SYSTEMS AS NATIONAL GARDENS

Each nation creates its own gardens. National gardens vary depending on the culture of the country and on the flowers that each country holds dear. There are beautiful gardens all over the world that vary according to the climate, terrain, weather, and plants and flowers that the citizenry believe represent their nation best. Gardens can be compared to a country's flag or coat of arms. When I think of England, for example, I see the beautiful, stately gardens surrounding Queen Elizabeth's palace. There is the Liu Yuan garden in China, France's Courances Castle garden, Italy's Isola Bella gardens, Russia's Tsarskoe Selo, and the beautiful Longwood Botanical Gardens near Philadelphia, in the United States—to mention just a few.

The educational system of each country is part of that country's national garden system. Such systems represent what seeds that nation has sown in education and what it has harvested as a people. When we look, therefore, at national achievement rates in reading, math, science, and problem solving, we see the fruits of the educational seeds that specific nations have planted. Based on the educational statistics presented in chapter 1 of this book, it is clear that American schools are not planting the kinds of educational seeds that will lead this nation to high achievement rates in reading, math, science, and technology. Although we were once leaders in the world in terms of academic achievement, our educational harvests have been less than stellar or desirable during the past decade and a half. For the most part, the decline in American achievement has been steady and has persisted across the generations. This chapter is, in part, about getting the United States to plant educational seeds different from those planted in the past because the harvest we are reaping has become less bountiful and less fruitful than what it used to be.

Whereas chapter 4 concentrated on the social-emotional component, this chapter examines the instructional program—the second major component of strengths-based schools. It analyzes how student academic achievement can be improved by shifting to a strengths-based model. I contend that the deficit model focuses on remediation that often stigmatizes young people and that produces disappointing achievement results. The question remains: can we produce academic excellence by emphasizing what is wrong with youth? I think not.

In the United States, it is recommended that each school develop its own strengths-based instructional program based on the curriculum standards established in that state. Therefore, this chapter does not propose any specific academic curriculum to be instituted across all schools. Instead, it offers principles and approaches to establish a strengths-based academic instructional program. For example, Part 1 of the chapter begins with a reminder of what is at stake if we continue to plant educational gardens that end up with young people achieving far less educationally than many nations of the world, especially those countries that we label as emerging nations.

It would seem that the term *emerging nations* is fast becoming a misnomer because some countries, such as India, China, and Korea, have already emerged. Their youth are outscoring American youth on international achievement tests in reading, math, and science.[1] The achievement of these young people has been responsible for their making significant technological advances, such that their countries' products are being exported all over the world. To some extent, Americans have acknowledged the emerged presence of these countries on the global community when they buy these countries' products and cars at a far higher rate than they do their own American products and cars.

Yet, the problem does not stop with these emerging nations obtaining a greater share of the world's financial market. American corporations are packing up their businesses in the United States and setting them up in emerging nations, partly because these nations' educational systems produce a citizenry strong in math, science, technology, and problem solving. The re-location of American companies to foreign nations can be traced partly to the low achievement of our educational systems across this great nation. Jobs are being outsourced to countries where the educational achievement rates surpass ours.

Part 1 of this chapter examines the low academic achievement of American students in comparison to the emerging nations and the established nations of the world.Part 2 presents a school's strengths-based instructional and educational philosophy. Principles related to strengths-based education are stressed. Part 3 analyzes educational issues such as learning styles and learning disability challenges (Individual Education Plans). Part 4 presents designing a strengths-based instructional model.

EDUCATIONAL GARDENS AND AMERICAN YOUTHS' ACADEMIC ACHIEVEMENT VERSUS GLOBAL ACHIEVEMENT

As noted in Chapter 1, the academic achievement scores of American youth in math and science have created deep concerns among both U.S. educators and political leaders. The headlines have become quite familiar: "U.S. Kids Mediocre in Math and Science";[2] "4th and 8th Graders in the U.S. Still Lag Behind Many Peers".[3] American fascination with these stories is partly driven by our national desires to be number one. Yet, recently American *policymakers*, business leaders, and educational analysts have pointed out that much more is at stake than boasting rights to being number one in academic achievement. These national leaders have argued that the nation's economic future depends directly on schools' ability to improve our current academic standing, particularly in math and science.[4]

Are American Youth Losing the Achievement Race?

Although the United States was once a world leader in higher education, it can no longer make that claim, primarily because of increasing investments in higher education abroad. Among OECD (Organization for Economic Cooperation and Development) countries, the United States ranks only 11th among 25- to 34-year-olds, while Korea ranks first;[5] and the United States has slipped to number 16 in high school graduation and 9th in postsecondary enrollments.

To obtain a critical perspective on the achievement of United States students by way of comparisons with students from other nations, the

United States participates at the international level in the Programme for International Student Assessment (PISA), the Progress in International Reading Literacy Study (PIRLS), and the Trends in International Mathematics and Science Study (TIMSS). TIMSS and PIRLS measures students' mastery of specific knowledge, skills, and concepts and are supposed to reflect curriculum frameworks in the United States and other participating countries and jurisdictions. PISA differs from the other evaluation programs by focusing on the application of knowledge in reading, mathematics, and science to problems with a real-life context.[6]

The Center for Public Education reported that there is a relative decline in American schools' effectiveness as youth age.[7] Reading, math, and science scores all declined as American students completed the K–12 educational system. For instance, the combined literacy scores are reported on a scale from 0 to 1,000, with a mean set at 500 and a standard deviation of 100. In the United States, 15-year-old students had an average score of 489 on the combined science literacy scale, which was lower than the OECD average score of 500. Students from the United States scored lower in science literacy than their peers in 16 of the other 29 OECD jurisdictions and 6 of the 27 non-OECD jurisdictions. In 2006, the average U.S. score in mathematics literacy was 474, lower than the OECD average score of 498. Thirty-one jurisdictions (23 OECD jurisdictions and 8 non-OECD jurisdictions) scored higher, on average, than U.S. students in mathematics literacy in 2006.[8]

Moreover, even the American adult population (ages 16 to 65) performed near the bottom on a six-nation assessment of literacy and numeracy. Adults in Norway, Bermuda, Canada, and Switzerland outscored the performance of similar adults in the United States. The United States literacy performance was greater only than Italy's.[9]

The High Cost of Low Academic Achievement

A number of factors have been given for the high academic achievement of some OECD nations—some of which are culturally ordained, such as greater respect for teachers, high national value placed on academic excellence, having all students from one ethnic and cultural background, and so on. Clearly, in the United States, the low achievement scores of African Americans and Latinos depress the average performance score on international tests. Yet, as was pointed out in Chapter 1, even if we eliminated all the low-performing scores of African Americans and Latino students, the scores of the average white American student would still fall below that for many OECD nations.

Even within the United States itself, white American students are often outscored by Asian American students. Although Asian American students often score similarly to whites and higher than that of other underrepresented minority groups in reading and verbal tests, Asian Americans outperform whites in terms of their overall average grades (GPA, grades in math, and test scores in math).[10] We need to find out what is it in Asian American approaches to education that is instrumental in their youths' higher achievement scores in math and science.

Clearly, scores for all American youth need to increase if we are to remain competitive on a global basis. A recent study conducted by PISA tried to tackle improving the scores of OECD membership nations and jurisdictions. The OECD member countries are: Australia, Austria, Belgium, Canada, the Czech Republic, Denmark, Finland, France, Germany, Greece, Hungary, Iceland, Ireland, Italy, Japan, Korea, Luxembourg, Mexico, the Netherlands, New Zealand, Norway, Poland, Portugal, the Slovak Republic, Spain, Sweden, Switzerland, Turkey, the United Kingdom, and the United States. Commenting on the wide difference in educational achievement, PISA stated:

> Results of the three-yearly PISA surveys reveal wide differences in the performance of education systems in terms of the learning outcomes achieved by students. For some countries, the results from PISA are disappointing, showing that their 15-year-olds' performance lags considerably behind that of other countries, sometimes by the equivalent of several years of schooling and sometimes despite high investments in education. However, PISA also shows that other countries are very successful in achieving strong and equitable learning outcomes. Moreover, some countries have been able to significantly improve their learning outcomes, in the case of Poland by almost three-quarters of a school year between 2000 and 2006 alone.[11]

This study used the technique of economic modeling to relate cognitive skills—as measured by PISA and other international instruments—to economic growth. It found that relatively small improvements in the skills of a nation's labor force can have very large impacts on the future well-being of that nation and its people. Moreover, the gains in a nation's labor force skills when put in terms of current gross domestic product (GDP) far outstrip the value of the short-run business-cycle management. The educational achievement of youth from all nations is a long-run approach to improving the economic growth of a nation, including its gross domestic product score. Citing the real economic benefits of improving a nation's improved scores on PISA, the report titled *The High Cost of Low Educational Performance* stated:

> A modest goal of having all OECD countries boost their average PISA scores by 25 points over the next 20 years—which is less than the most rapidly improving education system in the OECD, Poland, achieved between 2000 and 2006 alone—implies an aggregate gain of OECD GDP of United States dollars 115 trillion over the lifetime of the generation born in 2010 (as evaluated at the start of reform in terms of real present value of future improvements in GDP). Bringing all countries up to the average performance of Finland, OECD's best performing education system in PISA, would result in gains in the order of USD 260 trillion.[12]

Improving the educational system of the United States is not just a good thing to do—a platitude that one enunciates during a political campaign. It has real economic consequences for a nation—not only in the present, but also in the future. As a nation, Americans cannot afford to let the low academic achievement of African Americans and Latinos to become the norm in far too many communities.

The report continued by indicating that the reason some countries have not developed much economically is directly related to the role of human capital in economic development. The human capital influence on economic growth was best characterized by the relationship between direct measures of cognitive skills and long-term development. The report concluded that the evidence points to differences in cognitive skills as an explanation of a majority of the differences in economic growth rates across OECD countries.[13]

RELATIONSHIP BETWEEN HUMAN CAPITAL AND ECONOMIC GROWTH

"Higher cognitive skills of a nation offer a path of continued economic improvement.

Achievement deficits of nations, measured by average scores on PISA tests and other international tests of mathematics and science, point to serious shortfalls in economic performance compared to economic possibilities."

—*The High Cost of Low Educational Performance*, PISA (published by OECD)

The PISA report carries with it something of the idea that, within any given nation, either we all make it educationally to some acceptable degree or we all go under. A nation can have a few outstanding individuals; however, unless we all pull together, all of us might experience a less than desirable standard of living. Long-term or long-run issues involving the education of a nation far outweigh the value of any given short-run business cycle in an economic recession. To put it another way, America's economic recovery from the current economic recession has more to do with the educational level of the American workforce than giving businesses a tax break.

It is also worth noting that the PISA report placed quality of teacher instruction as the primary variable affecting the achievement levels of students within a given nation. If we take this finding to be true, then raising the achievement levels of American students—including African American and Latino students—has much more to do with the quality of teacher instruction than it has to do with the color of a young person's skin. In Finland, South Korea, and Singapore, teachers are those who graduated from the top of their classes. There is some evidence to suggest that the PISA conclusion is accurate for the education of African Americans. In the United States only 23 percent of teachers graduated from the top third of their class. In urban schools, only 14 percent were high academic achievers.[14] In their report Auguste, Kihn, and Miller stated: "When McKinsey & Company analyzed 'How the World's Best School Systems Stay on Top' (2007), we found a few common themes. Perhaps the most important was that 'the quality of an education system cannot exceed the quality of its teachers.' "[15] The studies in the next section indicate that when African Americans are exposed to greater technology, their math and science scores increase.

Technology in Schools: A Real Boost to Educational Achievement of Students

The strengths-based school places special emphasis on math, science, technology, and problem-solving courses, for these are the academic subjects American students are being outperformed in by students in nations throughout the world, but especially in Europe and Asia. Research has found that when Americans invest in education and in technology, there is a positive payoff for African American students.

In a study commissioned by the Software and Information Industry Association, Sivin-Kachala and Bialo[16] reviewed 311 research studies on the effectiveness of technology on student achievement. Their findings revealed positive and consistent patterns when students were engaged in technology-rich environments, including significant gains and achievement in all subject areas, increased achievement in preschool through high school for both regular and special needs students, as well as improved student attitudes toward learning and increased student self-esteem.

Research also shows that students in one-to-one computer environments are highly engaged and motivated and develop twenty-first-century skills. Michigan's Freedom to Learn[17] initiative, an effort to provide middle school students and teachers with access to wireless laptop computers, has been credited with improving grades, motivation, and discipline in classrooms across the state, with one exemplary school reporting an increase from 29 percent to 41 percent in Michigan Educational Assessment Program test scores for seventh graders and from 63 percent for eighth graders. Another advantage of being connected is that parents and caregivers are better informed through access to students' progress and achievement information.

Sharon Judge[18] studied the relationship between academic achievement of young African American children and access to and use of computers in their school and in their homes. The sample was composed of 1,601 African American public school children enrolled in kindergarten and first grade. The results showed that access to and use of a home computer, computer area in classrooms, child-to-computer ratio, software, and computers in school were positively correlated with academic achievement. Moreover, frequent use of software for literacy, math, and games was positively correlated with academic achievement during kindergarten. High achievers in kindergarten used software for literacy and math more frequently than both low and average achievers.

STRENGTHS-BASED EDUCATIONAL PHILOSOPHY

The strengths-based educational philosophy is based on the idea that focusing on a student's strengths functions to engage and motivate that student. Yet most students and teachers are unaware of their strengths, and they do not know how to use such strengths to promote their academic achievement. Developing students' strengths represents a form of learning that requires time, intentional planning, and student reflection on their strengths. Strengths-based educational programming confronts students with the challenge of being excellent

---

LEARNING AND THE HEART

"In order for the brain to comprehend the heart must first listen."
—David Perkins, "Smart Schools"

---

and being people of integrity by applying their strengths in ways that conform to their values and their sense of destiny. Strengths-based educational programming helps students to deal with beliefs about who they are and what their strengths and talents enable them to do best. Strengths-based educational programming assists students (1) to learn more about their strengths and talents, (2) to have increased personal confidence because they know what they can do, (3) to have increased academic confidence because they have apply strengths in study strategies and they know better where and how they can excel, and (4) increased motivation to achieve because they are approaching learning from a positive self-assessment. Some beliefs about students' rights in schools include:

- Every child has the right to be surrounded by a school culture of high expectations.
- Every child deserves good educational and career guidance to help them define the pathways for their future.
- Every child merits a rigorous academic curriculum and excellent teaching within a supportive educational environment.

Strengths-Based Learning Communities

Strengths-based schools are first and foremost learning communities. The term *learning community* has come to mean several things, for instance placing students in a classroom into meaningful group-directed tasks, or bringing community people into the school to enhance the curriculum, or engaging students, teachers, and administrators simultaneously in learning. A school learning community includes educators, students, parents, and community partners who work collaboratively to improve both young people's learning opportunities and the overall condition of the school. In contrast, a professional learning community stresses the teamwork of principals, teachers, and school staff to identify school goals, improve the curriculum, measure student progress, and promote the overall effectiveness of the school.

Creating schools that are learning communities is essential to closing achievement gaps across racial, ethnic, and socioeconomic groups. Learning communities generally structure the curriculum so that students are actively engaged in a sustained academic relationship with other students and faculty over a longer period of time than is possible in traditional courses.(http://lists.ctt.bc.ca/lo/learningcommunities .html). A formal definition is, "A "learning community" is a deliberate restructuring of the curriculum to build a community of learners among students and faculty. Learning communities generally structure the curriculum so that students are actively engaged in a sustained academic relationship with other students and faculty over a longer period of their time than is possible in traditional courses." http://lists.ctt.bc.ca/lo/learningcommunities.html. Such schools break down the barriers that isolate teachers. Teachers share ideas daily regarding important areas of instruction, curriculum, testing, and school organization. There is faculty training, parent involvement, and curriculum and report card redesign. Schools that are learning communities share common characteristics:

- A personal relationship exists between teachers and students; teachers know their students quite well.
- Classrooms focus on creating new knowledge; learning is viewed as a process in which teachers and students participate.
- Teachers and students have a commitment to collective learning; the learning community is comprised of a wide variety of people who contribute different skills and knowledge based on their experience and education.
- Students and teachers experience a sense of ownership for their learning.
- Strengths-based schools have a collectively determined common vision for the school and a shared sense of purpose.
- Learning takes place in a physically and intellectually safe environment, and students and others take risks regarding their learning inquiries.

Learning Is Relational

Strength-based learning is based upon research drawn from several research areas, including brain-based learning, learning styles, engaged learning, and differentiated instruction. The strength philosophy is that everyone can learn, and that each person's brain functions as a very powerful processor of information. Traditional schools often establish classrooms that inhibit learning by discouraging, ignoring, or punishing the brain's natural learning processes. All too often,

---

TEACHERS AND THEIR BELIEF IN YOU

"The dream begins with a teacher who believes in you, who tugs and pushes and leads you to the next plateau, sometimes poking you with a sharp stick called 'truth.'"

—Dan Rather

---

traditional learning is pain based and fraught with memories of feeling inferior or negativity. Both children and adults remember the pain that it took to learn their time tables or a particular fact from their social studies lessons. Some children remember being humiliated in front of a class when they could not seem to learn a particular fact.

Jana was recognized as an outstanding teacher of the year by her students and by her school principal. What made Jana stand out was that she had established a relationship with every one of her students—even the ones who acted out. She could put a halt to a student's acting-out behavior simply by reminding him or her about the strengths that lived inside them. I remember hearing her scold one student: "Derek, I know that with all the talents you have, there's something more constructive you could do with your time. I'm expecting good things from you. One day you'll come back and visit me, telling me that you are CEO of XYZ Corporation. You want that, too, now, don't you, Derek? Well, turn around and get busy using the talents you've been blessed with." Derek smiled, turned from his conversation with his classmate, and said: "Destiny is calling me. I might even give you a job . . . later."

To discipline Derek, Jana had elicited Derek's hope for a better future for himself. She believed in him—at least that what she said. As long as he had one person believing in him, that was enough for him.

ISSUES IN STRENGTHS-BASED SCHOOLS: LEARNING STYLES

Strength-based schools take into account students' learning styles. The theory in abbreviated form is that young people learn in one of three ways: visually, auditorily, or kinesthetically. Based on their learning style, they develop a preference for learning academic material in a certain way. Learning styles can promote fast learning where the young person's strengths lie, or they can impede learning when an area is weak and compensatory skills are lacking. Auditory learners are inclined to be better at language arts subjects such as English and social studies. Visual learners fare better at math and science, and kinesthetic learners perform well on hands-on or laboratory-type of learning instead of lecture-type instruction. Teaching based on students' individual learning styles is an effective way to ensure students' achievement and motivation.[19]

Young people with auditory weaknesses experience difficulty following spoken directions and tend to rely on visual cues, including watching other youth, to understand what to do. These are the kids in class who say: "What did she say to do?" Youth who experience challenges in auditory learning find it difficult to follow multistep directions. They may get lost at step three of a seven-step process. Therefore, it is important to place all steps on the blackboard, or to present them in a PowerPoint presentation. Youth who have auditory challenges become distracted sometimes when they are listening to a story; therefore, it is helpful if teachers provide visual cues and pictures to indicate the next step to take.

In contrast, youth who have visual limitations find it hard to remember places and locations, and they may need to be guided through class material that uses charts, graphs, diagrams, or other visual displays. These children have difficulty learning things by doing them.

When teachers observe young people either excelling or struggling with a class exercise, they should make a mental note of what is taking place in that specific learning environment. What caused the youth's success or lack of success with the activity? As students and teachers become aware of students' learning style, they can choose relevant learning strategies to master the material. The process of demystification helps children to overcome learning difficulties:

- Start the process by helping a child to understand his or her strengths. False praise should not be used to convey their strengths because children see such praise as the ultimate, condescending put-down. Let children know the things that they do well.
- Give children specific vocabulary to examine their learning challenges ("You have a problem getting the main idea of a paragraph; or you have a problem reversing certain letters when you read"; or "You are getting distracted by your own thoughts and that's why you forget what you started to say in your presentation"). Children work better when they can name specifically their learning challenge.

- Number the weak areas for the child (e.g., "There are two things that you need to work on to make you stronger). In this way, a child has hope that he or she can improve.
- Give the young person hope that he or she can correct the situation or minimize the challenges. Hope keeps the youth still willing to try.

Strengths-Based Schools and Learning Adjustment Challenges

Students who are labeled learning disabled have strengths that may not be measured by a school, if that school focuses only on linguistic and mathematic strengths. All too often, the strengths of children labeled learning disabled are smothered by an educational system that focuses more at what they cannot do rather than what they can do.

Statistics on the prevalence of exceptionality suggest that 2 to 5 percent of American schoolchildren can be expected to have a learning disability.[20] Their differences in learning may cause them to underachieve and to lose motivation. Learning disabilities are difficulties children have with skills such as listening, reading, writing, spelling, or speaking. These skill impairments may not necessarily affect a child's overall intelligence. Most learning disabled children have normal or high intelligence, and some may be gifted. Students with learning disabilities may have strengths in painting, drawing, music, drama, and athletics. Yet these gifts may be masked by the intense pressure for them to succeed according to linguistic and mathematical standards.

The more educators discover about learning disabilities in children, the more they understand that such disabilities do not have to limit children and their later achievement in life. Consider, for example, the condition known as dyslexia, which is a condition recognized most commonly for causing difficulties in reading, spelling, and detailed manipulation of words and numbers. Dyslexia is usually treated as a pathological or deficit problem—a learning disability. Although dyslexia does create problems and difficulties in certain areas for children, there are also positive aspects of this condition. Often, dyslexic people have above-average abilities in physical coordination, mathematics, creativity, and spatial visualization.

Some notable famous people who have been diagnosed with dyslexia include: Alexander Graham Bell, inventor of the telephone; Albert Einstein, creator of the theory of relativity; Pierre Curie, physicist and 1903 Nobel Prize winner; Sir Richard Branson, entrepreneur; Cher, singer and actress; Charles Schwab, founder of a brokerage firm; Jay Leno, television host; Tom Cruise, actor; George W. Bush, former

President of the United States; and Winston Churchill, former British prime minister.

Dr. Mel Levine,[21] a pioneer in the field of neurodevelopment and learning and professor at the University of North Carolina, has developed a theory involving eight constructs of neurodevelopment that influence learning. Each person develops a combination of all eight constructs; however, each person has different strengths and weakness areas. These eight constructs are as follows:

- Attention (what we focus on)
- Memory (long-term memory, short-term memory, working memory)
- Temporal sequential (how we sequence things in time).
- Spatial learning (how we arrange, space, and perceive objects)
- Language (how we take in and put out verbal information)
- Motor skills (how our body interacts with the learning environment)
- Social cognition (how we interact with others)
- Higher order cognition (how we solve complex problems, evaluate, innovate)

Each student is given a profile and the profile is shared with the student in a process known as demystification. As students are let in on information about how they learn, they become self-advocates for their own learning. The learning process become more manageable because areas of strength are highlighted.

Learning Strengths

It is important for teachers to have some method for uncovering and communicating with students their learning strengths. Teachers can use either Gardner's multiple intelligence framework or Levine's eight-construct process. I recommend using Gardner's approach because so much research has been conducted using this framework. After completing an assessment instrument using Gardner's multiple intelligence theory, the teacher might also give students an instrument to measure their learning style. Based on the information that the teacher has obtained from students' scores on a multiple intelligence inventory and a learning styles inventory, he or she then develops a learning strength profile for each student. The teacher discusses with each student his or her learning strengths, as measured by these two instruments. Table 5.1 is a learning strength profile I have developed based on Gardner's multiple intelligence profile. The profile is typically completed by the teacher. Students, however, should have access to their own chart of their learning strengths and learning style preferences.

Table 5.1 Learning Strengths Chart

Learning	High Strength	Medium Strength	Low Strength	Functional Competency	Weakness
1. Linguistic Intelligence (Verbal)					
2. Logical-Mathematical Intelligence					
3. Musical Intelligence					
4. Bodily-Kinesthetic Intelligence					
5. Spatial Intelligence					
6. Interpersonal Intelligence (Relationships with Others)					
7. Intrapersonal Intelligence (Self-Knowledge)					
8. *Naturalistic Intelligence					
9. Auditory Learning Preference (Learning by Hearing)					
10. Visual Learning Preference (Learning by Seeing)					
11. Kinesthetic Learning Preference (Learning by Doing)					

Note: Copyright © Elsie J. Smith.

Learning Strategies and the Bloom Taxonomy

Students are usually engaged only in lower order thinking—meaning that they receive or participate in routine educational practice. Typically, students do not go beyond the simple reproduction of knowledge. In contrast, when students engage in higher order thinking they transform information and ideas. This transformation takes place when students combine facts and ideas. As they do so, they begin to synthesize, generalize, or arrive at some conclusion or interpretation. Higher order thinking results in students' becoming producers of knowledge. The teacher's primary instructional task is to create activities or environments that allow them opportunities to engage in higher order thinking. During the 1950s, Benjamin Bloom[22] developed a taxonomy of cognitive objectives. Bloom's taxonomy provided a way to organize thinking skills into six levels from the most basic to the higher order levels of thinking. During the 1990s, Lorin Anderson (former student of Bloom) revised the taxonomy. Table 5.2 incorporates learning strengths, learning style, and Bloom's taxonomy of cognitive objectives as a handout that teachers might use with their students.

Tables 5.1 and 5.2 can be of immense help to teachers and students who desire to use students' strengths for their learning assignments. Strengths-based schools focus on the strengths of students who are categorized as learning disabled. Every Individual Education Plan and functional behavioral assessment should list a student's strengths that can be used to deal with the academic or social challenge. Teachers determine how the actual disability functions to limit the student's academic achievement, and then they develop strategies to limit the manifestation of the disability.

STRENGTHS-BASED EDUCATIONAL MODEL

This section examines several components of a strengths-based model. It discusses features of a strengths discovery and assessment program; instructional steps a teacher might use in implementing a strengths approach; KIDTAP,[23] a strengths-based approach to curriculum assessment; and a strengths-based report card and cumulative record. I provide a student strengths chart and a description of strengths memories.

Strengths Discovery and Assessment Program

All students are required to undergo a strengths discovery process as part of their yearly academic and personal growth program. All too

Table 5.2   My Own Learning Strength Chart

My Top 3 Learning Strengths
Strength 1:
Strength 2:
Strength 3:

I Can Describe My Strengths
My Description of Strength 1:
My Description of Strength 2:

I Prefer to Learn by:
Hearing:
Seeing:
Doing:

Difficult Ways for Me to Learn
1st Difficult Way for Me to Learn:
2nd Difficult Way for Me to Learn:
3rd Difficult Way for Me to Learn:

I Recognize When to Use My Strengths
I will use my _____ strength to complete my _____ assignment.
I will use my _____ strength to complete my _____ assignment.
I will use my _____ strength to complete my _____ assignment.

I Evaluate Learning Challenges I Face
My learning challenge in completing Assignment 1 is:
My learning challenge in completing Assignment 2 is:

Learning Strategy and Bloom's Taxonomy
Bloom's taxonomy deals with higher order thinking and lists the six types of
thinking that students engage in—from the most basic to the higher order levels
of thinking. Students should complete this chart by listing the kind of thinking
or learning strategy they will use.

**Remembering: I am able to recall, restate, and remember learned information.
I will check below each of the *remembering* learning strategies that I will use to
complete this assignment.**
I can recognize.
I can list.
I can describe.
I can identify.
I can retrieve.
I can name.
I can locate.
I can give an example.
I can repeat.
I can label.
I can memorize key points.

(continued)

Understanding: I am able to understand the meaning of the information I learned by interpreting and translating what has been learned. I will check below each of the *understanding* learning strategies that I use to complete this assignment.

I can interpret.
I can summarize.
I can paraphrase.
I can classify.
I can compare.
I can explain ideas and concepts.
I can discuss.
I can give the main idea.
I can outline.
I can define.
I can give a report.

Applying: I am able to make use of information I learned in a different context from the one in which I learned it. I will check below each of the *applying* learning strategies that I will use to complete this assignment.

I can use the information I learned in another situation.
I can illustrate what I learned.
I can demonstrate what I learned.
I can practice what I learned.
I can adapt what I learned to another situation.
I can translate what I learned.
I can solve problems related to what I learned.
I can calculate what I learned.
I can sequence what I learned.
I can manipulate what I learned.
I can paint a mural, make a game about the topic, make a model of what I learned.

Analyzing: I have learned to break information into its parts so that I can explore my understandings and relationships. I check below each of the *analyzing* learning strategies that I will use to complete this assignment.

I can discuss what I learned.
I can debate different sides of what I learned.
I can diagram what I learned.
I can make a flowchart to show the sequence or order of what I learned.
I can think deeply about what I learned.
I can outline what I learned.
I can conduct a survey related to what I learned.
I can uncover issues related to what I learned.
I can arrange what I learned.
I can question what I learned.

Evaluating: I can make in-depth reflection, criticism, and assessments related to what I have learned. I check below each of the *evaluating* learning strategies that I will use to complete this assignment.

 I can make judgments about what I have learned.

 I can make hypotheses about what I have learned.

 I can justify a decision or course of action related to what I learned.

 I can question what I have learned.

 I can appraise issues related to what I have learned.

 I can make predictions related to what I have learned.

 I can give a speech about what I have learned.

 I can evaluate what I have learned.

 I can compare what I have learned.

 I can contrast what I have learned.

 I can prepare a list of criteria to make judgments about what I have learned.

Creating: I know how to create new ideas and information using what I previously learned. I check below each of the *creating* learning strategies that I will use to complete this assignment.

 I can generate new ideas or ways of viewing what I have learned.

 I can see a possible solution to the problems described in what I learned.

 I can devise my own way of dealing with the issues presented in what I learned.

 I can develop a proposal related to what I learned.

 I can design an artistic product related to what I have learned.

 I can create a film about what I learned.

 I can create a new product related to what I learned.

 I can sell an idea related to what I have learned.

 I can write an advertisement about what I have learned.

 I can compose a song about what I have learned.

 I can write a jingle about what I have learned.

Learning Strategy for Assignment 1: _____

Learning Strategy for Assignment 2: _____

Learning Strategy for Assignment 3: _____

Strategies I Chose for Dealing with Learning Weaknesses

Strategy 1 for dealing with learning weakness in Assignment 1:_____

Strategy 2 for dealing with learning weakness in Assignment 2:_____

Note: Copyright © Elsie J. Smith.

often young people have no idea of their strengths or of what they really want to do. Instead, they have more of a sense of what they do not want to do.

Strengths-based assessment is needed to combat a deficit approach to assessment. Deficit-oriented assessments focus on a student's limitations, deficits, problems, pathologies, and weaknesses. Although deficit-oriented assessments provide important information, they tend to describe only one aspect of the student—what is wrong with him or her rather than what is right. Epstein and Sharma[24] have described strengths-based assessment "as the measurement of those emotional and behavioral skills, competencies and characteristics that create a sense of personal accomplishment; contribute to satisfying relationships with family members, peers and adults; enhance one's ability to deal with adversity and stress; and promote one's personal, social and academic development." Strengths-based assessments can be informal "strengths chats" or they can be formal assessments wherein a professional asks a series of questions about the family and a child. Included with this presentation is a publication, "Strength-Based Assessment Toolkit," which focuses on the guidance counselor's relationship with young people in schools and mental health settings.

Teaching Metacognition Skills: A Strengths-Based Approach to Learning

Strengths-based learning involves adopting the principles from *How People Learn: Bridging Research and Practice*,[25] especially that report's delineation of metacognitive strategies for learning. Defined most simply, metacognition is "thinking about thinking." The term *metacognition* is usually associated with John Flavel,[26] who asserted that metacognition consists of both metacognitive knowledge and metacognitive experiences. Metacognition helps students to be successful learners. It refers to higher order thinking, which involves active control over the cognitive processes engage in learning. Some metacognitive activities include planning how to approach a given learning task, monitoring comprehension, and evaluating progress toward the completion of a task.

LEARNING: A GAME OF CHESS

If you have ever played the game of chess, you learn to develop a strategy for winning.

Learning is a lot like playing chess. You have to develop your own personal strategy for learning.

You have to understand how you best learn—gain metacognitive skills.

Teachers in strengths-based school teach students how to use their intrapersonal knowledge to improve their learning. In a study with eight- and nine-year-old children who were low-achieving in English, Sellars[27] introduced them to a program specifically designed to promote their self-knowledge as learners and to establish how such self-knowledge may be used to improve their self-management skills in English. As students became aware of their own relative strengths, they used this information to negotiate their learning environment. More specifically, they identified learning strategies that worked for them, and they took increasingly more responsibility for their own learning.

Strengths-based teaching involves helping students to understand their strengths and how they best learn. Learning tasks are accomplished using a variety of different learning strategies; however, all too often teachers may impose a learning strategy on students that does not reflect how they best learn. Many students fail simply because they do not understand what works for them in the learning process. They use ineffective learning strategies that may reflect primarily their teacher's metacognitive strategy. Once students learn their strengths through a strengths discovery and assessment process, teachers introduce them to various learning strategies to help them determine what the best learning strategies are for them. Some metacognitive learning strategies are:

Strategy	Steps
Plan/Organize	Plan the content of the task to be completed.
	Set goals.
	Plan how to complete the assignment.
Manage Your Own Learning	Determine how you learn best.
	Establish conditions that help you to learn.
	Focus your attention on the task at hand.
Monitor	As you work on a task or assignment:
	Check your progress on the task.
	Check your comprehension of the language associated with the academic subject or task at hand.
	Are you understanding what you have to do? Do you know what might be blocking your understanding?
Evaluate	After finishing an assignment or task:
	Assess how well you have accomplished the learning task.
	Assess how well you have applied the strategies.

(continued)

(Continued)

Strategy	Steps
	Decide how effective the strategies were in helping you to accomplish this assignment/task.
Cooperate	Work with others to complete tasks, build confidence, and give and receive feedback.
Talk Yourself Through It	"I can do it." Reduce your anxiety by reminding yourself of your prior progress, the resources you have available to you, and your goals.

Strengths-Based Instructional Steps

The strengths approach to academic achievement involves five basic steps for teachers, school counselors, and parents. These steps form part of the academic curriculum and part of parental teaching of children.

Step 1: Communicate to the youth/adult a strengths attitude and belief in his or her ability to achieve academically or in other areas. Adopt a strengths-based attitude.

Step 2: Challenge negative thoughts and replace them with positive actions to take or solutions.

Step 3: Adopt a strengths focus to problem solving. The youth decides what strengths are needed to tackle the issue or academic challenge at hand. Perspective taking is central to this step.

Step 4: Teach students metacognitive skills; that is, teach them to discover how they best learn. Strengths-based teaching involves teaching young people intrapersonal knowledge about how they best learn and metacognitive skills to monitor their learning.

Step 5: Promote strengths-competency development. The youth uses strengths to deal successfully with an academic challenge or issue. Strengthen the brain neural pathways.

Step 6: Evaluate strengths. Help students to evaluate what strengths they used in completing a task and how effective the use of a particular strength was for them.

Strengths-Based Report Card and Cumulative Record

Strengths-based schools redesign student report cards to reflect their overall accomplishments and achievements. Report cards deal with students' strengths related to the 10 life skills as well as to their grades.

Cumulative records are also required to provide information about students' progress on strengths. Parents respond favorably when the strengths of their children are noted on their report cards.

Students should have cumulative record cards that follow them emphasizing strengths they have shown since their enrollment in school. In this way, teachers get an idea of which strengths have developed or been nourished by the school. Table 5.3 consists of a positive format that teachers might use in recording students' strengths.

Table 5.3   Student Strengths Chart

1.	**Academic:** English, Math, Science, Reading, Social Studies					
2.	**School Activities Strengths:** School Government, School Clubs, School Sports, Art, Drama					
3.	**Community Activities:** Community Service, Religious, Spiritual					
4.	**Family Bonding**					
5.	**Teacher Relationships**					
6.	**Problem-Solving Skills**					
7.	**Interpersonal Skills**					
8.	**Personal Appearance**					
9.	**Communication Skills**					
10.	**Inner Emotional Strengths:** Sense of Humor, Coping Skills, Resilience					
11.	**Inner Circle of Support Strengths:** Family, School Friends, Community Friends, Church					
12.	**Cultural and Ethnic Strengths**					
13.	**Spirituality**					
14.	**Creativity**					
15.	**Analytical and Cognitive**					
16.	**Wisdom**					
17.	**Relational and Nurturing**					
18.	**Survival**					
19.	**Other**					
20.						

Note: Copyright © Elsie J. Smith.

Creating Hope Symbols

Have students create hope symbols that they can refer to or carry with them. For instance, one student mentioned that a friend had given him a little elephant with the student's birthstone near the elephant's trunk. The student decided to use the elephant as his hope symbol. When he felt low in hope, he would take the elephant out and engage in positive self-talk about his dreams.

Strength Memories

Ask students to remember a time in their lives when they displayed good strength and to keep this image in mind while planning and working toward goals. For instance, one student had been an excellent soccer player during his youth, winning many medals. During a teacher-led learning circle, the student recounted playing soccer as one of his strengths. To engage the student in class and to help him deal with anxiety about his academic performance, the teacher asked him to get a picture in his mind of himself winning one of his prized soccer medals. Every time that he went for a job interview or took a step toward reaching one of his goals, he was asked to first take a few seconds to ready himself with his strengths memory.

KIDTAP: A Strengths-Based Approach to Curriculum Assessment

The KIDTAP[28] model is a strengths-based approach to curriculum development and assessment. The Virginia Department of Education has trained teachers in the use of the Gickling model of curriculum-based assessment. An important feature of this model emphasizes maintaining students at their instructional level or their comfort zone. The purpose of assessment is not to create fear or anxiety for the student but rather to discover what the student knows and can do. The Gickling or KIDTAP model provides a means of identifying student strengths to inform teacher intervention and instruction. The model is designed to find out what students know and can do so that instructional interventions can be designed to accelerate learning. The KIDTAP curriculum-based assessment model contains five questions:

1. *Know*: What does the student know? Prior student knowledge is considered the foundation of learning. To retain new information, students must be able to connect such material to prior knowledge. The issue of

what kinds of skills and information the student already has is a critical one.

2. *Do*: What can the student do? The task on which the student is to be assessed should represent and be linked with prior knowledge. If the task is too difficult, the student may not be able to show what he or she actually knows. When students are asked to perform at their instructional level, the teacher's assessment will indicate the kinds of skills they already have.

3. *Think*: How does the student think? The teacher asks students to think aloud and explain how they arrived at the answer. This question is based on the underlying assumption that by knowing how a student thinks, a teacher is in a better position to deal constructively with what the student needs to know.

4. *Approach*: How does a student approach what he or she is unsure of? The teacher observes the student on task and evaluates how persistent he or she is and how much frustration he or she can tolerate before giving up.

5. *Plan*: As a teacher, what have I learned that will help me plan for the student's instructional plan? The teacher examines what skills the student can perform, the demands of the task for the student, and any disparity or gap between the two. Instruction focuses on filling the gap between what the student can do and the demands of the learning task. Essentially, the instructional methods must connect with the student's strengths.

SUMMARY

Far too often schools have focused on correcting young people's weaknesses, and recording such weaknesses on student report cards and cumulative records. In our haste to correct these weaknesses, educators and parents have failed to note and nurture young people's strengths. Yet, what really matters in the adult real world are a person's strengths. Real achievement occurs in an area of a person's strengths.

This chapter reviewed four broad areas. First, statistical data on American achievement versus international achievement was examined. Our public schools are simply not working—at least not very well. For the most part, the average American public school was designed for an age that has long since passed—the industrial age. The world is now well into the computer and technology age. Numerous research studies have documented the declining performance of American students as they progress from K to 12. The deficit approach to teaching young people has just not worked very well.

Strengths-based schools can assume a major role in establishing a meaningful educational framework for working with students from diverse backgrounds. Teachers in such schools communicate to their students that "what is right about you is more important than anything that is wrong with you."

Our American national educational gardens are in need of replanting and recultivating to a different format. A strong connection was made between the poor performance of the American educational system and the prospects for our long-term national growth. More specifically, if the American people were to focus concerted national attention on improving the U.S. educational system, the long-term return on this investment would be great—in the trillions of dollars. If nothing is done to improve the academic achievement of American students in math, science, technology, and problem solving, the future does not look very bright.

The chapter discussed the role of learning styles and learning strengths on students' academic achievement. Strengths charts were presented to help teachers develop strategies for working with students. KIDTAP was discussed as a strengths-based approach to curriculum assessment.

Component 3: Caring and Empathic Classrooms

WHAT MAKES A GARDEN? WHAT MAKES A CLASS A COMMUNITY?

I remember the day I first planted flowers in front of my new home. I had always liked flowers. Once I started planting the garden, I found that I could not stop at just the one or two flowers that I had originally intended to plant to "spark" things up a bit. So I began adding a few more and then a few more of my favorites. One day, one of my neighbor's walked by and said, "You have a beautiful garden. Let's see." She stood back looking at it for a moment, then asked, "What shall I call it?" I looked in wonderment at her. I had not thought of what I had planted as a garden but simply as a bed of flowers.

"I know," she said finally. "I'll call it Elsie's garden." I stood there for a few seconds in the early summer sun, deeply pleased that she had called what I had created a garden and that she had even named the garden. Since I have planted that garden, people stop for a minute or two on their way to or from work usually or sometimes during their leisurely stroll, and they comment on the garden. Several people told me my garden gave them a sense of pleasure just watching it grow. My garden, bring feelings of happiness in others? Wow, that was a pleasant unintended reward. But that is the way gardens are. Gardens are not just for the people who create them.

I thought about at what moment my bed of flowers had turned into a garden. True gardens are more than an aggregation of individual flowers. My thoughts traveled to what I had read about Chinese gardens. Traditionally, Chinese gardens are designed to provide a spiritual shelter for its people, a place where they can be far away from

---

WHAT PROMOTES LEARNING

- Learning has more to do with emotions than with IQ.
- Students' strengths serve to motivate them.

---

their daily social lives and in touch with their real selves—a kind of back-to-nature life. Chinese people use plants as symbols. For instance, most traditional Chinese gardens use bamboo because it represents a strong resilient character. Pine is used to symbolize longevity, persistence, tenacity, and dignity. Another important staple of traditional Chinese gardens is the flowering plum, which represents renewal and strength of will. Whereas the chrysanthemum is placed in Chinese gardens to symbolize splendor, peonies symbolize wealth.

Gardens are almost invariably metaphors for something else. The same question that I raised about my own garden—when does a bed of flowers become a garden—can be raised about a teacher's class. When does a teacher's class become a classroom community rather than just a group of 20–30 kids required to stay there for so many hours during the day? I maintain that a class becomes a community when its members really care about one another, when they express empathy toward one another, and when the teacher treats the students as if they really matter to her or him and to the school.

This chapter focuses on the caring and empathic classroom as an essential part of a strengths-based school. The first section of the chapter defines empathy and a caring classroom. It involves input to the brain from different intelligences, including interpersonal intelligence and empathy. Downshifting takes place when a young person goes from the thinking mode to the survival mode. When students are in a survival mode due to emotions, they are unable to learn. Teachers should help create a climate that is conducive to learning. They must learn how to talk so that students listen. The second section of this chapter is on building a classroom community. A key feature of such a classroom community depends on promoting student relationship strengths. The concept of mattering is examined. Approaches to teaching empathy, especially the skill of empathetic listening, are discussed.

The biggest challenge facing educators is how to engage students. Student motivation is at the center of engaging students. It is the best predictor of academic success because it fuels student effort and persistence. Engaged learning is a positive energy invested in one's own

> ### THE CONNECTION BETWEEN EMPATHY AND STRENGTH
>
> We become stronger when we have the emotional resources to view the world as the other person sees it.

learning. It is evidenced by meaningful mental processing, attention to what is happening in the moment, and participation in learning activities. When teachers focus on students' strengths, students not only become focused but they tend to persist on an academic task. A strengths-based approach promotes students' achievement because strengths awareness leads to student' having self-confidence and a sense of self-efficacy, which in turn increases their motivation to excel and their engagement in the learning process.[1]

EMPATHY AND A CARING CLASSROOM

What Is Empathy?

Both Daniel Goleman,[2] renowned writer on emotional intelligence, and Howard Gardner,[3] author of the multiple intelligence theory, have written about the importance of empathy. Gardner listed interpersonal intelligence and empathy as part of his eight intelligences. According to him, we are also social animals who thrive and grow when we are involved with others. Gardner called this ability to interact with others, understand them, and interpret their behavior, interpersonal intelligence. Gardner described interpersonal intelligence as how we "notice distinction among others; in particular, contrasts in their moods, temperaments, motivations and intentions."[4] Interpersonal intelligence involves our ability to work cooperatively with others in a group as well as our ability to communicate verbally and nonverbally with them. People who have very high interpersonal intelligence have the ability to read other people's intentions and desires.

Moreover, the connection between interpersonal intelligence and the brain has been well established. Empathy is a right-brain activity. If damage is done to the frontal lobe, as was once the case with lobotomy patients, you damage that person's ability to interact well with others. Empathy constitutes an important part of effective relationships. Empathy helps us to create bonds of trust with others, and it provides insights into how others might be feeling or thinking.

Empathy can be defined as "putting yourself in someone else's shoes or seeing things through someone else's eyes."

Interpersonal intelligence allows us to influence others by understanding them; without it, we are severely restricted in our interactions with others. People who score high in interpersonal intelligence excel at group work and collaborative projects. This type of intelligence is highly correlated with empathy for another's feelings, fears, and beliefs. Some of the people who are said to be high on interpersonal intelligence are counselors, politicians, salespeople, and teachers.

Basing part of his work on Gardner's theory of interpersonal intelligence, Goleman has outlined three kinds of empathy: cognitive, emotional, and compassionate. *Cognitive empathy* involves simply knowing how another person feels and what they might be thinking. Goleman reported that a study at the University of Birmingham revealed that managers who were good at perspective taking inspired workers to give their best efforts. Gardner points out, however, that there can be a dark side to this type of empathy. Narcissists, Machiavellians, and sociopaths are talented in *cognitive empathy* but they lack sympathy for their victims. For most crises, cognitive empathy alone is insufficient.

The second type of empathy is called *emotional empathy.* This form of empathy takes place when you feel physically with the other person, as if their emotions are contagious. *Emotional empathy* helps you to become sensitive to another person's inner emotional world. There is a downside to *emotional empathy* when we are unable to detach ourselves from the emotions that are taking place in another person's life. Hence, *emotional empathy* can lead to professional burnout in the case of teachers and counselors.

Compassionate empathy or empathic concern takes place when we not only understand another person's situation and feel with them but also are moved to help, if needed. Counselors are required to demonstrate empathic concern in that they enter the client's world as if it were their own, but always remain professionally detached in order to help the client.

When people have empathy competence, they have a good awareness of others' emotions, concerns, and needs. The empathic person senses emotional currents in a room, picking up on nonverbal clues such as a person's tone of voice or facial expression. Empathy awareness also requires that a person have self-awareness or self-understanding. Our understanding of the feelings of others emanates from our awareness of our own feelings. Typically, young people with well-developed empathy bond well with parents and significant others. They form and maintain healthy social relationships. They acknowledge and communicate effectively with others on both a verbal and a nonverbal level. They acknowledge the feelings, thoughts, and motivations of those with whom they come into contact. What does empathy help students to do? The ability to empathize helps students to:

- Demonstrate an understanding of (and respect for) others' point of views
- Appreciate how others might be feeling
- Understand that their actions might affect other people in both positive and negative ways
- Be able to read the verbal and nonverbal signals of a person, and be able to change their approach in response to those signals.
- Realize that all people have different feelings based on their experiences.
- Understand that their feelings may be manifested in different ways, depending upon the circumstances.

Empathy as a Relationship Strength

Empathy is a relational strength. It involves the ability to form high-quality, deep, personal understanding and relationships. Empathy is powerful because when you give it to others, they feel deeply understood. Although it may be difficult to listen to the pain of others, they will feel deeply indebted to you. Students respond to teachers because they care about their students and because they are able to demonstrate that they understand their students' feelings. A student walked into my class one day and slammed her books on her desk. "I hate this school," she said. "I absolutely hate this school." Realizing that she was upset about something, I asked her if it were okay for us to talk about what had happened. She started to cry—big sobs—and the rest of the kids were walking into the class and wondering what was going on. I asked the class if we could have a private moment, and the two of us walked outside the classroom, standing next to the door. When we came back in, one of the students looked at her and said, "Hey, don't sweat it," and gave her a smile. I was grateful that the class understood that the student needed my time and that they allowed me to give attention to her undisturbed. The student appreciated the fact that no one was laughing at her as we walked back into the classroom. On the contrary, the class understood that she was experiencing difficulties, and students put themselves in her place—empathy.

SCHOOL CONNECTEDNESS

The school connectedness bond is second only to the power of parents on young people.

School connectedness changes the life trajectory of youth.

When teachers show empathy for their students, they establish a caring classroom. Kids feel that they can truly express their feelings. They feel a sense of trust and relationship with the teacher and their classmates. Teacher empathy is also closely related to student strengths development. Strengths development takes place most easily within the context of a trusted relationship. When teachers express empathy for students, they indicate that they understand their students' feelings, desires, and hopes.

Empathy and School Connectedness: Two Sides of the Same Coin

Empathy is closely aligned with school connectedness. Both provide a sense of bonding for a young person. School connectedness is defined as student belief that adults in the school care about their learning and about them as individuals.

School connectedness has become a major area of research for educators because studies have shown its importance in students' lives. When students feel connected to their schools, they achieve better academically, and they evidence better overall health.[5] According to Robert Blum and his associates, kids who feel connected to school smoked less, drank alcohol less, had a later age of first sexual experience, and attempted suicide less frequently.[6] Blum stated, "There is something in that bond, in that connection to school that changes the life trajectory—at least the health and academic behavior. It is very powerful—second only in power to the bonding with parents. In some contexts it's more powerful than parents."[7]

Yet, connectedness is not just for students. When teachers do not feel connected to a school, it may be hard for them to help their students feel connected to the school. A similar situation exists for school personnel, including custodians, cafeteria workers, paraprofessionals, and secretaries. In addition, parents need to feel a sense of connection with their children's schools, and community members must be engaged with students for youth to feel connected.[8]

What Is the Significance of Positive School Connectedness?

The answer to this question is provided in part by the Adolescent Health Study, a comprehensive school-based study of the health-related behaviors of adolescents in the United States. The study was conducted between 1994 and 1995 for more than 90,000 students in Grades 7–12 who attended 132 U.S. schools. These students answered questions about their lives. Likewise administrators at the participating schools also completed a questionnaire. As researchers analyzed the data, they found compelling evidence for school connectedness. Michael Resnick and his colleagues[9] report that school connectedness was a protective factor for young people. The Add Health study measured school connectedness based on students' responses to the following on a five-point scale from "strongly agree" to "strongly disagree":

"How strongly do you agree or disagree with each of the following statements?

- I feel close to people at this school.
- I am happy to be at this school.
- I feel like I am part of this school.
- The teachers at this school treat students fairly.
- I feel safe in my school.[10]

School connectedness affects almost every area of a student's life, not just their academic performance. Students who experience a sense of connectedness to school are:

- Less inclined to use alcohol and illegal drugs
- Less inclined to engage in violent or deviant behavior
- Less inclined to become pregnant
- Less inclined to experience emotional distress and suicidal thoughts
- More likely to earn higher grades and test scores
- Less likely to drop out of school

Dimensions of Connectedness

School connectedness is influenced by three major factors: (1) individuals (students and school staff), environment (school climate and school bonding), and (3) the culture of the school (social needs and learning priorities). Heather Libbey[11] conducted an extensive review of the research literature and found that there were consistent factors that indicated students' sense of connectedness at school.

- *Student academic engagement*. This variable involves the extent to which students are motivated to learn and do well in school.
- *Student sense of belonging*. This factor includes being proud of one's school, feeling respected, being able to talk to teachers, and feeling like school staff are interested in students.
- *Student perception of fairness in discipline*. Fairness perception deals with the extent to which students perceive the rules of the school to be enforced fairly.
- *Student feeling that they like their school*. Students feel positive about their school and they looked forward to going to school.
- *Student participation in extracurricular activities*. Students participate in after-school activities.
- *Student belief that they have a voice in the running of the school*. This variable includes giving students opportunities to participate in decision making.
- *Student perception of positive peer relations*. Students have friends at the school and experience positive relations with their classmates.
- *Student belief that they are safe in school*. Students report that they feel safe in school.
- *Student perception of teacher support and caring*. The most common theme that emerged from the literature review was whether or not students feel close to or valued by teachers and school staff.

Developing a Strengths-Based School Culture

One way of investing in children is to develop a strengths-based culture where they feel encouraged, heard, and supported. A strengths-based culture is one where there is a shared vision that teachers and students are a team. Teachers let young people know that the problem is the problem; the *person is not the problem*. Caring schools start with the premise that most young people have good intentions and that they have tried sometime in the past to deal with the problem behavior. Teachers point out to young people that problems can blind them from noticing and appreciating their strengths.

In an effort to create caring schools, some schools have instituted practices such as looping (teachers stay with the same students for two or more years) and block scheduling to connect students with their schools. Strengths-based schools have a foundation of caring that is achieved by the schoolwide program of 10 skills of life, as well as by circles of learning and classroom meetings. A key feature of the caring school is establishing mutual respect between teachers and students and among the student body. In addition, caring schools establish schoolwide activities and goals that bring students and teachers together.

In establishing caring, strengths-based schools, school personnel should take into account the developmental stage and age of the children. Elementary school students place a great deal of importance on their relationships with teachers. Does my teacher like me? Does my teacher care about me?[12] Middle and high school students feel most connected to schools when they have opportunities for autonomy as well as opportunities to demonstrate competence, and that they receive caring and support from adults.[13] They tend to be interested in how their peers perceive them. They want to know that their peers like them and perceive them as competent and as worthy of respect. These children are inclined to be preoccupied with answering questions such as:

- Do I fit in with my group?
- Do my classmates accept me?
- Do I have friends?
- Am I competent?
- How do I measure up to my classmates?

To achieve acceptance by their peers, children and adolescents must acquire social and emotional competence. That is, they must be able to identify and regulate their emotions, to relate positively to others, and to make friends. Children who have social-emotional competence achieve at a higher level than those who lack such competence. Social skills linked to academic success include a young person's ability to:

- Express feelings
- Recognize feelings in others
- Share ideas with others
- Listen when others are speaking
- Take turns and share
- Accept different points of view
- Respect each other's belongings and physical space

Social competence is best developed when children are young— before negative and disruptive behavior patterns have become entrenched. When children do not develop social skills during their early years, they stand a greater chance of becoming disruptive in the classroom, failing to do their work, attacking their peers, and subsequently dropping out of school. Once negative acting-out behaviors become entrenched within a young person, difficulties with the law tend to emerge.

BUILDING A CLASSROOM COMMUNITY

What Is a Classroom Community?

Sue Bredekamp and Teresa Rosegrant[14] have defined community as a place where people share common values, goals, and activities. Each member assumes different roles to provide services so that the community's goals are reached. In a community, individuals establish social bonds. Similar to communities within a society, every classroom has its own distinct culture, values, and rules. Empathic, caring, strengths-based schools endeavor to build a classroom community.

Haley David and Robert Capraro[15] have proposed that a classroom community should provide each child "with space to develop specific capabilities and to experience a sense of inner balance and wholeness in a community with others." Children experience a need to participate as a contributing member of a community. A classroom community addresses young people's basic needs, encourages their resilience to life's difficulties, teaches them the values of respect and responsibility, and promotes their social and academic competence. Teachers build a classroom community when they help develop a child's sense of positive self-esteem, make their classroom expectations clear, and model caring and empathic behavior for their students. According to David and Capraro, "students should develop a process of understanding, sharing, compassion and empathy." Teachers should refer to "our classroom" rather than "my classroom."

Building Inclusive Classrooms

Building a classroom community should involve creating a classroom atmosphere of inclusion for all students, especially those with disabilities. Students with diagnosed disabilities also have strengths, just as other students have strengths. All too frequently, however, the emphasis is on the weaknesses of a child with special needs. Typically, educators spend years of remedial work trying to fix a child's learning disability rather than capitalizing on his or her strengths. Dr. Robert Brooks, child psychologist and recognized authority on attention deficit hyperactivity disorder, has talked about children with disabilities having "islands of competence." Brooks noted that he and his colleague Dr. Sam Goldstein conceived of the term more than 20 years ago after listening to young kids who were struggling with learning problems and who had experienced a great deal of frustration and failure in their lives. Some of their comments reflected a sense of help-lessness and hopelessness. A sample of their statements includes:

- "I was born with half a brain. Do you know how to fill in the other half?"
- "I feel stupid. I feel I will never learn."
- "I think I'm not smart enough to ever get a job."
- "I can't think of anything that I am good at."[16]

While reflecting upon such negative comments, Brooks and Gold-stein came up with the phrase "islands of competence"—that is, areas that have been or have the potential of becoming sources of pride and accomplishment for a young person. The metaphor was intended to evoke an image of shifting one's focus from young people's weak-nesses to their strengths. Young people with learning problems often struggle with depression and feelings of low self-esteem. If a young person has a learning disability, teachers should consider behavioral supports that encourage him or her, and they should explore every area in which the youth has performed well. Teachers might focus on testing students' knowledge, not their disability.

Sometimes technology can provide a great boost to students who have learning disabilities. Youth who are easily distracted can evidence focused attention when their eyes are watching a computer screen. Moreover, youth with writing problems can show rapid improvement if they use a computer. The technology contained within the computer levels the playing field for young people with disabilities.

If teachers focus on the strengths of students who have learning dis-abilities and are in a mainstreamed class, then class members are inclined to be more accepting of the student. Moreover, the teaching of respect for all students in strengths-based classrooms reduces instances of name-calling and ridiculing of students with disabilities.

Building a Classroom Community with a Wall of Strengths

Just as every garden has its strengths, so do classrooms. Strengths-based teachers work under the assumption that every student has at least one strength to offer the class. The teacher begins by asking students to identify one strength that they have. Teachers also engage in a strengths discovery and assessment process as discussed in chapter 5.

A major goal is to develop the theme of classroom strengths. Teach-ers need to be able to identify the strengths of the entire class. For in-stance, a classroom strength might be class members' ability to get along with each other or to work quietly, regardless of whether the teacher is in the classroom or just outside the door. Classroom strengths tend to come from the manner in which the class interacts interpersonally as a group. However, classroom strengths can also relate to academic achievement or achievement in the arts. For instance, our class was instrumental in developing the props for the school play or providing the singing and dancing.

The first step in building a community of classroom strengths is to build a strengths-based profile for each student. Such a profile provides important data for communicating with that student, parents, and other school staff. Identifying strengths can be done in a number of ways depending on the teacher's end goals. Each student has his or her name, picture, and a brief strength profile next to their picture. Teachers not only post students' strengths on the classroom wall of strengths, but also they refer to them when appropriate during class. Table 6.1 provides an example of a way of examining students' strengths and goals.

Table 6.1   Student Strengths and Goals

Hello, my name is _____
My top three strengths are:
    1. _____
    2. _____
    3. _____
My strengths help me to:
    1. _____
    2. _____
    3. _____
My goal(s) this year are:
    1. _____
    2. _____
    3. _____
I intend to use my strengths to help me achieve my goals:
    Goal 1 Strength to be Used _____
    Goal 2 Strength to be Used _____
    Goal 3 Strength to be Used _____
Domain strengths:
    1. I use this strength to help me learn in school _____
    2. I use this strength to help my family _____
    3. I use this strength to help my community _____

Note: Copyright © Elsie J. Smith.

Table 6.2 Our Classroom Wall of Strengths

- We treat each person with courtesy and respect.
- We communicate effectively and listen to each other.
- We work together cooperatively.
- We honor each person's strengths and diversity.
- We are the achieving class.
- We are the most respectful class in the school.
- We are the hardest-working class in the building.

Teachers can also use journal writing to encourage students' awareness and understanding of their strengths. They might have students keep a strengths-based journal or portfolio to help them document their feelings and ideas related to self-concept, personal strengths, and awareness of the strengths of classmates. Students might be asked to write an essay about their favorite person and what strengths he or she demonstrates. In the later grades, student reading of autobiographies provides an opportunity to examine the strengths of others.

After a teacher has helped students to identify at least two strengths, he or she works to create a classroom wall of strengths. By emphasizing classroom strengths, young people are encouraged to view the strengths of others and to celebrate those strengths. There is also the message being conveyed that our class is strong because it has strengths. We recognize our own individual strengths and those of our classmates. The classroom wall of strengths is placed on a large bulletin board. See Table 6.2 for an example wall of strength.

Strengths-Sharing Circles

Strengths-sharing circles form another way of building a classroom community. Teachers establish a classroomwide practice of recognizing the strengths of others. Students might discuss strengths they have used to solve a problem or strengths they have observed in a fellow classmate during the week. Strengths-sharing circles promote students' empathy and interpersonal intelligence, as they listen to and observe the thoughts, feelings, and behaviors of their classmates. For instance, one student mentioned that he helps his younger brother get ready for school. The teacher helped the student identify that strength as a nurturing strength, and class discussion focused briefly on how he might use that strength in other situations and for choosing a career later on in life.

CULTURE OF ACADEMIC ACHIEVEMENT

Is characterized by students who:

- Are intrinsically motivated to work hard for academic achievement
- Know and use their strengths to achieve academic success
- Collaborate with peers for mutual learning
- Establish academic goals for themselves and ways to reach them
- Use their strengths to deal effectively with academic weaknesses
- Take responsibility for their mistakes and learn from them.

Building a Culture of Academic Achievement

To motivate students to achieve academically, teachers need to establish a classroom community based on academic achievement. The ultimate goal is to have a class of motivated students who take the initiative for their own learning. A classroom community founded on academic achievement establishes high expectations for students, emphasizes teamwork and unity, and values student effort. A teacher models a culture of achievement by being highly organized in the classroom and by presenting a classroom goal, a schedule, and plans for student growth and learning.

The strengths-based teacher communicates a clear and simple academic vision for the class. Jon Saphier and Rowent Gower,[17] authors of *The Skillful Teacher: Building Your Teaching Skills*, maintain that teachers must send clear academic messages. For instance, they must communicate that they believe that each student has the ability to achieve and to succeed in that class. Teachers do not just value a final grade on a test or on an activity. Instead, they send the message that effort, persistence, and growth matter. Teachers communicate the idea that true academic achievement requires hard work and that, further, academic achievement leads to opportunity. In other words, they convey the message: "You can do it. It might take you a little longer, but you can do it." Teachers model the message that we have the power and the ability to solve our problems.

Class chants are another way of encouraging students to achieve at their highest academic level. Although chants are usually used at the elementary level, they can be used at each grade level. For instance, a teacher might inspire students with the chant: "_____ made a mistake, and that's OK, because as long as he [or she] learns from it, we say hurray." A teacher might require students to learn the following creed:

I believe in myself and in my ability to succeed.
I can learn. I will learn. I am learning.
I will listen, read, and write.
I will do my best and persist till I get it right.
I am too smart to waste any part of today and my life.

Class Meetings as a Way of Building a Class Community

Classes can turn into beautiful gardens when the class is treated as the center of community life. The message that is conveyed is "This is our class, our community." Young people learn what it means to be part of a community when they participate in class or group meetings and exchange ideas and listen to one another. Each community, regardless of where it is located, must establish rules regarding members' ability to speak and listen effectively, procedures for members to make choices and reach decisions, and ways for members to resolve conflict.

Meetings establish a forum for young people to participate in group discussions on a number of topics. During such times, teachers can model and teach communication skills, such as how to listen respectfully when others are talking and how to solve problems and contribute to the group/class. Meetings to start the day are usually convened to help children make the transition from home to school. In elementary school, teachers write a different welcoming message each day, pointing out what will take place during that day. The content of the message varies on the teaching goals for the day. For an example of a fourth-grade class morning message, see Table 6.3.

Table 6.3   Morning Message

Good Morning, Class.
Today is November 14, 2010.
We will recite our class creed.
Review your math homework with your math patner.
We will review your collage for English.
Our word for this week is *courage*.
What does courage mean to you?
Music and gym will be provided to you today.

Other Tips for Building a Classroom Community

There are a number of other techniques teachers can use to build a classroom community. For instance, the teacher might discuss with students the characteristics of a team, or choose a team-building vocabulary word for each week, such as *cooperation, dependability,* or *responsibility.* The class might work on a project together, and each team or member would be responsible for completing one part of a project.

Another approach is to have young people participate in a puzzle-making exercise called "We all matter." The teacher begins a discussion about the different shapes and colors of a puzzle. If one piece is missing, no matter how small, the puzzle is incomplete. The teacher tells the students that he or she has taken the pieces of the puzzle and written down a student's name on each piece so that when the puzzle is complete it has all the class members' names on it. Each student is given a piece of a puzzle with another student's name on it. The student is asked to interview the student whose name is on the puzzle piece and write one interesting item or strength about that student. In front of the group, each pair of students introduces his or her partner, states a strength his or her partner has, then pins the puzzle piece on the board where it fits.

Another classroom community-building technique is to have a *gratitude box.* The teacher takes an ordinary box and puts a slash in it. Plastic Kleenex boxes also work well. The box is labeled "Gratitude." If students see one of their classmates performing a good deed or an act of kindness, they write the student's name down with a brief note about what the student did for another member of the class or for the class, then place it in the box.

Team-building games provide fun activities for building a classroom community. Teachers might consider playing a noncompetitive game designed to give everyone a chance to have fun together. Have students work on a math problem. Divide the class into small groups or teams. Assign specific responsibilities to each member. Ask the group come up with a team name or logo. Another technique is to have them write a story about their team and then design a poster with the team name and a self-portrait of each member.

SUMMARY

This chapter has examined what constitutes a caring school. Empathy and interpersonal intelligence were discussed as ingredients of a strengths-based, caring school. Empathy and school connectedness were analyzed as two sides of the same coin. Both give youth a sense of bonding with others and with their peers in a school setting. School connectedness was defined as students' belief that adults in the school care about their learning and about them as individuals. The research is very clear. Kids who feel connected to their schools smoked less, drank less alcohol, attempted suicide less frequently, and achieved at a higher academic performance level. Forming school connectedness is very powerful and second only to the bond one forms with parents. A pervasive theme throughout this chapter was that teachers must build a classroom community. It is insufficient to treat a class of 30 students as simply a group of unrelated students. Instead, teachers should seek to build a caring classroom community that emphasizes empathy, respect for others, and high academic achievement.

Component 4: Preventing Failure

WEEDING THE EDUCATIONAL GARDEN

Most gardeners are concerned about how to prevent weeds from intruding into their gardens. They do not want to spend most of their time in the garden pulling up, cutting, and disposing of weeds on a daily or weekly basis. Gardeners seem to agree that before you can plant your new garden, you have to remove any existing weeds and to prepare the soil with organic compost or with manure. We can encourage plants to grow to full size by fertilizing.

Every school has weeds. If children are to achieve academically and to mature emotionally, educational leaders must continuously remove weeds from their school garden. In effective schools, teachers and principals become vigilant for persistent weeds with deep roots that destroy the school's academic garden and the learning motivation of young people. Some deep-rooted educational weeds include low teacher expectations for student achievement, poor and inadequate school curriculum, teachers who cannot teach and who have little understanding of how to establish caring classrooms, substandard school discipline, and school violence. Strengths-based education is designed to weed out deficit-based educational thinking and ineffective schools.

PREVENTION AS A POWERFUL WEEDER

Prevention is the fourth component of the strengths-based approach to education. When you pull weeds, be sure that you are getting the entire

---

STUDENT STRENGTHS AND PREVENTION

Students' strengths are often camouflaged, distorted, and blocked by the weeds growing in their lives.

---

root system out of the ground. If you do not get the entire root, it will simply grow back. When I first began gardening, I used to just pull the weeds out of wherever they were located. As most gardeners know, pulling up weeds is a never-ending process. If you do not kill a weed at its roots, it almost always comes back to visit you, as if to say: "You thought you really got me. You'll have to do better than what you did to get me to leave for good." I soon developed an entire arsenal for combating weeds in my garden, including Weed-Be-Gone, Weed Wacker, and a host of other tools that promised if I bought them and used them correctly, I would never see another weed in my garden.

Gradually, I learned that life is a matter of dealing with weeds—that pulling them up and using Weed-Be-Gone and the rest of my arsenal would not ensure complete freedom from weeds. The wind carries the seeds of weeds on its very breath, and they lodge in our gardens imperceptibly. The best we can do is to not get upset when some weed seeds have found their way into our gardens. Instead, have a strategy for dealing with weed prevention. I thought about some of the classes that I have taught and the weeds that my students had to confront. Teachers have to be mindful not to be overcome by the weeds in their students' gardens.

DEFINITION OF PREVENTION

Prevention can be defined as a school's active process of creating conditions and/or personal attributes within students that promote the well-being of youth. It is a process of intervention designed to change the circumstances associated with student problem behaviors. Effective prevention programs decrease these problem behaviors and later difficulties that children and adolescents experience in school and in the community. The current research suggests two related approaches to prevention. The traditional first approach was to focus on preventing high-risk behaviors among young people, such as substance abuse, early sexual activity, dropping out of school, and violence or bullying. During the past two decades, a second approach to prevention has come to occupy center stage. This approach is geared toward identifying *protective factors* that serve to prevent young people from engaging in high-risk behaviors that can sidetrack their healthy development as contributing members of a society. When schools help strengthen the protective factors in young people's lives, they reduce the potential impact that highly toxic risk factors might have on them.

According to Gottfredson and associates,[1] a school prevention program consists of an intervention or a set of interventions designed to reduce problem behavior in a school. Examples of prevention activities include school policies, instructional activity, supervision, coaching, and other interventions with youths or their families, schools, or peer environments. Typically, school prevention programs target problem behaviors that may lead to later criminal activity. For instance, such programs may establish schoolwide programs to prevent alcohol and substance abuse, risky sexual behavior, violence, or bullying. Prevention programs are usually located within the school building, and they may be directed toward the entire school population (primary prevention) or toward a defined subpopulation that is at particular risk for a problem behavior like drug use or violence.

Prevention programs are designed to find a deficit and to remedy it by using an intervention program. Effective prevention practices decrease student problem behavior. In general, research has found few causal connections in the social sciences. Nevertheless, understanding factors that put young people at risk for school failure and antisocial behavior can help teachers and school administrators to work better with youth. Reviewing all the major prevention programs that are in existence in this country is beyond the scope of this book. This chapter approaches the topic of prevention by examining the major problems that prevention programs are designed to prevent—namely school failure, school dropouts, and problematic social behavior such as bullying and substance abuse.

WHY CHILDREN FAIL IN SCHOOL

There are a number of reasons that young people fail in schools. Some of the more common reasons include lack of parental involvement and parent absenteeism, poor study skills, lack of connectedness to school, lack of basic academic skills in reading and math, and lack of social skills, including the ability to get along with their peers.[2]

A disproportionate number of children from ethnic minority groups experience school failure. This may be due, in part, to the fact that many of these students come from cultures and backgrounds quite different from their teachers. It may also be because many of these children test low on most academic achievement tests because they are poor and come from schools that lack sufficient resources to provide quality education services.[3]

In a February 2009 Fact Sheet titled "High School Dropouts in America," the Alliance for Excellent Education[4] pointed out that there is no single reason that students drop out of high school; however, research indicates that difficult transitions to high school, deficient academic skills, and a lack of student engagement are high on the list as barriers to high school graduation. The report highlights the following on why students drop out:

- By the middle grades, most dropouts are already on the path to failure, and they engage in behaviors that correlate highly with dropping out of school—including low school attendance and failing grades.
- Ninth grade functions a as turning point for many students who begin their freshman year only to discover that their academic skills are insufficient for high school-level work. Approximately 40 percent of ninth-grade student in the 15 cities with the highest dropout rates repeat ninth grade; only 10 to 15 percent of those repeaters actually graduate.
- Academic success in ninth-grade course work is highly predictive of eventual high school graduation, and over one-third of all high school dropouts are lost in the ninth grade.
- The 6 million secondary students who fall in the lowest 25 percent of academic achievement are 20 times more likely to drop out of high school than are students in the top-performing quartile.[5]
- Both academic engagement and social engagement (school bonding and connectedness) are major components for high school graduation. Research studies show that a lack of student engagement predicts their dropping out, even after controlling for academic achievement and student background.[6]

Many of the points made in the Alliance for Excellent Education's Fact Sheet were echoed by the Institute of Education Services' (IES) September 2008 publication on dropout prevention.[7] The researchers who worked on this project made five recommendations to prevent high school dropouts. These are incorporated in the 16-session

Strengths-Based School Program (© Elsie J. Smith) presented later in this chapter. The recommendations were as follows:

> *Recommendation 1*: Use data systems that provide a realistic diagnosis of the number of students who drop out and that help identify individual students at high risk of dropping out (diagnostic).
>
> *Recommendation 2*: Assign adult mentors or advocates to students at risk of dropping out (targeted intervention).
>
> *Recommendation 3*: Give academic support and enrichment to improve students' academic performance (targeted intervention).
>
> *Recommendation 4*: Implement schoolwide programs to improve students' classroom behavior and social skills (empathy training, listening skills, etc.—schoolwide intervention).
>
> *Recommendation 5*: Give rigorous and relevant instruction that actually engages students in learning and that provides the skills they need to graduate and to succeed in adult life.

While some of these recommendations are anchored in the risk factor, remedial approach to education, others are not. The strengths approach incorporates part of the risk factor approach under the rubric of managing weaknesses as illustrated in Figure 4.1. The next section discusses briefly the risk factor approach to prevention of school failure. Some noteworthy strengths-based approaches to prevention of school failure are discussed.

THE RISK FACTOR APPROACH TO ESTABLISHING PREVENTION PROGRAMS

Although chapter 4 of this book highlighted the importance of understanding risk factors in young people's lives, this chapter uses risk factors to examine a cycle of failure that many young people encounter. Children's homes and families provide one of the earliest indicators of potential academic failure and subsequent school dropout.[8] Research studies have found consistently a connection between poverty and school dropout for both regular and special education students.[9] Children and adolescents who are at risk often come from families that have low academic skills in reading and math and where multiple family stressors may be present (e.g., alcohol and other drug abuse, divorce, child abuse and neglect).

How do risk factors affect young people's lives? Home, community, and school risk factors are intertwined. Children who live in poverty districts frequently do not experience a great of verbal interaction with their parents. Therefore, their vocabularies tend to be far more restricted than children who come from middle-class homes.[10] These children then are faced with the prospects of having middle-class teachers who use a complex vocabulary to teach and who assume that the children have a level of familiarity with educational materials. As a result, academic failure takes place. *Early academic failure is second only to poverty in predicting subsequent school failure.* Although the risk factor approach is grounded in the deficit approach to education, it does offer some benefits. Problematic student behaviors get targeted and addressed with a program designed to eliminate that behavior. A disadvantage of risk factor programs is that students often see themselves as problems rather than as assets. They rarely get a chance to focus on their strengths.

STRENGTHS-BASED APPROACH TO PREVENTION OF SCHOOL FAILURE

Schoolwide interventions for prevention can be implemented using a strengths-based approach. Strengths-based interventions are proactive and positive. Such interventions focus on clarifying expectations and on teaching students the skills needed for success, instead of just waiting for student misbehavior to take place and responding with punishment or a remedial treatment plan.

Schoolwide strengths-based programs are geared toward evaluating the school environment to determine when, where, and in what contexts student problems are likely to take place. The goal is to create strategies that prevent problems by focusing on the positive, the strengths that young people bring to school. The strengths approach responds to inappropriate social behaviors as errors. Instead of emphasizing punishment, the goal is to use positive behavioral supports to reteach the skill that is lacking.

Researchers and the popular media have maintained that prevention of school failure is especially important for African American male students, who tend to lag behind their white counterparts in academic achievement.[11] The strengths approach to prevention is especially relevant to closing the achievement gap between African American male students and white students as well as between boys and girls.[12] National data indicate that boys are experiencing more academic difficulties and are achieving at lower levels across most school subjects than are girls.[13] In addition, boys are reported to have a significantly higher incidence of attention deficit hyperactivity disorder, special education referrals and placements, behavior issues, and school suspensions.[14] Mary Ann Clark and her fellow researchers[15] have conducted research that shows that boys as a group do not seem to believe that school is as important in their lives as do girls. In a longitudinal national survey of U.S. 12th graders for a decade, researchers found that girls stated that they saw the importance of their schoolwork as related to their futures and that they found school more meaningful and interesting than did boys.[16]

Possible selves theory has been used to explain the difference in boys' and girls' academic achievement.[17] This theoretical approach focuses on the motivational power of students' views of themselves in the future. Possible selves can be either positive or negative. Students can separate their possible selves into different categories, such as possible selves for academic, social, and physical life domains. In general, boys tend to have possible selves that are oriented in the present, while girls have possible selves that are oriented in the future. Whereas girls are inclined to have a possible self that is academically oriented, boys do not. If students are to achieve, it is important for them to have well-defined visual pictures of positive selves within the academic domain.

Mary Ann Clark and associates[18] used a strengths-based approach to enhance African American middle school boys' possible selves in the academic and positive planning toward the future. A group of 17 boys were identified because they were deemed to have high academic potential based on statewide test scores and teacher recommendations but had lower than expected grade point averages. Some boys had been referred for disciplinary problems and were viewed as having low motivation for academic success. Over half of the boys came from economically challenged homes and communities and were on the free/reduced-price school meal program, and many were from single-parent homes. Each boy was individually contacted and agreed to participate in a strengths-based group with 12 sessions. Some of the goals for the group included increasing their motivation in school, decreasing school disciplinary referrals, and identifying their strengths and those of group members. The 12 sessions dealt with such issues such as healthy life choices, organization and time management, mediation and negotiation skills, memory strategies and test-taking tips, and preparing for high school (Parts 1 and 2).

Clark and her associates found that discipline referrals for this group were reduced; however, whereas the grades for 88 percent of the mainstream boys increased during the last marking period, the grades of the gifted boys did not improve. The authors found that strengths-building activities that engage adolescent males are essential to helping them develop into motivated, achieving young men. The researchers concluded:

> Helping the eighth-grade boys envision their futures, offering skills and information on topics of importance to them, and assisting them in communicating positively with their peers and adults have been important strengths-building activities as they learn to become more independent and responsible for their actions and envision future possible selves. We have learned that strengths-building efforts need to be made on an ongoing basis to build and maintain the support systems that adolescent males need in their lives.

Taking a strengths-based approach improves not only students' academic achievement but also their general functioning. Students benefit from learning when their strengths are highlighted.[19] The Achieving Success Identity Pathways program,[20] uses a systemic frame that targets youth from low-income and culturally diverse backgrounds by asking them to identify barriers to their achievement at the macro- (societal level), exo- (linked), and microsystemic (individual) levels. Students are encouraged to identify their strengths at the microsystemic level.

The Boston Connects Program represents another approach for using students' strengths to prevent school failure.[21] This program is a school-community partnership designed to promote learning and healthy development. The Boston Connects Program is located in 14 Boston public elementary schools representing two diverse and low-income neighborhoods. Its university partner is Boston College, which has developed a data-driven approach to the delivery of comprehensive support services. According to its researcher leaders, "Boston Connects does not merely tack on supplementary supports for students, but rather it modifies schools' structures so that effective student support becomes an essential component of the educational mission of the schools."[22]

The Boston Connects Program implements two schoolwide programs in each school that promote a strengths-based approach: (1) a social competence, and (2) a health promotion curriculum. During the academic year, students are given weekly lessons that focus on such social competence skills as good decision making and different dimensions of health, such as nutrition. A health lesson on nutrition teaches children how to read nutrition fact labels. These lessons are delivered in each classroom by certified teachers in coordination with Boston Connects school counselors.

The Boston Connects Program also uses a whole-class review process, which is a "focused strategy to identify the strengths of all students as well as to identify community-based enrichment and support opportunities for each student."[23] The data-driven findings indicate that the Boston Connect Schools have experienced an increase in the range of resources and services to which young people are referred and a change in referrals from remedial services to referrals for services that build strengths. The results of the program are quite impressive. The need for intensive remedial services, especially in counseling, have been significantly reduced. An analysis of counselor activity in the Boston Connects Program showed that counselors use 23 percent of their time engaging in prevention and 29 percent of their time linking students with community agencies.[24]

Wendy Logan and Janna Scarborough[25] have proposed helping students to increase their connectedness to school by establishing a schoolwide clubs program. These educators established a "Connections Through Clubs" program to promote a strengths-enhancing school environment. Each faculty member, including the school principal member and secretary, was asked to design his or her own club and submit a club name and description, plus a request for materials. Based on this request, more than 40 school clubs were established in such diverse areas as jewelry making, scrapbook, TV production, chess, money makers, math club, guitar, and law enforcement. A database was constructed that listed the clubs and students' club interests. Club meetings were held on Fridays for 45 minutes a week.

Logan and Scarborough articulated three overarching goals of the club program: (1) to promote positive personal and supportive connections between teachers (or another caring adult club leader) and students based on a mutual interest; (2) to build positive and cooperative connections between students; and (3) to give students an opportunity to explore their interests, gain skills, and have fun through a different learning experience of their choosing.

The results of the club connected approach were impressive. Students indicated overwhelmingly that they had developed a positive relationship with club leaders and their peers. After completing the third year of the clubs program, Logan and Scarborough increased the amount of club time from 45 minutes to one hour, the day of club meetings was changed from Fridays to Wednesdays, and club leaders began to think of themselves as mentors and, therefore, focused on the process of working with students (e.g., facilitating conversations, fostering relationships with peers) rather than on the content or the completion of a project. Club leaders were given several team-building lessons at the beginning of the school year to help them build school connections with students. Requests for donations to the club program resulted in $3,000 in donations from the community. Based on informal reports from students and faculty, Logan and Scarborough concluded that the schoolwide club program had been a success in helping to build student connections with their school.

A 16-SESSION STRENGTHS-BASED SCHOOL PROGRAM (© ELSIE J. SMITH)

In this section, I propose a 16-session strengths-based school program that addresses many of the issues discussed in this chapter regarding what is needed to prevent school failure. A detailed presentation of the 16 sessions is available to a teacher, guidance counselor, and student workbook from the author. The 16-session strengths-based program is time limited, usually 45 minutes to one hour of instructional and class time. In addition to these 16 sessions, I also advocate implementing a number of schoolwide programs. Sixteen sessions are just not enough to change an entire school climate and focus.

Brief Description of the Components of the 16 Sessions

The 16-session strengths program is based on the strengths domain framework first described in chapter 4. These 16 sessions cannot by themselves substitute for schoolwide programs; rather, they are used in conjunction with the sessions that are outlined below. The following key components have been identified for the 16-session strengths-based school program.

> Key Component 1: The school establishes a schoolwide strengths discovery program.
> Key Component 2 is the strengths-based learning program.
> Key Component 3 is a mentoring program that uses a club program, adults within the school and community, and older students for a schoolwide mentoring program.

Key Component 4 is a life skills component.

Key Component 5 is a multicultural diversity focus.

Key Component 6 is student career program that involves students in career awareness, counseling, vocational education/technical training, and extracurricular activities.

Key Component 7 is a schoolwide social-emotional learning program that seeks to increase students' self-regulation and emotional intelligence. This component is reflected best in the life skills part of the 16 strengths session.

Schoolwide Strengths-Based Programs

Several schoolwide programs support the 16-session program described herein. In addition to a schoolwide strengths discovery program, I recommend a strengths-based learning program based on the concept of multiple intelligence and learning style.

Key Component 1 involves a schoolwide strengths discovery program. The 16- session model deals with this component under domain one—strengths of the individual. Three of the 16 sessions are devoted to student strength discovery.

Four of the 16 sessions described under the Smith model deal with *Key Component 2*, a strengths-based learning program. These four sessions address the school domain involving students' strengths.

In response to *Key Component 3*, a schoolwide cross-mentoring program is established. Previous research has found positive effects for mentees as well as for mentors. This schoolwide intervention is designed to help school personnel to promote students and leadership and collaboration skills, while at the same time promoting elementary and middle school mentees' connectedness and academic achievement.[26] Cross-mentoring and community mentoring programs offer students the opportunity to have a one-to-one relationship focused on interpersonal development or academics. In addition, tutoring has been found to be an effective way for addressing specific needs in a number of academic competency areas.

Key Components 4 (life skills) and *5* (multicultural component) are represented under the sessions that deal with life skills. Students learn to respect themselves and those from other cultures.

Key Component 6 deals with the career development of students. I suggest that schools adopt a schoolwide career development program to give students meaning and a sense of purpose. Such a program helps students make connections between what they are doing in their classes and what they might be doing to earn a living as an adult. A number of research studies have found that people with a strong sense of meaning and purpose in life report greater happiness and fewer psychological problems.[27] Helping students develop a sense of purpose in their career development fosters a deeper level of commitment and persistence in school. According to Erikson,[28] the major task of adolescence is identity development, and the formation of one's career identity is an integral part of Erikson's identity versus role confusion stage of development. When students are involved in a purpose-centered career development program in school, their active engagement in identity formation is promoted and they are given a sense that their lives matter. There is purpose to their lives.

A schoolwide career development program promotes meaningful conversation between students and adults and even among students themselves. When students are engaged in a career development program, they are encouraged to think about their strengths and how they might use them to provide a living for themselves and their families. A schoolwide career development program can be linked with school clubs and a school mentoring program. Career development is developed under the establishing goals session of life skills.

Key Component 7 deals with the social-emotional curriculum. The content of a schoolwide social-emotional curriculum or program was described in chapter 4 as the first component of a strengths-based school. In the 16 sessions delineated next, four of the life skills sessions focus on the social-emotional development of students.

Description of the 16 Sessions

Strengths Domain 1: Strengths within the Individual, Such as Creative, Resilience, etc.

This domain has three sessions, all of which deal with strengths within the individual. The goal is to engage in a strengths discovery and assessment process.

Strengths Session 1

Session 1 involves helping students to find their own *strengths zones.*

Description of the Strengths Discovery Process: Use the Strengths-Based Inventory [SBI], Strengths Checklist, and the Identification of Students Strengths Zones. Every student is given a copy of the

---

STAY IN YOUR STRENGTHS ZONES

Students learn their strengths zones and how to stay in their
strengths zones to accomplish their goals.
Students' strengths energize and motivate them to achieve.

Strengths Pyramid (see Figure 4.1), and students engage in a discussion of the pyramid. They are taught what constitutes a strengths mindset and what constitutes a deficit mindset. During this discussion, teachers/counselors use Table 2.1, Summary of Deficit and Strengths Mindset. *Students are encouraged to examine their feelings about themselves and about their school performance in terms of the deficit/ strengths mindsets.* Teachers take an active approach to help students identify their strengths. Instead of focusing on student misbehavior, teachers focus on "catching students doing something positive" either within the class or within the broader school community. Students are asked such questions as:

> What motivates you to action?
> What accomplishments are you most proud of?
> What makes you feel happy?
> Name at least one strength you have.
> What things have people praised you for?
> How have you helped other people?
> What strengths were involved in your helping others?

Strengths Session 2

Continue individual strengths identification. This session also includes strength sharing with students—the teacher shares strengths with students on an individual and group basis. Teachers document the strengths of students and the amount of time that they are actually on task in the classroom. Teachers ask themselves: when does this student tend to demonstrate his or her strengths? The teacher includes multiple observations when things are going well for the student to assess potential strengths and environmental supports. Informal assessments can involve drawings and other art forms, such as musical performance or a dance routine.

Strengths Session 3

Students write their own strengths profiles (see Table 5.3, Student Strengths Profile). They post their strengths profiles with a picture of themselves on the bulletin board and around the classroom. *Students learn how to stay in their strength zones.*

Strengths Domain 2: Strengths within the Family, Such as Family Communication, Family Protection, etc.

Strengths Session 4

Session 4 has to do with parental, caregiver, and family involvement. Parents are invited into the school. Students identify and share family strengths with family and classmates. Using a multicultural framework, students are asked to think about with whom they identify as a significant other. The presence of parents and other adult mentoring relationships is a developmental strength that promotes a young person's academic and life success. Possible questions to be used during this session include:

> Who is the person within their family that they connect with best? Students are asked to identify their family strengths.
> Students are asked to identify their cultural/spiritual strengths.

Strengths Domain 3: Strengths at School, Such as School Bonding, Sense of Belonging, Academic Achievement

The focus of these next four sessions is on identifying individual learning strengths and learning style, metacognitive learning strategies, and identifying classroom strengths.

Strengths Session 5

Session 5 involves Identification of students' learning strengths and learning style.

   Teachers and/or counselors administer the following instruments to students:

- Multiple Intelligence Instrument
- Learning Style Instrument
- Metacognitive Strategies Instrument

After administering these instruments, teachers/guidance counselors work collaboratively with students to complete Table 5.1 (Learning Strengths Chart), and Table 5.2 (My Own Learning Strength Chart), and Table 5.3 (Student Strengths Chart).

The following is a brief exercise you can use to set the foundation for introducing students to the concept of learning style. It is called the *Paper Airline Exercise*. Students are given three sheets of paper. Based on the teacher's instructions, the students are to build three different paper airplanes. For students' first attempt at making a paper airplane, the teacher reads verbal directions to the students. After the students listen to the verbal instructions, they are asked to make an airplane. For the second attempt, the teacher gives only visual instructions without any words. For the third attempt, the teacher demonstrates each attempt while the students fold their paper airplanes. Then students are told they can fly the airplanes for one minute. The teacher then engages in a discussion about auditory, visual, and kinesthetic learning styles and how these learning styles may be applied to them. Which directions did the students prefer and why?

Learning Style Writing Exercise: After the learning style exercise, the teacher asks students to write in a few sentences or a paragraph:

What is your learning style?
I learn best when the teacher . . .

Videos on multiple intelligences and a CD-ROM titled "Exploring Our Multiple Intelligences" are available from the Association for Supervision and Curriculum Development, Alexandria, Virginia, 22314, 800-933-2723 or 703-549-9110.

To identify classroom strengths, students based their beginning discussion on Table 6.2 (Our Classroom Wall of Strengths).

Strengths Session 6

Session 6 involves the identification of students' learning strategies, that is, their metacognitive strategies. In many classrooms, reading comprehension instruction in teacher-generated questions which actually measure comprehension of specific text rather than developing metacognitive strategies for comprehending all text. Students need to learn how to go about learning reading comprehensive strategies to help them read more accurately. Linda Eilers and Christine Pinkley[29] (2006) taught students various metacognitive strategies to help them better comprehend their text. Students were taught such metacognitive strategies as making text connections, predicting what was going to happen in the passage, and sequencing (i.e., establishing a chronological sequencing of events in the reading passage), was evaluated for its usefulness in improving reading comprehension in a first-grade classroom. The researchers found a significant difference in students' awareness of comprehension strategies and comprehension of text as measured by the Index of Reading Awareness and the Beaver Developmental Reading Assessment before and after the intervention. These findings suggest that students in primary grades may benefit from explicit instruction in reading comprehension strategies at the same time they are learning to decode words. I remember teaching a class of students who lived in the inner-city of a large Northeastern city. The students were failing because they had no idea of how they learned. To hook the students' interest, I boasted that I could teach them a scientific equation within a matter of minutes using specific techniques. Before doing so, I explained the symbols used in the equation. I used the technique of repetition—of saying e=mc squared rapidly within a two-minute time span. Students were laughing because they were surprised that all could say the formula and all understood what it meant. Then I asked them to use another strategy to increase their learning—put the equation in the form of any popular song they chose. The point I am making is that students had no idea of how they learned. Learning was a mystery to them. They discovered that some of them learned best by using the strategy of repetition, while others learned best by using mnemonic devices.

Strengths Session 7

Session 7 focuses on the assessment and evaluation of students' learning strategies—that is, their metacognitive strategies. Students assess the extent to which their metacognitive learning strategies are or are not working for them.

Strengths Session 8

Session 8 involves the development of new individual metacognitive learning strategies and identification of classroom strengths.

Strengths Domain 4: Strengths with Peers and Teachers (Prosocial Peers)

Researchers have found that the most successful, empirically-based dropout prevention program created meaning bonds between

---

STRENGTHS ARE NEVER ENOUGH

British poet and lexicographer Samuel Johnson once stated:
"Almost every man wastes part of his life in attempts to display qualities that he does not possess."

To realize your strengths, you have to focus on them. It is the development, refinement and application of strengths that make a difference in a person's life.

---

students and teachers, and connected students to an attainable future. A schoolwide clubs program can serve to strengthen the connections between students and teachers.

Strengths Session 9

Session 9 deals with issues that pertain to social decision making, problem solving, and friends. The teacher might construct a class discussion or lesson that deals with the following questions:

How did I choose my friends?
Who are my friends?
What does it mean when someone does not like me?
What is a relationship?
What is empathy?
How can empathy make be a good friend?

Strengths Session 10

Session 10 deals with conflict resolution and bullying.

Strengths Domain 5: Strengths within Neighborhoods and Communities, Such as Safe Neighborhood, Opportunity to Participate in Community Activities

Strengths Session 11

Session 11 focuses on the identification of community resources and the linking of students with community services. Students are asked to identify resources within their communities. They are given an opportunity to participate in service learning or a community project.

Domain 6: Strengths from Faith, Spirituality, and Culture, Such as Spiritual Identification, Church, Synagogue, or Mosque Social Support

Strengths Session 12

Session 12 involves the identification and discussion of multicultural issues and spirituality strengths in students' lives.

Domain 7: Strengths from Mastering the 10 Skills of Life

Strengths Session 13

Session 13 deals with Life Skills 1, 2, and 3:

> *Life Skill 1—Power of Self-Esteem*: Students participate in Exercises to help them build their self-esteem.
> *Life Skill 2—Power of Attitude*: Students participate in exercises related to positive attitudes.
> *Like Skill 3—The Power of Understanding One's Own Strengths and Weaknesses*: Students participate in exercises designed to help them understand their own strengths and weaknesses.

Strengths Session 14

Session 14 deals with life skills 4 &5:

> *Life Skill 4—Power of Learning How to Communicate*: Students are taught basic listening skills
> *Life Skill 5—Power of Being a Problem Solver and a Person Who Can Cope*: Students are taught coping skills. Teaching children and adolescents coping strategies provide them with some measure of immunity or resistance against anxiety disorders.

Strengths Session 15

Session 15 deals with Life skills 6, 7, and 8:

> *Life Skill 6—The Power of Building Supportive Relationships with Others*: Students are taught how to build relationships within the school via clubs and other activities.
> *Life Skill 7—The Power of Finding Your Purpose in Life*: This lesson is connected with the schoolwide career development program.

Life Skill 8—The Power of Establishing Goals and a Life Plan of Action: Students are asked to establish three goals for the academic year. One goal must relate to their academic program.

Strengths Session 16

Session 16 is the summary and deals with Life Skills 9 and 10:

Life Skill 9—The Power of Persistence: Adopting a "Whatever It Takes" Attitude

Life Skill 10—The Power of Establishing a Life of Integrity and Moral Behavior: Teachers use Lawrence Kohlberg's theory of moral development to work with students.

SUMMARY

This chapter has presented Component 4 of the strengths-based school, which focused on prevention. Every educational garden needs weeding if it is to continue grow and flourish. Prevention of learning and behavior problems is critical to students' academic and life success. The chapter focused on a strengths-based approach to prevention. A 16-session strengths-based program was outlined.

8

Component 5: Increasing Home, School, and Community Partnerships

SCHOOL AND COMMUNITY OF GARDENS

I am always pleased when I walk through a community that is supposed to be one that has almost 100 percent of its students on free school lunches, and I see flower gardens breaking the dreariness of the landscape. "Who plants these gardens?" I muse to myself. "I'd like to talk with the person who planted this beautiful garden." Why? The answer is because I know that in the midst of poverty there is hope. The person who planted the garden has hope that what he or she has planted will bear fruit. Plant a garden in a neighborhood, and you plant hope—not just for yourself but also for the people who walk by and watch something beautiful growing. Plant a community garden, and you initiate a conversation in a neighborhood about "we" and "our."

Every community, no matter how challenged it might be economically, has the potential for growing a garden. All we have to do is to plant the right seeds; then water and nourish the garden. I believe that every school should plant a community garden because it builds a bond between the school and the people who live in the neighborhood. Digging a school garden brings out the best in people and helps to erase the rigid boundaries that separate students from faculty and faculty from parents. There is not a principal or teacher out there digging in the soil, but rather just people trying to make a better community. A school/community garden is something that everyone—students, parents, faculty, and community members—worked on together.

COMMUNITY STRENGTHS

Every community has the potential for growing a beautiful garden.

Building a school garden nourishes students' naturalistic intelligence.

Schools live within communities and neighborhoods of families trying to make life worth living. No matter how desperate the economic situation of a community, there are strengths. I remember working in a school that came was surrounded by gangs, prostitutes, and drug addicts. No one gave the kids in the school much chance of success. The kids in the school were treated as if they were disposable, throwaway kids that stayed for a while and provided jobs for primarily middle-class women—both white and African American—and a sprinkling of men teachers here and there.

As part of the guidance team, we had won a grant of considerable money. We were quite proud of ourselves. Yet, we had failed to ever contact the parents of the children whom we were seeking to serve. Much to our surprise, a group of parents showed up on the school's doorstep demanding that the program be halted until the parents could have a say in it. They were tired of people coming into their neighborhoods with programs that seemed to benefit only the school administration and the teachers, rarely the kids.

Initially, the school responded to the parents with an attitude of "Why you ungrateful . . . , we're only trying to help you people." Yet as I sat across from some very forceful and intelligent African American mothers, I knew that the parent group was no joke. These mothers were determined to be included in what the school was planning for their children. Although the school met with the parents, they were given "our plan" for their children. The parents called the federal agency that was funding the grant project. The grant was halted. We saw the parents' power, and they were treated with greater respect. After all, we were talking about a grant of a quarter of a million dollars over a four-year time period.

I informed the principal that I thought the best solution was to sit down and talk with the parents—form some sort of parent-teacher-guidance/school coalition. Finally he relented, and a group was formed. Despite all the negative surroundings—the prostitutes, drug addicts, and gangs—there were families living in those homes who wanted the best for their children and who saw education as the only way out for their children.

Over the course of the year, I got to know the parents quite well, and my respect for them grew. What they were fighting for—to be heard and to be taken into consideration—was considered routine for children in more economically favorable districts. Major changes were made in the school. A partnership grew among the families and the community with the school that did not previously seem possible. The school went from being on the state's endangered list of failing to one of the president's schools of excellence.

I was taught a valuable lesson that somehow I had forgotten in college—that all communities have strengths, no matter how impoverished they may seem, and that most families want the best for their children, even when they are not able to give them the best that life has to offer. Schools should be about forming partnerships with the families of the students and the surrounding community. If we see only the deficits in families—what is wrong with them rather than what is right with them—we will miss opportunities for partnerships and for finding diamonds in the rough.

Even in the most desolate situations, there are strengths. I remember working with one student whose mother was on drugs. As we talked, I said to him "How do you get up in the morning and get ready to come to school?" "Oh, my mom, no matter how messed up she is the night before, she always gets up and gets us breakfast." Despite the negative set of circumstances, I heard a strength in the boy's description. So, I said to him: "No matter how messed up your mother might be the night before, she loves you kids enough to get up to fix breakfast and to get you off to school." The boy looked at me as if he had not thought of conceptualizing the situation through the lens that I had used. "Well, I guess you could say that. I never thought about her loving us enough to get up to fix us breakfast."

I take the view that if a family can get a child to school, there is a strength somewhere. I actively look for that strength because I want

---

FAMILY STRENGTHS

Every family has strengths, even those facing the most challenging of situations.

to build upon it. I also want to convey to that family that I see one of their strengths.

Strengths-based schools encourage and promote home, community, and school partnerships (i.e., giving families an opportunity to be informed about their children's academic instruction and to assist them as well they can). They increase community involvement and support by conducting outreach to garner community involvement and support, thereby increasing the number of school volunteers.

THE OVERWHELMING POSITIVE BENEFITS OF PARENT/SCHOOL/ COMMUNITY INVOLVEMENT: A GENERATION OF EVIDENCE

In 1981, Anne Henderson and Nancy Berla published the first in a series of *Evidence* reports. In the first report, Henderson and Berla reviewed 35 studies that documented the positive benefits between parental involvement in a child's education and measurable benefits for children, their families, and schools. They reaffirm their earlier conclusions in the third installment of their ongoing literature review on parental involvement. The authors state: "The evidence is now beyond dispute. When schools work together with families to support learning, children tend to succeed not just in school, but throughout life" (p. 1).[1]

Henderson and Berla found that the benefits of parent and family involvement with their children's schools included higher test scores and grades, better attendance, more completion of homework, more positive attitudes and behavior, higher graduation rates, and greater enrollment in higher education. Even though parental involvement is strongest at the elementary level, it still should be continued throughout the middle grades and high school. When the responsibility for children's learning is shared by the school, home, and community, children have greater opportunities for meaningful, engaged learning; that is, they are able to make the connection between what they are learning in school and the skills required of them in the real world.

In *Home-School Relations: Working Successfully with Parents and Families*, Glenn Olsen and Mary Lou Fuller[2] have found additional benefits of home, school, community connections. These are listed according to the stakeholder.

1. *Benefits for the Children*
   - Children achieve higher academically, regardless of ethnic or racial background.[3]

- Children consistently complete their homework.
- Children have higher self-esteem, are more self-regulated, and evidence higher aspirations and motivation toward school.
- Children's positive attitude toward school translates into improved behavior in school and fewer suspensions for disciplinary reasons.[4]
- Fewer children are placed in special education and remedial classes.
- Junior high and high school students whose parents remain involved with their education tend to make better school transitions, and they are less likely to drop out of school.

2. *Benefits for the Parents*

- As parents acquire more knowledge of child development, they tend to use more affection and positive reinforcement and less punishment with their children.[5]
- Parents gain a better understanding of the teacher's job and school curriculum.
- Parents are more inclined to help when their children's teachers ask them to become more involved in their children's learning activities at home.

3. *Benefits for the School and Educators*

- When schools have a high percentage of involved parents, teachers and principals experience a higher sense of morale.
- Consistent parent involvement promotes improved communication and relations among parents, teachers, and administrators.
- Teachers and principals report an increase in job satisfaction.
- Schools that actively involve parents and the community have better reputations than those that do not establish such relations.
- Schools that have strong parental involvement engender greater community support.
- Schools that have programs that involve the community and parents tend to have higher-quality educational programs than those that do not include these groups.

BUILDING HEALTHY CONNECTIONS: SCHOOL, FAMILY, AND COMMUNITY

Is the student connected to the community or homeless and marginalized? It is important that schools work to help build young people's connections to their own identity, culture, and community. Some young people might require assistance in understanding who they are, where they come from, and what their heritage offers them. Armed with this new understanding, young people can appreciate their own identity, understand how historic al issues affected them, and use this knowledge to make positive changes in their lives.

The strength-based approach recognizes that young people are assets to their communities. Positive programs engage young people as community workers and leaders on issues that matter to them. I recommend that in each school students be involved in developing and running small projects that connect them to their communities. Research suggests that the following things make a difference in young people's lives: physical and psychological safety; appropriate structure; supportive relationships; opportunities to belong; positive social norms; opportunities for skill building; and integration of family, school, and community efforts.[6]

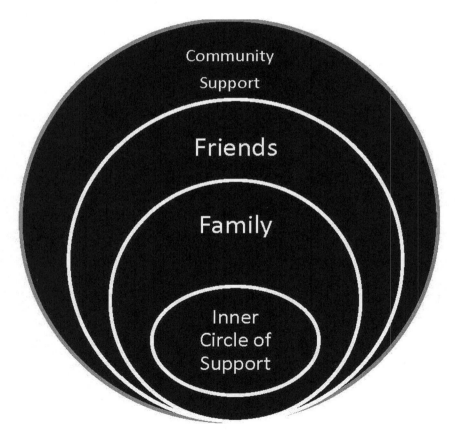

Figure 8.1   Circle of Support

HOME/SCHOOL/COMMUNITY PARTNERSHIPS AND STUDENTS' CIRCLE OF SUPPORT

In strengths-based schools, all students are asked to create a circle of support (see Figure 8.1) to promote their learning and to experience a purposeful and meaningful life. Students are asked to consider the following questions during sessions that focus on their social emotional learning: Did I look at my circle of support this week? What sources of support did I use this week? Did my source of support help me? How can I change my circle of support to make it better? Can I add any other sources of support to my circle?

SCHOOL LEARNING COMMUNITIES: NATIONAL NETWORK OF PARTNERSHIP SCHOOLS

A school learning community includes educators, students, parents, and community partners who work collaboratively to improve the school and to promote students' academic achievement. School learning communities should have an organized program of school, family, and community partnerships that are connected with the school's mission and goals. Research shows that such partnerships improve schools, strengthen families, increase community support, and promote student academic achievement.[7]

Since 1996, more than 1,200 schools, districts, and state departments of education in the National Network of Partnership Schools at Johns Hopkins University have collaborated with researchers to develop and implement programs of school, family, and community partnerships. One result of the National Network of Partnership Schools is that many research materials have been developed for elementary, middle, and high schools.[8]

It is difficult for schools to improve without significant improvement in the level of community support and engagement in the schools. Community engagement can be defined as the degree to which the school has developed a constructive relationship with its surrounding community. The term describes the extent to which the school can count on community support from parents and community members as well as the extent that the community feels a sense of pride about the school's accomplishments. Tschannen-Moran, Parish, and DiPaola[9] found that middle school students were more inclined to show academic achievement on state tests where teachers felt that parents and community members were working together with their schools to promote student success. When school administrators and teachers engage their surrounding communities in positive ways, their students are likely to achieve academically.

In building partnerships with schools, it is important to designate culture brokers and community persons of influence.[10] When powerful allies become part of the school/community partnership, schools benefit. To build strengths-based partnerships, schools must locate assets in the community (e.g., community members, businesses, community organizations). Some community organizations that schools might consider forming partnerships with are: Big Brother Big Sister, McDonald's, Sam's Club, law firms, and restaurants. Colleges and universities can provide critical tutoring and mentoring services for young people.

In their book *Building Communities from the Inside Out*, John Kretzmann and John L. Mcknight[11] have proposed that youth can be important contributors to the well-being of a community. Projects that connect young people productively with other youth and adults are the foundations upon which healthy communities can be built.[12] Youth must be rediscovered as community assets. Many young people desire to contribute meaningfully to their community and flourish when they are given an opportunity to do so.

Kretzmann and McKnight have examined the how neighborhood leaders can mobilize their assets and turn them into meaningful assets for community building. These researchers outline a four-step process for connecting youth with their communities:

Step 1: Make a detailed capacity inventory outlining all the various skills and assets for each youth involved in the community/school partnership.

Step 2: Compile an inventory of the community, as in local leaders, associations, and institutions. Community assets should fall in the following four categories: (1) citizens associations and not-for-profit organizations of all types; (2) publicly funded institutions such as hospitals, parks, libraries, and schools; (3) the private sector and small businesses, banks, and local branches of larger corporations; (4) local residents and special interest groups such as seniors and artists.

Step 3: Use the information that has been gleaned from the inventories in Step 2 to form partnerships with youth and individuals, organizations, and associations within their communities.

Step 4: Use the partnerships formed to establish new partnerships for youth with resources that exist outside the immediate community.

Table 8.1 represents a schematic framework for mapping a community's assets.

Kretzmann and McKnight provide an example of how youth in one school mapped the capacities of their neighborhood and used this information to make an important contribution to the community in which they lived. The fifth and sixth grades participated in an innovative curriculum at their school that involved their walking around their neighborhoods to learn about the buildings and the process of community planning. They saw the vacant lots and much discarded wood. One outcome of this project was that the students established a successful firewood venture. The young people became productive contributors to their communities because they understood how to use "mapping" techniques to discover that even old unused buildings and illegally-dumped scrap wood can become marketable assets for the community. Students must first gain knowledge about existing community assets in order to connect with the positive assets of their neighborhoods. To achieve this goal, the school sponsors an educational program in which young people learn about their own community and the process of community building. Next these students participate in a walking tour and slide presentation of their community. Information gained from a walking tour is used to construct goals for school and community partnerships.

Table 8.2 is a community profile that schools can use to represent the information they have gathered from mapping a school's assets.

SCHOOLS PARTNERING WITH FAMILIES AND COMMUNITIES MAKE A DIFFERENCE

Researchers associated with National Network of Partnership Schools (NNPS) have conducted studies on the impact of family involvement on various student outcomes (Epstein, 2005).[13] These studies found that family involvement contributed to positive results for students from kindergarten through high school on the following variables: higher academic achievement, better attendance, more course credits earned, more responsible preparation for class, and other indicators of success in school.[14] The *Focus on Results* studies revealed that when educators communicated clearly with families on targeted content

Table 8.1   Mapping Community Assets and Strengths

Directions: Asset mapping involves locating and making a "capacity inventory" of the talents, skills, strengths, and resources of individuals, associations, and institutions in a community. It helps to paint a community profile. It helps a school to determine the assets it can draw upon for specific strategic issues.

The following is a chart that allows your school to map the sources of the neighborhood/community in which your school is located. For each category, identify a specific individual, association, government, and/or cultural association that might be of assistance to your school for the purpose of developing partnerships with the school.

Individual Assets	Institutional Assets	Associations Assets	Government (City, State, and Federal) Assets	Physical and Land Assets	Cultural Assets
People demographics People occupations	Churches Colleges and universities	Community centers Radio/TV stations	City government State government	Agriculture Energy resources	Museum Cultural associations
Income of people	Libraries	Small businesses	State education agency	Industrial areas	Ethnic associations
Skills of people (clerical, construction and repair, maintenance, food, child care, music)	Police department	Neighborhood associations	Small business administration	Natural resources, lakes, ponds	Heritage groups
Leadership of people	Hospitals and clinics	Nonprofit organizations	Economic development department	Parks, recreation areas	Historic groups
Resources of people	Mental health facilities	Banks, corporations	Social services	Vacant land	Art groups
Mentoring	Fire department	Business associations	Senior agencies	Waste resources	Music groups

Table 8.2 Community Profile

Directions: Using the information gathered in your collection of mapping assets, complete a community profile that provides an overall view of the community in which your school is located.	
Population Description	
Major Ethnic, Racial, Cultural Groups	
Household Type/Presence and Age of Children and Youth	
Educational Attainment	
Median Household Income	
Unemployment Rate	
Key Industries	
Biggest Employers	
Major Occupations	
Major Civic and Nonprofit Organizations	
Churches/Religious Organizations	
Social Service Agencies	
Technology Use in the Community	
Schools and Educational Resources	
Recreational and Leisure Time	
Cultural Associations and Highlights	

about school attendance, the participating partnership schools' rates of average daily attendance increased, while students' chronic absence decreased from one year to the next.[15]

Studies conducted by researchers in the National Network of Partnership Schools reported the positive impact of parents on students in a number of other areas. When educators communicated effectively, and family and community members participated in activities related to student behavior, schools reported fewer disciplinary actions with students from one year to the next.[16] Similar positive results were obtained regarding students' academic achievement. In schools where educators implemented math homework that required parent-child interactions and offered math materials for families to take home, students' math proficiency scores increased from one year to the next. Studies have found repeatedly that family involvement with students' reading positively affected their reading skills and scores across the grades.[17]

Two of the best things a parent can do for his or her children are to help them identify their strengths and then nurture them in those areas. Often children fail their parents' dreams for them because such dreams were built on the parents' strengths rather than on those of the children. When parents tailor their parenting to their children's strengths, special bonding and closeness takes place between them. Children are happy, and parents feel they have done a good job in parenting. Everyone wins when parents help their children discover and nurture their strengths. Family involvement in students' academic and behavior success at school is integrated throughout the strengths-based school from kindergarten through Grade 12.

A SCHOOL/COMMUNITY PARTNERSHIP MODEL FOR STRENGTHS-BASED SCHOOLS

The National Network of Partnership Schools has established a research-based approach to arranging school partnering programs. Schools are asked to develop an Action Team for Partnerships that consists of teachers, administrators, parents, and community partners that is linked with members from the student council or school improvement team. The Action Team writes yearly plans for family and community involvement. It also implements and evaluates these activities.

Annual action plans utilize a research framework of six types of involvement—parenting, communicating, volunteering, learning at home, decision making, and collaborating with the community to develop home/school/community partnerships. When schools design activities for all six types of involvement, they can assist parents in becoming involved at school and at home with their children.[18] The six types of involvement are:

- *Parenting*: Help families with parenting skills, family support, understanding their children's psychosocial development, and forming home conditions to support learning at each age and grade level. Help schools in understanding families' backgrounds, cultures, and goals for children.
- *Communicating*: Schools communicate with families about school programs and student progress. Create different ways that schools and parents can communicate.
- *Volunteering*: Enhance recruitment, training, activities, and schedules to involve families as volunteers, and help educators work with volunteers for the benefit for students.
- *Learning at home*: Engage families with their children in academic learning at home, including homework, goal setting, and other curriculum-related activities.

- *Decision making*: Involve families in school decision making, governance via school improvement teams, committees, and parent organizations.
- *Collaborating with the community*: The school works to coordinate resources and services for families, students, and the school with community groups, including businesses, agencies, cultural and civic organizations, and colleges and universities.

In support of its program, the National Network of Partnership Schools has described positive school-family relationships. For instance, the Madison Junior High in Naperville, Illinois, has constructed a welcoming family program by implementing activities for all six types of family involvement.[19] Madison High held evening discussions about adolescence to help parents learn effective parenting strategies and to network with one another on published newsletters and other topics. They instituted a "Thursday Things" program, which was a weekly activity for sending things home. In addition, the school created a database of volunteers, held honor roll breakfasts, conducted family literacy nights, and built connections with business partners.

In St. Paul, Minnesota, Roosevelt Elementary School organized the Second Cup of Coffee Program,[20] which is a monthly morning activity during which parents meet with teachers, administrators, and other parents to discuss such diverse issues as testing, homework, and reading programs. This program has been helpful for families coming from culturally diverse backgrounds. Other parent and community programs developed by the National Network of Partnership Schools include the following:

- Atenville Elementary School, Harts, West Virginia, developed the Parents as Educational Partners program to overcome the geographic isolation of families in this rural coal-mining community.
- Buffalo Public Schools, Buffalo, New York, a large urban district, opened the Buffalo Parent Center to increase family involvement.
- Cane Run Elementary School in Louisville, Kentucky, in which a large proportion of students are eligible for free or reduced-price lunches, established a Family Resource Center and involves families in the school's decision making.
- Christopher Columbus Family Education Academy, New Haven, Connecticut, a public school with a large percentage of Latino students, developed the Parents as Educators program and opened a parent center.
- Ferguson Elementary School, Philadelphia, Pennsylvania, which serves an inner-city area of low-income families, hired a full-time school-community coordinator, constructed a parent center, and provides adult education classes.[21]

Two major national school partnership programs are *All Pro Dads* and the *Gentlemen's Club* and *Ladies' Club*. All Pro Dads (http:// www.AllProDad.com) is part of the fatherhood program of Family First. It consists of a monthly breakfast meeting of fathers and children. All men are invited, including fathers, stepfathers, uncles, brothers, and guardians (and mothers and grandmothers for children who do not live with their fathers), to have breakfast with their children at school. A major goal of the program is to forge stronger relationships among fathers/mothers and children and to increase the involvement of fathers in their children's education. Usually, either McDonald's or Chick-Fil-A provides breakfast, and prize drawings are held at each breakfast. During each meeting, parents and families discuss their children's strengths. Although typically parents share why they are proud of their children, students may also share why they are proud of their dad or mom. Community guest speakers present on the importance of fatherhood, successful parenting, and academic success.

One major benefit of All Pro Dads is that the breakfasts: (1) promote strengths-based instead of problem-focused conversations between teachers and parents; and (2) establish an encouraging environment for youth. Teachers have reported that All Pro Dads has increased parent involvement in the school.

The Gentlemen's Club and Ladies' Club (http://www .stephenpetersgroup.com) is a mentoring and after-school enrichment program. Stephen Peters[22] created the clubs to help poverty-stricken youth to avoid falling through the cracks. There are Gentlemen's Clubs and Ladies' Clubs in more than 100 schools throughout the United States, and the programs have been featured on the *Oprah Winfrey Show*. The goals of these programs are to: (1) instill hope and purpose in young people and to educate them about options for their lives; (2) help them learn that they do not have to be ruled by the rhythm of the streets; and (3) teach them the social skills and etiquette necessary to comport themselves like gentlemen and ladies. Programs have reported that Gentlemen's Clubs and Ladies' Clubs are student favorites and that those who participate in these programs like being taught how to be a gentleman or a lady. Students participating in these programs tend to show improvement in their grade point averages.[23]

Teachers can also use individual approaches to increasing the connection between families and the school. They can engage students in creating a *Scrapbook of Family Strengths* or a collage of family

> ## NO DISPOSABLE OR THROWAWAY KIDS
>
> The strengths-based approach says that we have to work toward recovering students who are diamonds in the rough.
> Deep down inside, young people want to become gentlemen and ladies

strengths. Teachers can introduce this project by asking such questions as:

- List three strengths that your family has.
- What family strengths hold your family together?
- How does your family use its strengths to overcome adversity?
- How might your family's strengths help you to deal with a difficulty you are currently facing?

STRENGTHS AND THE SCHOOL COMMUNITY INVOLVEMENT AND SERVICE LEARNING

Service-learning programs exist in every state in the union. The term *service learning* refers to a method that allows students to learn and develop through active participation in an organized service that is coordinated by a school and a community organization. Such activities are designed to foster civic responsibility among students. Service-learning projects are integrated into and enhance the core academic curriculum, and they provide structured time for the students to reflect on the service experienced. Typically, the major components of service learning include: active participation, thoughtfully organized experiences, focus on community needs and school/community coordination, academic curriculum integration, and development of a sense of caring for others. Essentially service learning is a teaching strategy that links community service experiences to classroom instruction.

There is a strong research base for including service learning in strengths-based schools. Studies have found repeatedly that service learning has a positive effect on the personal development of public school youths. Middle and high school students who participated in high-quality service-learning programs showed increases in measures of personal and social responsibility, communication, and sense of educational competence.[24] Service learning helps students to develop academic skills and knowledge. Students in more than half of the high-quality service-learning schools studied had moderate to strong gains on achievement tests in language arts or reading. Students reported that they learned more in service-learning classes than they did in other classes, and such learning was also associated with increased student attendance. Strengths-based schools incorporate service learning as an integral part of their academic curriculum based on the consistent reports that service learning improves students' sense of civic responsibility, their academic grades, their attendance, and their caring for others.

SUMMARY

The research evidence for building positive relationships between schools, parents, and communities is incontrovertible and long-standing. Besides the quality of teacher instruction, there are no more important variables than forming partnerships with parents and the local community. If you are in a low-achieving school district, you would be better to forge meaningful connections with the students' families and the communities in which they live than trying to get a fancy new approach to learning. The research is clear. First, get quality teachers working with young people, and they will achieve academically. Second, forge meaningful and quality relationships with the students' parents, families, and community, and you have done a great deal to increase the academic achievement and social-emotional development of youth.

9

Assuring Teachers Understand Their Own Strengths

In teaching you cannot see the fruit of a day 's work. It is invisible and remains so, maybe for twenty years.

—Jacques Barzun

One looks back with appreciation to the brilliant teachers, but with gratitude to those who touched our human feelings. The curriculum is so much necessary raw material, but warmth is the vital element for growing plant and the soul of the child.

—Carl Jung

GARDENS TEACHERS CULTIVATE

Teachers cultivate the gardens of children's mind and learning. In this respect, every classroom is a learning garden. Our favorite teachers are those who cultivated our gardens in some kind of special way. One of my favorite teachers was my geometry teacher, Mr. Gebler, a six-foot-two white man with pepper gray wavy hair. He was a 50- to 60-year-old engineer who had left a lucrative career in corporate America and came to teaching because he wanted to do something meaningful with his life. Geometry and I did not get along very well, but Mr. Gebler made it interesting somehow. I cannot remember Mr. Gebler ever having disciplinary problems in his class. We all believed that he cared about us. Why did we think this? I do not know. Maybe it was because he was available to meet with us for extra help. I think what came through was his very caring voice and attitude.

I can remember going in to see Mr. Gebler during lunch hour and working with him, who usually had a sandwich in his hand. One day I came in, and Mr. Gebler handed me a paper that he wanted me to read before we got started on the extra-credit problems. It was a teacher recommendation form that I did not even know that teachers completed on each one of us. "Read it, Elsie," he said. "I want you to know what I said about you." I read it and I was quite surprised about the many positive things that he said about me. After all, I was not one of his "A" students who always had the answer before he could complete the question. I was coming in for extra credit and "enrichment," as he nicely put it.

I do not recall all that he said, but I remember the handwritten comments that he wrote at the end of the checklist on the bottom of the page. He said: "Always gracious, always a lady." I have carried those words inside me for all of my life. I had never seen myself as trying to be a lady or gracious. Why, I could mix it up with the best of them. Yet Mr. Gebler had seen qualities in me that I had never seen in myself. His kind words motivated me to achieve and to consider how I was presenting myself to the world. He cultivated my learning garden about geometry and life itself. "Wherever you are, Mr. Gebler, thank you"; and I bow graciously to honor you as one of my favorite teachers.

The best teachers do more than instruct. They inspire us to believe in ourselves. They see strengths that are just beginning to dawn in our awareness. This statement is supported by research on favorite teachers. Recently, the Horace Mann Educators Corporation of Illinois asked 1,099 adults a series of questions about their favorite teachers. Some of the questions included: Whose image comes to mind when you see the phrase "your favorite teacher"? What was it about this teacher that has kept a hold on your memory in such a positive way for all these years? What was so great about him or her? What did you take from this teacher that has lasted? The findings of the Horace Mann survey revealed that the most enduring teachers were "not the ones with the most facts in their heads or who delivered the most information. They were not those who held the firmest or the deepest grasp of knowledge. Instead, favorites were those who had displayed a personal interest in their students caring and engaging dynamics, genuine love for their role as a teacher, and who continually offered encouragement and praise."[1]

Teachers have an enormous impact on young people from their first enrollment in kindergarten through Grade 12. Some years ago, Werner and Smith[2] found that children's most frequently mentioned role

---

THE VALUE OF TEACHERS

"Modern cynics and skeptics ... see no harm in paying those to whom they entrust the minds of their children a smaller wage than is paid to those to whom they entrust the care of their plumbing."

—John F. Kennedy, former president of the United States

---

model, outside their circle of family members, was a favorite teacher. These mentioned teachers were often referred to as "turnaround teachers." They were described as caring individuals who developed relationships with their students. Students portrayed such teachers as being interested in them, actively listening to them, and validating their feelings, knowing their strengths, and conveying the sentiment that "you matter."

For the average young person, teachers are more than instructors for academic skills. They are role models that a young person uses to guide his or her behavior. Good teachers use such knowledge as a beginning point for teaching. Strengths-based teachers also tend to hold high expectations for students' achievements.

This chapter begins with a brief review of studies on the qualities of effective teachers. I focus primarily on what students say are the qualities of effective teachers. Next, it examines the role of teacher expectations on student achievement. Following this section, the skills for strengths-based teachers are offered. Finally, I present material on how teachers can discover their teaching strengths, and I present effective teaching strategies.

BRIEF REVIEW OF STUDIES ON QUALITIES OF EFFECTIVE TEACHERS

Jennifer Rice[3] reported that five broad categories of teacher attributes related to teacher quality are: "(1) experience, (2) preparation programs and degrees; (3) type of certification, (4) coursework taken in preparation for the profession, and (5) teacher test scores." Barnett Berry[4] examined the criteria that lead to a designation of highly qualified teacher. Although he agreed generally with Rice's finding, he contended that highly qualified teachers must also know "how to organize and teach their lessons in ways that assure diverse students can learn those subjects ... Highly qualified teachers don't just teach

---

CULTURE OF ACADEMIC ACHIEVEMENT

Strengths-based teachers establish a culture of academic achievement as is defined by students who:

- Are motivated to work hard for academic success
- Set high academic goals for themselves
- Take steps to find ways to reach those goals
- Take responsibility for their mistakes and learn from them
- Collaborate with classmates for high academic achievement

---

well-designed, standards-based lessons. They know how and why their students learn."

Donald Cruickshank, Deborah Jenkins, and Kim Metcalf[5] concluded in their book *The Act of Teaching* that effective teachers are caring teachers. The authors state:

> Most people would agree that good teachers are caring, supportive, concerned about the welfare of students, knowledgeable about their subject matter, able to get along with parents . . . and genuinely excited about the work that they do . . . Effective teachers are able to help students learn.

Nel Noddings[6] has provided a definition of what constitutes a caring teacher. According to her, caring is shown in a number of ways, including being attentive and receptive. Nodding stated: "A caring teacher is someone who has demonstrated that she[he] can establish, more or less regularly, relations of care in a wide variety of situations . . . [and] will want the best for that person." (pp. 100–101)

QUOTATIONS FROM TEACHERS

"The only reason I always try to meet and know the parents better is because it helps me to forgive their children."

—Louis Johannot

"If you promise not to believe everything your child says happens at school, I'll promise not to believe everything he says happens at home."

—Anonymous

Susan Thompson, John Greer, and Bonnie Greer,[7] all from the University of Memphis, conducted a study on characteristics every teacher should possess. The study examined the reflections of university students on the characteristics of their favorite teachers. The results show that there were 12 common characteristics central to what students considered good teaching. The characteristics are strongly related to the theme of caring for students, both academically and personally. They are as follows: (1) fairness, (2) positive attitude, (3) preparedness, (4) personal touch, (5) sense of humor, (6) creativity, (7) willingness to make mistakes, (8) forgiving, (9) respect, (10) high expectations, (11) compassion, and (12) sense of belonging. The authors concluded, "These traits have proven to increase student achievement."

THE ROLE OF TEACHER EXPECTATIONS AND YOUNG PEOPLE'S ACHIEVEMENT

Teacher expectations can have a powerful influence on whether a youth's strengths will be used to achieve academically or to overcome adversity in his or her environment. In 1968 Jane Elliott,[8] an Iowa teacher, conducted a classroom experiment on tolerance with her students. She divided her class of all white students into two groups, those with brown eyes and those with blue eyes. The experiment involved her manipulating the two groups into either superior or inferior categories based on their eye color. On one day, she would tell the group that the students with blue eyes were the superior ones, and on another day, she said she had made a mistake and those with brown eyes were really the superior ones. The superior group would receive special treatment that the inferior group did not. The results of Ms. Elliott's experiment revealed that the "superior" group was confident and performed better academically than they did when they were told they were in the inferior group. The inferior group was sullen and withdrawn and performed lower academically, regardless of whether they had brown or blue eyes.

Without intending to do so, some schools place children into inferior and superior groups, and then they wonder why the children are low-achieving, angry, and violent. As Ricardo Stanton-Salazer and Stephanie Spina[9] maintained, educators must better state how the forces of exclusion and social oppression have been routinely normalized within every institutional structure within which minority families and youth live. "We must seek to better articulate how the forces

THE POWER OF EXPECTATIONS

"High achievement always takes place in the framework of high
  expectation."

—Jack Kinder

"A master can tell you what he expects of you. A teacher, though,
  awakens your own expectations."

—Patricia Neal

"High expectations are the key to everything."

—Sam Walton

of exclusion and social oppression have become normalized within
every institutional structure which minority families and youth must
routinely negotiate (e.g. public schools, housing, job market, judicial
system)" (p. 000). These researchers point out that the needs of marginalized youth must be addressed in a culturally appropriate manner
that is responsive to the barriers they encounter. Educational and counseling interventions must identify young people's needs and provide
opportunities for them to engage with their own cultures and communities in positive ways.

Stanton-Salazer and Spina's work have particular relevance to African American male students. African American males encounter
circumstances in schools that challenge their academic success in
school. In an extensive review of the literature, Ronald Ferguson[10]
found that teachers tend to hold lower expectations for African American males and that their lower expectations contributed to their disengagement. Ferguson noted:

> Teachers in integrated schools can be 'biased' in ways as simple as
> reinforcing a propensity of White children to speak more often in class
> (e.g., see Katz as cited in Brophy & Good, 1974; Irvine, 1990). Black stu-
> dents may assume that this means teachers think Whites are 'smarter'
> or like the White students more. Ways that teachers communicate about
> academic ability, especially in integrated schools where the perfor-
> mance of Whites is superior, can affect the degree to which Black stu-
> dents disengage from the pursuit of excellence or stay engaged and
> aim for mastery. (p. 483)

Terrell Strayhorn[11] found that teachers have lower expectations for
black males in comparison with white males and black females. He
used a sample of adults and asked them to reflect back on their high

school years. In comparison with white males and African American females, black male adults reported that teachers tended to recommend that they choose work rather than college.

Clearly, teachers cannot control everything that a young person does or perceives. Teachers can control, however, what they themselves do—what they say, how they respond, and how they present their expectations for students and for themselves. It is important that teachers set high and explicit expectations for student work and achievement. Teachers must also establish high standards for students' behavior. Teachers strive to maintain student dignity and do not punish or humiliate them publicly.

Here is a brief exercise you can do to help clarify your teaching expectations. Generate a list of student expectations by completing the statement: "In my classroom, I expect students to _____."

Prioritize your teaching expectations from highly important to least important. After you have accomplished this part of the exercise, have your students list their expectations of you, of themselves, and of the class as they relate to learning and interpersonal relationships within the class. Have them rank their expectations from highly important to least important. Discuss with your students their expectations in those three areas. Does your personal list of expectations match your students' list? What did you learn from discussing your students' learning and interpersonal expectations for your class? Share your list with students and have them rank your list from highly important to least important.

Importance of Believing in a Child

Closely connected to teachers' expectations is the idea of believing in a child. I remember working with a student who was writing a paper for her high school psychology class. She had been giving her parents quite a bit of difficulty—hanging around with the wrong kids, mouthing off in disrespectful ways, and not keeping her room clean. She called me on the telephone to read her papers for English and psychology.

The paper in psychology dealt with her own searching for who she was. She had been adopted from birth, and she told me that she felt bad because she did not look like either of her

> ## GARDENERS DO NOT TAMPER WITH THE SEED
>
> All of us who work with youth are gardeners who must nurture not tamper with the seed . . . because there is a flower inside.

parents—one African American and the other white. Her parents had told her that her mother was a Puerto Rican and her father German. "That's a really beautifully written paper," I said after listening to her intently. "You think so?" she responded. "I know so, Jana. I don't have to think about it. Your paper is beautifully written." I encouraged her to consider becoming a psychology major because of the insights that she had shown. She questioned me: "Do you actually think I am going to make it to college?" In response to her apparent self-doubt, I replied: "I believe in you. I think that you could do just about anything that you set your mind to do."

Jana began to cry. For a moment, I just listened to her tears. "Tell me what your tears are all about, Jana." Crying softly, she replied: "You said you believe in me. No one has ever said that he believed in me— not my mother, not my father, not my brother. They're always telling me what's wrong with me—I'm too loud, too sloppy, too mouthy . . . but you said that you believe in me." Believing in a child or youth is very important, especially when he or she is trying to establish an identity for him- or herself. Research has found that if just one person holds firm to his or her belief in a child, it can make a significant positive difference in how that child feels about him- or herself.[12] In fact, Bonnie Benard[13] has written that a parent's, counselor's, or teacher's belief in a child can be a part of his or her dynamic change for the better. Using a garden metaphor related to belief, Benard stated:

> I suggest that we need to begin with belief in the innate resilience of every human being, and with the metaphor that all of us who work with youth are gardeners, whose young people are the flowers in our care. . . . In our role as gardeners we do not tamper with the seed—the flower is in there. (p. 113)

Jana did not live in the inner city. Her parents were, by all standards, middle-class if not upper-middle-class professionals. Ye, the pain of her parents' and her teachers' lack of belief in her brought tears. Experience has taught me to recognize pain—whether it is in a middle-class kid who has many of the material comforts of life or an inner-city kid struggling to deal with serious trauma that would make you wonder how he or she can manage how to get out of bed every day and go to school. As Anne Masten[14] has pointed out, children and adults who have experienced pain and suffering almost invariably develop some ideas, capacities, skills, values, and/or traits that help them to tackle challenges in later development. Self-understanding of one's ability to deal with stress sometimes serves as the building blocks—the bricks and mortar for building a better life. When working with students, it is important for teachers and counselors to find out from students the trials they have encountered and the lessons they have learned and strengths they have developed from their ordeals.

Teachers must learn how to engage their students in a process of strengths discovery. You can engage students in a strengths discovery process by letting them know that you are interested in their talents and strengths, as well as their hopes and dreams. In addition, encourage your students to tell and to write about their stories—their journeys toward academic achievement and their search for self-esteem. Even as students tell stories that involve significant real-life challenges, listen carefully to hear their strengths—meaning the times in which they met challenges, avoided destructive or harmful behavior, or overcame adversities successfully. After listening to your students' stories, reflect back to them their strengths. Help them began to acquire a language of strength rather than one of defeat—a language that affirms and appreciates their strengths. Some questions that promote students' thinking about their strengths include: What is it that you like most about yourself? What do others like about you? What things have you done that you feel really good about? Dealing with their ability to survive difficult situations, you might ask: Given everything that you have had to face, how have you managed to survive? Which of the challenges you have faced has helped you to develop strengths that you will use again in life? How have you become stronger as a result of the difficulty that you faced?

What are other ways teachers might promote students' strength development? As mentioned previously, listen for their strengths in the stories they tell about their lives. Believe that your students have a self-righting capacity—that is, they have the ability to "right themselves," to pick themselves up from difficult life experiences. Display students' strengths publicly in your classroom and throughout the school. Help students become involved constructively in your school—as mentors, advisors, school leaders, and tutors. The strengths-based teacher sees him- or herself as a collaborator in building students' hopes.

STRENGTHS-BASED TEACHERS: NEEDED SKILLS AND COMPETENCIES

In strengths-based schools, it is important that school administrators recognize teachers' unique talents and strengths. When we provide opportunities for teachers to demonstrate their strengths, we improve our schools. Strengths-based education involves educators discovering and unfolding their own strengths and applying them to help students learn and to reach a high level of personal excellence. It represents a different way of working with students and developing programs and educational services for them. If teachers cannot see their students' strengths, then how can they guide them to achieve their best academically and in later life?

It is important for teachers to take into consideration students' theories of what it means to be intelligent because such views can affect their performance. Studies have found that students who think that intelligence is a fixed entity are more likely to be performance oriented than learning oriented; that is, they want to look good rather than take risks making mistakes while learning. Such students are inclined to bail out when tasks become difficult. In contrast, students who believe that intelligence is malleable are more willing to struggle with challenging tasks because they are more comfortable with risk.[15]

In addition to establishing a learner-centered classroom, strengths-based teachers create a knowledge-centered classroom environment that focuses attention on what is taught (information and subject matter), why it is taught (understanding), and what competence or mastery looks like. One of the conclusions in *How People Learn: Bridging Research and Practice*[16] is that in order for people to achieve a level of expertise, they must have been exposed to well-organized knowledge that supports understanding and that learning with understanding is important for students' development of expertise because it makes new learning easier. It is not easy, however, for teachers to teach so that students learn with understanding. It is more difficult to accomplish learning with understanding than simply memorizing. Sometimes teachers fail to engender learning with understanding because they present too many disconnected facts in too short a time. The problem is further exacerbated when tests reinforce memorizing rather than understanding. How teachers teach and the types of classrooms they organize—either teacher centered or learner/student centered—is a function of their own strengths, which may or may not be evident to them.

STRENGTHS

"Everyone—every child, every individual, every family, every group, every community, and yes, every teacher and school—has assets, resources, and capacities."

—Dennis Saleebey

Why Is It Important for Students and Teachers to Learn Their Strengths?

Strengths not only pave the way for your success in an endeavor, but they also energize you.

They create positive emotions, which create new channels for learning and complex problem solving. When we use our strengths, we are also more inclined to invest greater time and effort because strengths are self-reinforcing. Barbara Fredrickson's[17] studies have provided insight regarding why it is important for both teachers and students to learn their strengths. Fredrickson and her colleagues investigated the impact of positive emotions in a variety of situations. Some of her studies showed that positive emotions have a unique capacity to put people's bodies at ease. In contrast, negative emotions, such as anger, fear, anxiety—even sadness and crying—arouse individuals' autonomic nervous systems, and produce increases in their heart rate, vasoconstriction, and blood pressure, among other changes.[18] Laboratory experiments have found that experiences of positive emotions can quiet or undo the lingering cardiovascular effects of these negative emotions. In comparison with neutral distractions and sadness, positive emotions produce faster returns to baseline levels of cardiovascular activation following negative emotional arousal.[19]

In the book *Positivity: Groundbreaking Research Reveals How to Embrace the Hidden Strength of Positive Emotions*, Barbara Fredrickson[20] describes 10 forms of positivity: joy, gratitude, serenity, interest, hope, pride, amusement, inspiration, awe, and love. According to Fredrickson, (1) positivity makes you feel good; (2) it changes how your mind work; (3) it transforms your future; (4) it puts the brakes on negativity; (5) it obeys a tipping point; and (6) you can increase your positivity. Consultant and researcher Marcial Losada has helped Fredrickson discover a tipping point in the positivity ration. The positivity ratio is the ratio of people's positive experiences to their negative ones. There is a tipping point at which flourishing starts and below which it does not. This positivity ratio tipping point is 3:1. When individuals experience three times or more as many positive experiences than they do negative ones, flourishing begins with all of its benefits. Fredrickson also proposed a second tipping point of 11:1, which is the upper bound of flourishing. Above this upper bound, there may be too much positivity. She maintains that there will always be a useful role for some negativity. Fredrickson found that most people have more positive than negative experiences, but they are below the 3:1 tipping point. There are many ways to raise your positivity so that flourishing is attainable for most people.

Fredrickson has captured much of her theory about the effects of positivity on people in what she labels as her broaden-and-build theory. This theory states that your experiences of positive emotions broadens your thinking and helps you build enduring personal resources, which helps to transform you and to produce upward spirals in your development.

The significance of Fredrickson's human strengths theory and strengths-based education cannot be overestimated. Our awareness of our strengths leads to positive emotions, which broaden and build complex thinking on our part. The complex thinking on our part then leads to a response repertoire that contains feelings of our own self-efficacy, which in turn, increase our motivation to excel.

The Case for Students

What does all of this mean for learning and strengths-based education? When students learn about their strengths, they are inclined to engage in complex thinking and feelings of self-efficacy—"I can do this"; "I can learn this; "I can achieve this." The resultant formula is that students' awareness of their strengths leads to their feelings of self-efficacy, which in turn increase their motivation to achieve in school. As students engage in a pattern of strengths development at their schools, they discover different *strengths pathways* to achieve their goals. The positive effects of strengths development produces feelings of hope. Students' application of their strengths leads to academic achievement. When students learn how to apply their strengths to new situations or challenges, they develop resilience and coping skills.

Students develop interpersonal intelligence and a sense of community when they learn how to recognize strengths in others and how

> ## LOOK FOR STUDENTS' STRENGTHS RATHER THAN THEIR WEAKNESSES
>
> Strengths-based teachers take a nonpathological approach to problem solving, which makes students' problems seem solvable.

their strengths function to promote relationships. The view that students develop based on their development of strengths pathways and their strengths application leads them to develop a *strengths or a deficit mindset*. Students' development promotes complex and higher order thinking on the part of students. Strengths awareness also tends to promote better interpersonal relationships in the classroom as students may experience a positive tipping point. A positive tipping point quells negative student emotions, such as anger, fighting, etc. When students learn to apply their strengths to their areas of weakness, they stand a greater chance of achieving success even with their weak areas.

The Case for Teachers

Teachers also benefit from knowing their strengths—in much the same way as do students. That is, as teachers become aware of their strengths, they experience positive emotions toward themselves and their students. These positive emotions encourage teachers to establish caring, learner-centered classrooms. Recognizing the value of their own strengths awareness on their lives, teachers seek to help their students achieve this same benefit. The net result is that teacher-student relations become more positive and more nurturing.

In addition, teachers' awareness of their teaching strengths helps them feel more confident in their ability to teach. When teachers are confident in their own teaching ability, they are inclined to feel satisfied and happy with their jobs. Teacher confidence in their teaching ability leads to better and more competent instruction in the classroom.

A brief example illustrates the importance of teacher strengths awareness and lack thereof. *Teacher 1* has spent most of student teaching focused on what he or she did wrong. He or she is careful to avoid falling in the trap of the weaknesses that the supervising teacher identified. *Teacher 2* has undergone a strengths awareness and discovery program, which has caused him or her to feel a sense of self-efficacy and competency about teaching. *Teacher 1* dreads having the principal or supervising teacher make a teacher observation. Fear, a negative emotion, is the dominating emotion. *Teacher 2* welcomes the principal and the supervising teacher in his or her classroom because such observations provide an opportunity for strengths application and excellence. Teacher 2 can be compared to a musician who wants to share his or her music with the principal.

When teachers are aware of their strengths and can apply them successfully in the classroom, students are inclined to feel connected to the teacher, and they learn better than when they have a teacher who does not know his or her teaching strengths. Teacher application of teaching strengths leads to a positive classroom climate and fewer behavioral problems.

Now that I have considered some potential benefits of teacher and student awareness of their strengths, the next section discusses ways that teachers can identify their teaching strengths.

IDENTIFYING YOUR TEACHING STRENGTHS

It is not easy to identify your own teaching strengths. This section contains several different ways that you can discover them. Think back on the best lesson that you ever taught. What motivated you as you were teaching? What passion was elicited within you? What strengths were operating during your teaching? What knowledge were you dealing with during that session? Now consider a challenge you face in your teaching. How might you use your strengths to counteract that weakness/challenge? You might also complete the sentences: My greatest teaching strength is _____. My greatest weakness as a teacher is_____. Consider having your students generate their own list of positive teacher characteristics and strengths. Ask them to fill in the blank for the following statement: "I think the best teachers are those who_____."

Teaching Strengths Checklist

In Table 9.1, I have developed a teaching strengths checklist to provide you a means to evaluate your use of the strengths perspective in your teaching. The checklist is not exhaustive. As you teach and discuss

Table 9.1   Teaching Strengths Checklist

Directions: This checklist has been developed to help you to begin thinking about your teaching strengths. There are no wrong or right answers. Use this inventory as your own private checklist for teaching. After you complete this checklist, ask yourself if you are meeting the learning needs of your students.

For each of the items listed below, write the number that most closely corresponds to the degree to which you believe this is a strength for you.

High Strength = 5; Medium Strength = 4; Low Strength = 3; Functional Competency =2; Weakness = 1

_____1 I am passionate about my teaching.

_____2. I am a good listener.

_____3. I know how to engage students in the learning process.

_____4. I have high expectations for my students.

_____5. I establish a learner-centered classroom rather than a teacher-centered classroom.

_____6. My lessons are well organized.

_____7. I show students that I care about them and that they matter to me.

_____8. I have a fair system for assessing and grading students.

_____9. My homework assignments are meaningful.

_____10. I build upon students' strengths during my lesson planning and execution.

_____11. I encourage my students to perform their very best.

_____12. I activate my students' prior knowledge in order to build new material on what they already know.

_____13. I show a sense of humor when I am teaching.

_____14. I nurture students' strengths and talents.

_____15. I have good classroom management skills.

_____16. I use a variety of instructional strategies to help teach a diverse classroom of learners.

_____17. I have excellent subject matter mastery.

_____18. I use excellent creativity in my teaching.

_____19. I communicate well with students.

_____20. I incorporate and teach problem-solving skills in my activities so that students have an opportunity to learn how to make informed decisions.

_____21. I involve students in helping to create in helping to create some of the rules and consequences of behavior in the classroom so that they experience greater responsibility for their own behavior.

_____22. I identify and reinforce the strengths of students.

_____23. I use hands-on activities in my classroom.

_____24. I build sound relationships with students.

_____25. I have high expectations for my students and am able to motivate them with my high expectations.

_____26. I teach to multiple learning styles.

(continued)

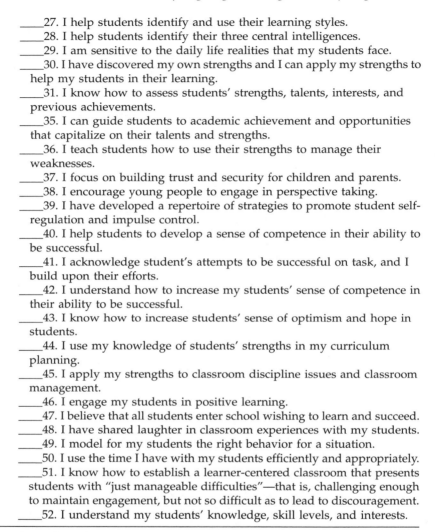

____27. I help students identify and use their learning styles.

____28. I help students identify their three central intelligences.

____29. I am sensitive to the daily life realities that my students face.

____30. I have discovered my own strengths and I can apply my strengths to help my students in their learning.

____31. I know how to assess students' strengths, talents, interests, and previous achievements.

____35. I can guide students to academic achievement and opportunities that capitalize on their talents and strengths.

____36. I teach students how to use their strengths to manage their weaknesses.

____37. I focus on building trust and security for children and parents.

____38. I encourage young people to engage in perspective taking.

____39. I have developed a repertoire of strategies to promote student self-regulation and impulse control.

____40. I help students to develop a sense of competence in their ability to be successful.

____41. I acknowledge student's attempts to be successful on task, and I build upon their efforts.

____42. I understand how to increase my students' sense of competence in their ability to be successful.

____43. I know how to increase students' sense of optimism and hope in students.

____44. I use my knowledge of students' strengths in my curriculum planning.

____45. I apply my strengths to classroom discipline issues and classroom management.

____46. I engage my students in positive learning.

____47. I believe that all students enter school wishing to learn and succeed.

____48. I have shared laughter in classroom experiences with my students.

____49. I model for my students the right behavior for a situation.

____50. I use the time I have with my students efficiently and appropriately.

____51. I know how to establish a learner-centered classroom that presents students with "just manageable difficulties"—that is, challenging enough to maintain engagement, but not so difficult as to lead to discouragement.

____52. I understand my students' knowledge, skill levels, and interests.

Note: Copyright © Elsie J. Smith.

with your students positive strengths they see in you, you will most likely add items to the list.

Identifying Teaching Strengths from Peak Classroom Experiences

Evaluate your teaching strengths by examining peak teaching periods. Describe an example from your experience for each of the categories listed below. *Your responses will give you insights into your teaching strengths.*

1. *A student learning breakthrough*: Describe a time when your teaching led to a student having an "aha" moment or an insight about concepts you had been teaching.
2. *A student relationship breakthrough*: Provide an example of a time in which you knew you had really "connected" with a student or with a class.
3. *A lesson you wish your supervisor had observed for a performance evaluation*: Think of a time that the lesson you taught was hitting on all four cylinders. You used several instructional strategies, engaged the students, and accomplished your teaching and learning objectives.
4. *Student encouragement*: Provide an example of a time when your praise or encouragement lifted or motivated a student.
5. *Creative improvisation*: Provide an example of a time when you had to change your plans and improvise—and it worked!
6. *Teacher role modeling*: Provide an example of a time when you modeled for students the right behavior or response to a situation.
7. *Shared classroom laughter*: Provide an example of a situation where you and your students shared a laugh or amusement together.
8. *A class surprise*: Provide an example of a situation where the students pleasantly and unexpectedly surprised you.

Table 9.2 provides a chart teachers can use to assess their teaching strengths and teaching strategies.

PROFESSIONAL DEVELOPMENT AND SHARING WITH TEACHING COLLEAGUES

Strengths-based teachers improve their strengths by participating in their own professional development, which usually involves their sharing and working with teaching colleagues. One way teachers can improve upon their teaching strengths is to share videotapes of their teaching with each other. Each teacher videotapes two teaching sessions, reviews those tapes, and then answers the following questions:

- If you were a student in his or her class, would you have learned from this teacher?
- Is this teacher engaging and personable to the class as a whole?
- Is this teacher qualified in the subject area?
- How would you describe the teacher's teaching style?
- Was the teacher's presentation organized and well planned?

Table 9.2 My Teaching Strengths and Strategies

Directions: Identify five teaching strengths. For each teaching strength, indicate how you use the teaching strength in lesson preparation, classroom management, instruction, and mentoring and working interpersonally with students.

Teaching Strength (Describe Strength)	How I Use This Strength in Lesson Preparation	How I Use This Strength in Class-room Management	How I Use This Strength in Teach-ing and Instruction	How I Use This Strength in Mentoring and Working with Students
First Teaching Strength				
Second Teaching Strength				
Third Teaching Strength				
Fourth Teaching Strength				
Fifth Teaching Strength				

Note: Copyright © Elsie J. Smith.

- Did the teacher's lesson engage the students' learning?
- What strengths did the teacher demonstrate in this lesson?
- What areas of weakness did the teacher show in this lesson?
- Did the teacher spend the appropriate amount of time dealing with the primary learning objectives of his or her lesson?

Developing Your Key Strengths Teaching Statement

Sometimes it is difficult to arrive at your teaching strengths. In fact, most teaching interviews ask this very question. If you are a teacher in training, be prepared to answer it. Regardless of whether you are at an interview for a teaching job or being evaluated by your teaching supervisor, it is helpful if you think of specific situations where you worked with students successfully.

A "Key Strengths" statement is a summary of your most powerful skills and attributes. It can be given at a performance evaluation of your teaching with a supervisor or during your interview for a teaching position. Your Key Strengths teaching statement:

- Highlights your most important skills and abilities
- Distinguishes you from the group of other teachers or teacher applicants
- Avoids generalizations
- Gives examples of your teaching achievements or peak teaching experiences
- Should take no more than three minutes

It is important for prospective teachers to be able to answer teaching strengths questions because if you do not know your strengths as a teacher, how effective can you be in the classroom? Would you hire a medical doctor who did not know his or her strengths or a plumber who was not sure of what he or she could do? I doubt it. Likewise, school districts are reluctant to hire teachers who cannot articulate their teaching strengths. During an interview for a teaching position, the interviewer may ask a teaching strengths question in several different ways. For instance, he or she may ask:

- What are your three primary teaching strengths?
- Why should our school district hire you?
- What can you contribute to our students and our school district?
- What would you say to convince me you are the right person for our school district?
- What is the goodness of fit between your teaching skills and the needs of our students?
- How might you go about establishing a strengths-based classroom?

Summary of Benefits of Strengths-Based Teaching

Strengths-based learning goes beyond what is usually found in schools. It requires more time, energy, intentional planning, thought, action, and reflection than most young people are used to investing. In strengths-based schools, teachers must be enabled and encouraged to establish a community of learners. These communities provide a sense of comfort to students as they become more interested in questioning rather than knowing the answer.

Teachers who use a strengths-based approach develop ways of linking classroom learning to other aspects of students' lives. They elicit parent support for the core learning principles and parent involvement in the learning process. On average, students spend 53 percent of their time in their homes and communities; 33 percent is spent sleeping, and 14 percent in school. If teachers focus only on the hours that students spend in school, they will have overlooked many opportunities for guided learning in other settings. Below is a summary of the benefits of strengths-based teaching for children and adolescents based partly on Fredrickson's broaden-and-build theory of positive emotions. It is left up to the principal or the chief academic officer to [missing word(s)] take these potential benefits into account when deciding whether or not to develop a strengths-based school.

Benefits of Strengths-Based Teaching for Children/Adolescents

Personal Self-Knowledge

The benefits in personal self-knowledge for children and adolescents who engage in strengths-based learning are:

- Have increased awareness of their strengths
- Evidence increased personal self-confidence
- Learn strengths behavior patterns that make them effective
- Learn strengths thought patterns that empower them to succeed
- Learn strengths-based attitudes that sustain their efforts toward achievement and excellence
- Understand themselves better
- Apply strengths in their daily personal lives

Academic Learning

With regard to academic learning, children and adolescents who engage in strengths-based learning:

- Demonstrate increased confidence in their academic abilities
- Use their strengths in study and learning strategies
- Believe that they can and will earn higher grades
- Know better where they can excel academically
- Are more positive toward learning and adopt positive study habits

Goals and Motivation/Making Connections

With regard to goals and motivation/making connections, children and adolescents who engage in strengths-based learning:

- Learn what motivates them to take action and how to maintain the energy required to achieve
- Are more willing to work for goals when they use their strengths
- Become more optimistic about their futures
- Make clear plans and goals
- Make connections between their strengths, academic achievement, and career goals

Improved Interpersonal Understandings and Relationships

With regard to interpersonal understandings and relationships, children and adolescents who engage in strengths-based learning:

- Learn how to view others in terms of their strengths
- Express a desire to help others discover their strengths
- Notice strengths in others
- Make an effort to relate to the strengths they see in others
- Tell their peers, family members, and others about their strengths
- Children and adolescents use their strengths to help others

Benefits for Teachers, Educators, and Guidance Counselors

Strengths-based education:

- Helps teachers, educators, and guidance counselors see students in a more positive light
- Represents a positive way for teachers, educators, and guidance counselors to view themselves as a professional
- Assists teachers to establish caring classrooms
- Improves their teaching effectiveness and their instructional learning strategies
- Helps teachers design strategies for engaging students meaningfully in the learning process
- Helps teachers to improve students' levels of academic achievement

- Motivates and engages students in their own learning process so that they are able to attain their best performance
- Creates classroom activities and assignment that help students to explore and develop their strengths related to specific academic tasks and assignment
- Helps teachers apply their strengths to each aspect of their teaching, such as preparation and course design, interactions with students in class, mentoring and advising students, and evaluating and giving feedback to students.

SUMMARY

This chapter has discussed the importance of teachers learning their teaching strengths. The chapter began with a discussion of teachers as cultivators of students' learning gardens. Research on favorite teachers was examined, and a set of common characteristics of favorite and effective teachers were identified. The role of teacher expectations on student achievement was analyzed. Using Fredrickson's research on positivity and her broaden-and-build theory of positive emotions as a foundation, I presented a model for asserting the importance of identifying students' and teachers' strengths.

The chapter contains a section on identifying your teaching strengths. I offered an instrument designed to give teachers some ways that can discover their strengths. A section on identifying teaching strengths by examining peak teaching experiences was presented. The chapter concluded with a summary of the benefits of strengths-based teaching for students and teachers.

Creating and Communicating a Strengths-Based School Vision: Getting Involved

I would give all the wealth of the world, and all the deeds of the heroes, for one true vision.

—Henry David Thoreau[1]

It is a terrible thing to see and have no vision".

—Helen Keller[2]

We do not need more of the things that are seen, we need more of the things that are unseen.

—Calvin Coolidge[3]

CREATING A GARDEN VISION

Every garden begins with a vision. It is difficult, however, to think about a vision for your garden when you are in the throes of winter and the ground is covered with six inches of fresh snow. Who thinks about gardening in the dead of winter? I do, and so do large numbers of gardeners who have hopes for planting beautiful gardens that blossom in the spring. Often, the most beautiful gardens are those that have been planned, conceptualized in your head long before spring greets you with warm temperatures and sunny skies. Visions for our gardens are begun in our hearts and viewed in our mind's eye. Whenever I look at a garden, I realize that someone took the time to have a dream of what might be—long before it was. We have to know what we want in our garden. Then we have to plant the right seeds, then cultivate—and that takes having a vision of what we desire.

Just as it is hard to think about gardening in the dead of winter, it is likewise difficult to think about creating a school vision when our schools are failing and being challenged by nations that just 50 years ago faced their own unique set of challenges. American schools are long overdue for a revamping. American schools need to change because they are not only failing our students but also failing our nation. A major paradigm shift is needed to move us out of a deficit-based remedial framework.

One major problem is that schools are being asked to carry burdens they were never really intended to shoulder. For instance, still enduring the lingering effects of the recession, many inner-city kids come to school just to have two full meals a day, some heat, and a place where they can camp out for six hours without someone asking them to move along. In poor neighborhoods, American schools help to hide what would be soup lines for our children. For these children, American schools have become daytime shelters. The soup lines are in the school cafeteria—hidden from the view of the American people. We have yet to come to terms with poverty in the United States, with homeless children living under bridges and in shady hotels that should have been demolished long ago. As stark poverty has increased in our nation, so has the academic achievement of our youth decreased precipitously.

Yet the problem with low American educational achievement is more than just one of poverty. There is large-scale poverty in India—much worse than what we have in America—but academic achievement in India is higher than in the United States. Korea has poverty; yet students from that nation have some of the highest math and science scores in the world. Hence, while poverty is a major problem that interferes with academic achievement, we have to look beyond poverty to consider the educational framework that we are using to teach our youth.

Schools in the United States are experiencing their winter of discontent. One might ask: Whatever happened to what was, in the past, one of the best educational systems in the world? Did we become too complacent with our past academic successes? Did we simply ignore problems that had been festering for far too long? Or, did we fail to change our educational system in light of our increased knowledge and the demands of a world driven by technology and computers?

It seems clear, to me at least, that American schools need a new vision to guide it. Too much of the American educational system is based on a model that is clearly out of date and not functioning very well—the deficit and remediation model. This entire book has been about moving the American educational system from a deficit-based to a strengths-based educational system. Why? Because the deficit-based educational system is simply not working—not for our kids, not for our schools, and not for our nation—which needs well-educated youth to retain a place of leadership within the world.

Strengths-based education is not just about fluff—some goody-two-shoes notion about making kids feel good about themselves. The rationale for a strengths-based education has already been firmly established in some of our research on the brain and on human responses to positive emotions, as exemplified by Barbara Fredrickson's[4] broaden-and-build theory discussed in chapters 3 and 9. We know, for instance, that a child's brain develops better when it is in a loving, nurturing environment. Learning is fostered by our increased self-knowledge about our strengths and how we can apply our strengths to deal with academic and personal problems. The greatest achievers in the world are those who have focused on developing their strengths rather than their weaknesses. Both Bill Gates, developer of Microsoft, and Steve Jobs, CEO of Apple, dropped out of college to pursue their strengths, and the world is a better place for their efforts to apply their strengths to computers and technology. Perhaps if schools were organized so that they helped students identify their strengths, develop them, and apply them, there might be more people like Bill Gates and Steve Jobs.

The purpose of this chapter is to discuss creating and communicating a strengths-based school vision. The first section of the chapter examines the differences between a vision statement and a mission statement. It highlights why it is important for a school to create a school vision. The second section discusses principles that school officials can use to guide the development and implementation of strengths-based school programs. It answers such questions as: What is the difference between having a school program that just identifies students' strengths and one that develops a strengths-based program? What principles should guide a schoolwide strengths-based educational program? The third section of the chapter analyzes barriers to creating a strengths-based school. I maintain that the process of changing to a strengths-based focus should be a well-thought-out

---

IMPORTANCE OF VISION STATEMENTS

"Where there is no vision, the people perish."
                                        —Proverbs 29:18.
"Leadership is the capacity to translate vision into reality."
                                        —Warren Bennis
Where there is no vision, schools flounder and so do their
    students.

---

process—one that involves more than just a few lessons on talking about students' strengths and then going back to business as usual.

COMPARISON OF MISSION AND VISION STATEMENTS

What is the difference between a mission statement and a vision statement? In general, a mission statement describes what business you are in, what products and services your organization provides, and the purpose of your organization. A mission statement is a short statement that explains, in simple and concise terms, an organization's purposes for being. Large companies spend many years and millions of dollars developing and refining their mission statement, with many of these mission statements eventually becoming household phrases. A mission statement can last for decades if it captures the essence of an organization.

In contrast, a vision statement is about where an organization is headed and how it will act. When I think of the word vision in relation to schools, I visualize something that holds the school together and that keeps school administrators, faculty, students, parents, and community members moving in the same direction. A school's vision statement can be compared to gravity that pulls the water in a stream down the mountain or to an area of low pressure that pulls the wind relentlessly in a particular direction. Schools need to have a vision that binds all of their stakeholders together and that keeps them moving in a desired direction.

A vision statement for a school is transformative. It aligns people in activities throughout the organization. A school's vision is important because it helps school officials to set priorities. It indicates what a school stands for, and it promotes goal setting and planning. The first step toward developing a strengths-based vision is to describe the

---

VISIONS AND ACTIONS

"Vision without action is a daydream. Action without vision is a nightmare."

—Japanese proverb

---

school you seek to become. During this process, key stakeholders identify where they want the school to go in relation to where they are. This information helps a school to identify the areas it desires to improve.

A shared school vision should be based on a set of core beliefs that your school community values. Your school's vision statement should reflect your school district's vision and goals and the state standards for academic development. When a school community identifies its core beliefs and describes how their schools should look, it becomes empowered. The lack of a school vision statement leads to settling for whatever happens, whereas creating a vision and staying true to a vision makes things happen. As Steven Covey, A. Roger Merrill, and Rebecca Merrill[5] have pointed out we have to change if we want to get different results in our lives. : "If we keep doing what we're doing, we're going to keep getting what we're getting."

A school's vision statement should be short and to the point. A short school vision unites the stakeholders in a school and motivates them to work toward the school being the best possible school it can be. Short and simple school vision statements stand a good chance of being adopted by the stakeholders—meaning school officials, teachers, students, and parents will remember it. For instance, *the vision statement of Strengths-Based School X is to help students identify, assess, and develop their learning and personal strengths for the purpose of engaging them in the learning process and for helping them to achieve academic and personal excellence.*

To be successful, schools need to share their vision and help others recognize their importance to the realization of the vision. Each day should be a step toward making the vision a realized dream. School administrators become aware of and avoid, reduce, or neutralize those forces that steer the school away from its vision. They should concentrate on envisioning the implications of successfully achieving the vision. A vision must indicate what must change as well as what must not change. A school's vision is an articulation of its desired future that is better in some significant way than what existed in the past.

The following are some exercises for identifying core beliefs that make up a school's vision statement. *I believe that . . .*

- A school teaches. . . .
- A good school is one that . . .
- A successful student is one who is able to . . .
- A quality instruction program should include . . .
- An effective school faculty . . .
- My ideal school is one that has faculty doing . . ., and students being involved in . . .

There is no one magical formula to be used to establish a strengths-based vision for all schools. In formulating a school vision, so much depends upon where the school is currently in terms of its students and their academic and personal achievement. The next section discusses some general principles to be taken into consideration in establishing a school's strengths-based vision statement.

PRINCIPLES TO BE CONSIDERED IN ESTABLISHING A SCHOOL VISION

Principle 1: Start from the End Goal and Work Forward

Prior to beginning a strengths-based program, schools should evaluate carefully the specific learning and social-emotional goals that the program is designed to promote.[6] It is important to begin with the end in mind, what the school hopes to accomplish by instituting such a program and how it might influence its academic curriculum. All too frequently, school administrators who desire to integrate a strengths approach in their school launch such a program without first determining why they are instituting the program.

School officials should ask themselves: what specific learning goals will we achieve by instituting a strengths-based approach to learning? For instance, a school can institute a strengths-based program throughout the school to increase student learning engagement, promote the sense of bonding and community within the school, or to help students gain self-knowledge necessary to guide their learning. A principal might say: "I am introducing a strengths-based approach in my school because I believe that self-knowledge is critical to learning how to learn and because I believe that students' metacognitive strategies are based on their self-knowledge." Another principal might say: "I am instituting a strengths-based approach throughout the school because I believe that students learn best by understanding, developing, and applying their strengths rather than by focusing on their weaknesses." Still another principal asserts: "I use a strengths-based approach to increase students' sense of academic and personal self-competency and self-efficacy," or "I have instituted such a program to bring about a sense of community among teachers and students and to reduce such negative occurrences as bullying." Think about the needs of the school and how a strengths-based program might address those needs. Think from the end—what you want to achieve and how the school might be if such a program were instituted.

After school officials have gained a clear understanding of why they are instituting a strengths-based approach within their school, they are now in a position to consider how the school's curriculum will be impacted by using this approach. How does the school intend to assess or measure students' strengths? Upon what known educational body of research is the strengths program based? For instance, I recommend using a framework that includes an assessment of multiple intelligences and different learning styles—plus 11 strengths categories discussed in chapter 4. The concept of strengths domains and life skills development can also serve as a unifying strengths-based framework for schools.

Schools might also consider adopting the Strengths Pyramid as a beginning framework for a strengths-based school philosophy; that is, we identify our strengths and use them to achieve and to manage our weaknesses. The development of a strengths-based school program should be predicated on sound educational research that takes into account recent knowledge on brain-based learning, the power of positive emotions to change students' behavior, for instance, Fredrickson's "broaden-and-build-theory"[7] and Dweck's[8] work on mindsets, and metacognitive learning strategies.

Principle 2: Self-Knowledge and Its Connection to Learning Are Important

The strengths-based vision maintains that every student will be aware of his or her strengths. Such a school highlights the importance of self-knowledge in the academic and personal learning process. For instance, a student who understands that he or she performs better on multiple-choice tests than on essay tests has some metacognitive self-knowledge about his or her test-taking ability. One of the signs of experts is that they know when they do not know something and have to rely on general strategies for finding the desired information. In other words, self-awareness of the breadth and depth of one's own knowledge base is an important aspect of self-knowledge. Students need to be aware of the different types of strategies they can use in learning.

On a number of occasions, I have worked with university students who were valedictorians of their high schools, which were located in small and/or rural communities or, in some instances, were inner-city schools. When the students faced the competition at a large, major university, they were astonished and disheartened to find out that their academic skills were not as good as those of many other students. One student tearfully said to me: "Dr. Smith, I can't do this work. I was getting all As at my school. My entire block had a college day for me, and I am failing in every subject." Although I tried to convince her to hang in there and get academic support services and tutoring, she left the university discouraged. Her self-knowledge did not reflect an understanding of what she did not know and what she knew in comparison to others at the university.

A strengths-based school vision should be based on connecting the importance of student self-knowledge to learning and personal relationships within the class and school. As Ryan and Deci[9] pointed out in their self-determination theory, individuals function at optimal levels and are most authentically motivated when three psychological needs are met: competence, autonomy, and relatedness. When teachers help students understand the connections between their strengths and goals, and they help them learn how to apply their strengths successfully to accomplish goals, they elicit students' feelings of competence and they provide them with opportunities for autonomy and self-direction.

Principle 3: Create an Individualized Strengths Development Plan

A school that adopts a strengths-based educational focus understands that while it may be advantageous for students to learn their educational and personal strengths, focusing just on identifying students' strengths is insufficient. Quick one- or two-day programs that introduce students to their strengths is not what a strengths-based school is all about. In reality, learning about your strengths is just a starting point. *The end goal is for students to learn how to develop and apply their*

STRENGTH DEVELOPMENT

While learning about students' strengths is an important step in the right direction, it is usually insufficient as an end goal. A more desirable end goal is to teach students how to develop their strengths and to apply them beneficially and successfully within the school's learning environment, within their communities, and within personal lives.

---

strengths in learning and life situations. Simply identifying students' strengths may lead to the false impression that identification of strengths is all they have to do. There are many people who know what their strengths but who fail to develop them or to apply them in life situations that count.

Consider, for example, the sport of basketball. In some neighborhoods, there are many excellent basketball players camped out in front of the corner stores of the neighborhoods. What makes a Le Bron James, Michael Jordan, or a Larry Bird? When asked this question, both Larry Bird and Michael Jordan have stated that it has taken thousands of practiced basketball shots before they can know with any degree of confidence that the ball will swish through the hoop during the last few seconds of the game. "Gimme the ball, gimme the ball," I've heard Larry Bird say when his team was down by one point during the final seconds of a championship game with the Lakers. When one of the reporters asked him how he knew the shot would go in, he responded, "Because I had practiced it going in a thousand times this week." Strength comes from practice, from honing one's abilities, from practice and refinement, and more refinement of one's strengths.

Students learn the impact of their personal effort in developing their strengths. Schools provide students with opportunities to evaluate which resources, skills, knowledge, relationships, and experiences can promote their strengths growth. Would it be helpful for them to become involved in a mentoring relationship designed to develop that identified strength? What community resources might help students to apply or to refine their strengths?

Every student should have an individualized strength development plan contained within his or her cumulative school record that indicates how the student plans to develop, practice, and refine his/her strengths. Teachers understand that the ultimate objective of a "strengths-based initiative is to help students consider their own responsibility in deliberately, attentively developing their strengths through practice and engagement in novel experiences."[10]

Principle 4: Developing and Nurturing Teachers' Strengths Should Be Ongoing

Teachers are less likely to be able to promote strengths-based education if they are unaware of their own strengths as human beings and as teachers. What are their strengths in terms of teaching students? What is their best teaching style? What kind of feedback do they give to students? Teachers need to be exposed to in-service training that helps them develop a classroom learning environment that promotes students' awareness of not only their own strengths but also the strengths of their classmates.[11] The goals of the strengths-based philosophy for teachers are simple:

- Support, identify, and maximize the strengths and self-reflective abilities of each individual teacher on staff.
- Strengthen the collaborative teaching relationships of the entire teaching faculty.

Principle 5: Develop Meaningful Connections and Partnerships Between the School, Home, and Community

Young people need opportunities to be connected positively with their families and communities. In establishing a schoolwide strengths-based program, school administrators identify a community's assets and discover ways to link them to the school's educational program. A school administrator's commitment to mapping a community's assets helps the school to become aware of the gifts and capacities of individuals and of citizens associations and local institutions. The fully mobilized community is one that is in a position to answer the question: "What resources do we have to solve this problem ourselves?"[12] Each time residents of a community are linked with others for problem-solving purposes, the community becomes stronger. Every time an association of citizens connects with a local school, and every time a local business builds ties with the youth of the community, the community becomes stronger and more capable, such that people come to believe that they are problem solvers.

Using Data from Effective Schools to Establish High-Achieving Strengths-Based Schools

Throughout this chapter, I have emphasized that the benefits of focusing on students' strengths is supported by brain-based research and the broaden-and-build theory of psychology. I likewise believe that strengths-based schools must be grounded in what we know about the characteristics of effective schools. *This We Believe: Keys to Educating Young Adolescents*[13] is the landmark position paper from National Middle School Association in which the association presents its vision for a successful school for 10- to 15-year-olds. The paper outlines16 characteristics of effective schools. The characteristics are grouped in three general categories: (1) curriculum, instruction, and assessment; (2) leadership and organization; and (3) culture and community.

16 Characteristics of Effective Schools
Curriculum, Instruction, and Assessment

1. Educators value young adolescents and are prepared to teach them. Teachers understand the developmental uniqueness of this age group, the appropriate curriculum, effective learning and assessment strategies, and their importance as models.
2. Students and teachers are engaged in active, purposeful learning.
3. The curriculum is challenging, exploratory, integrative, and relevant.
4. Teachers use varied and ongoing assessments to advance and measure learning.
5. Educators use multiple learning and teaching approaches.

Leadership and Organization

1. The school has a shared vision that has been developed by all stakeholder and that guides every decision.
2. Leaders are committed to and knowledgeable about this age group.
3. Leaders demonstrate courage and collaboration.
4. The school has ongoing professional development that reflects best educational practices.
5. The school's organizational structures promote purposeful learning and meaningful relationships.

Culture and Community

1. The school environment is inviting, safe, inclusive, and supportive of all.
2. Every student's academic and personal development is guided by an adult advocate.
3. Comprehensive guidance and support services are provided to meet the needs of students.
4. Health and wellness are supported in the school's curriculum and related school policies.
5. The school actively involves families in the education of their children.
6. The school includes community and business partners.

The five components of the strengths-based school outlined in this book fit well with what researchers have found out about effective schools. The strengths-based model maintains that self-knowledge is at the heart of all learning and that further knowledge about our strengths motivates us to learn and causes us to persist in the learning process. Virtually all of the more recent educational and psychological theories emphasize the importance of strengths and self-knowledge in some way. Gardner's[14] work on multiple intelligences was developed from Project Zero, working with inner-city kids and discovering that they had intelligence in areas that most of our achievement tests do not measure. His multiple intelligence theory is a major cornerstone of educational practice today. The theory essentially says that we must look for the strengths of young people in diverse areas and help them to develop those strengths.

Likewise, Daniel Goleman's[15] theory of emotional intelligence and his finding that emotional intelligence is a greater factor than academic intelligence in achieving life success has at its core the principle that self-knowledge, especially knowledge about one's emotional strengths and weaknesses, is critical in achieving goals, in coping, and in actualizing one's hopes and dreams.

Dweck's research on mindsets and the notion that students' mindsets can either promote or hinder their learning is valuable. Similarly, Fredrickson's broaden-and-build-theory that says positive emotions about ourselves cause us to relax and to engage in higher order thinking that helps us recover better and more quickly from medical operations and that leads to learning is another confirmation of the value of helping students discover their strengths.

Moreover, the entire wealth of hundreds of studies on metacognition tell us that students need to learn information about themselves—how they best learn and what their best learning strategies are. For instance,

I can remember working with one youth from the inner city who was struggling to learn in school. In fact, he was failing. Brian had no knowledge of how he could learn. All he understood was that the teacher gave him math problems that he could not complete, and another gave him English papers that he could not really write.

My approach with Brian was to first find out how he went about learning. "Usually, I take out my books at the dining room table, and I just feel overwhelmed." "Why?" I asked. "Because I know that I can't do the work." "How do you know you can't do the work?" I asked? Because I usually fail," he said. "Because no matter how many times my mom and my dad try to help me, I usually can't get the work."

As I sat next to him with my arm around him, I said: "You feel like you can't learn?" "Yeah," he replied, and his eyes filled with tears. "What if, what if I could show you that you can learn? Would you feel better?" "Yeah, sure," he responded. "Who are you . . . the tooth fairy?" I joked with him about putting something under his pillow before he left me.

To make a long story short, I began to examine every little thing that Brian did to learn, starting from his opening up his book with the expectation that he was going to learn and that he had strengths that he was not using. I engaged Brian in deep-breathing exercises to relax him, and I began to ask him about the things that he was most proud of. "Tell me something about yourself, Brian. What are you most proud of yourself for?" Brian told me that he played a piano mostly by ear, that he took care of his younger sister, and that he had memorized the 23rd Psalm. When I challenged him to recite the 23rd Psalm right there on the spot, and he did so perfectly, I knew that I had found my way to engage him and to disprove his theory that he was stupid and could not learn.

I asked Brian how went about learning the 23rd Psalm by heart, and he told me. "Well," I said, "we are going to use those same strengths that helped you to memorize the 23rd Psalm to help you learn your schoolwork." I had hooked Brian into a relationship with me and into the expectation that he could and would learn.

Here is another strengths-based principle. Healthy, caring relationships—whether provided by teachers or parents—promote the

---

STRENGTHS AND RELATIONSHIPS

Strengths are always developed within the context of a caring and nurturing relationship.

development of young people's strengths. It is very difficult to teach young people without first establishing a relationship with them. That is why I believe in relational teaching—teaching that uses the force of my being, my caring, and my knowledge to help a child or an adolescent

It is difficult to teach young people from some cultures without first establishing a relationship with them. Students who come from people-oriented and group-oriented cultures, such as African Americans and Asians, to name a few, emphasize the quality of the relationship between teacher and student.

Getting back to Brian, I worked with him for several weeks, teaching him some tricks that I used to learn academic information quickly. I discovered that Brian could learn if the information was broken down into small steps and if he experienced success with those small steps. We used note cards for just about everything—even for math. Brian liked the fact that he could design the way that he was going to approach a topic and learn. He now understood how to learn, and he could check his learning himself.

For a number of years I lost track of Brian, but met him somewhat unexpectedly at a gathering. He informed me that he was a medical doctor and that he had used the note cards and some of the other strategies we worked on to get through medical school. Talk about being affirmed! I felt as if my bank account had just been filled with a new deposit. When we help others, it comes back to us in ways that enlarge us.

Another important strengths-based principle is that learning is a mystery for most children and adolescents. They do not understand how they learn. Sometimes their parents tell them that they learn because they are smart, have a high IQ, or whatever. Most kids do not have many clues regarding how they learn until they have spent many years in a school, observing and getting feedback on what worked for them and what did not work for them. Yet, again, such learning is self-knowledge about learning—that is what metacognitive teaching and learning is all about. Students who know their own strengths and weaknesses can adjust their own thinking to promote learning. For instance, if a student realizes that she does know a lot about a topic, she might pay more attention to the topic or use different strategies to make sure that she understands the concepts underlying the topic. In contrast, students who are less knowledgeable about their own learning strengths and weaknesses are usually less inclined to adapt to different situations and to regulate their own learning in them.[16]

> Self-knowledge forms the basis of all learning. If students have little or no knowledge of their strengths and how they best learn, they are inclined to only achieve mediocre, and in some instances, disappointing academic results.

Similar to Brian, young people make judgments about their motivation ("I'm lazy or I try really hard") and judgments about their capability to perform a task (self-efficacy), their goals for completing a task (learning or just getting a good grade), and the interest and value the task has for them (high interest and high value versus low interest and low value). Despite the fact that the motivational beliefs are not usually taken into account in cognitive learning models, there is an increasing substantial body of literature that shows important links between students' motivational beliefs and their cognition and learning.[17]

Because of the importance of self-knowledge about our strengths to the learning process, every school should be required to graduate students who know their strengths.

Every school should have a Strengths Coat of Arms. The Strengths Coat of Arms should consist of four quadrants—one for students, one for teachers and administrators, one for parents, and one for community stakeholders. Each of these quadrants should list the major strengths of each stakeholder group. For instance, the coat of arms quadrant for teachers might list "caring teachers" or "highly qualified teachers."

Strengths Mapping and Schools

One way to develop a school's coat of arms is to map its strengths. Just as every student has strengths, so schools have their own unique strengths. Strengths mapping is essential for schools to know what assets they can use to achieve the school's vision. There are five steps to schools' strengths mapping.

Step 1: Map the school's strengths and assets in four primary domains: (1) students, (2) teachers, (3) faculty, principal, or administrative leadership, (3) parents, and (4) community. The school is interested in answering the question: what resources does the school have to help young people achieve academically and to succeed in life?

Step 2: Map a School's Relationship Strengths. Strengths mapping involves developing relationships among teachers and students, principals, parents, and the community within which a school is located. It is primarily within the context of a relationship that a strength can identified, developed, and cultivated. Dr. James Comer came from a working-class African American family in East Chicago, Indiana. He earned medical and public health degrees and worked at the Yale's Child Study Center. His responsibility was to go into two elementary schools in New Haven on a Ford Foundation program. Out of the 33 schools in New Haven, Dr. Comer's[18] schools were ranked number 32 and 33. The schools not only had the worst attendance, but also the student behavior problems were overwhelming.

Almost all of the nearly completely new staff brought in for the project were gone by the end of the year. Comer's first reaction was that he had to change the environment; children could not learn and develop in that chaotic situation. After five years, one of the schools was dropped and replaced by another. Gradually the two schools in the community development project achieved the third and fourth highest-level mathematics and language arts test scores and the best attendance in the city. It took seven years for the schools to reach this level of achievement.

During the past two decades, Dr. Comer and his associates have worked in almost a thousand schools. He notes that when he and his associates begin working with a dysfunctional school, they do not expect improvement in fewer than five years. What contributes to Comer's success? According to him, the answer is "relationships, relationships, relationships."Comer maintains that good between people in a family and community influence the quality of a child's life, largely home and school, make good child and adolescent rearing and development possible. When family members have good relationships with each other, children are able to focus more effectively on their academic courses.

Step 3: Mobilize for School Improvement and Information Sharing. The pathway for school improvement involves mobilizing all of the school's strengths/assets for two important purposes: improving the academic achievement of all students and strengthening the school's ability to better serve its students in life skills development and citizenship. It is important that all school stakeholders exchange information.

Step 4: Convening the School Stakeholders to Develop a Vision and a Plan. This part of strengths mapping deals with such questions as: Who are we in this school? What do we value most? Where would we like our school to go in the next 5, 10, 20 years? Without a commonly held school identity and a broadly shared vision, it is difficult to create a caring school learning community.

Step 5: Obtain or Leverage Outside Resources to Support the School. During this stage, all of the stakeholders have been inventoried for strengths. The stakeholders have begun to examine their relationships with one another. A broad representative group of school stakeholders have begun to solve problems together and to hammer out a shared vision and set of strategies. Only after these goals have been achieved should the school begin to consider leveraging resources from the outside.

The Benefits of School Strengths Mapping

Every school should engage in school strengths mapping—if only to discover what diamonds in the rough lie within its four walls. Schools can bloom in even the most difficult of situations. Geoffrey Canada is president and CEO of the Harlem Children's Zone (HCZ) and president of the HCZ Promise Academy Charter School, which is one of the highest-achieving charter schools for African Americans in New York City. Parents cry when they find out that there is no more room for their children at the Promise Academy Charter School. The HCZ Promise Academy shows that schools can blossom wherever they are—in the richest communities of our nation or in poor neighborhoods where parents believe that education is their only hope for their children. Flowers blossom where they are planted—sometimes even within the most challenging environments.

On April 22, 2010, Dr. Canada testified before the Senate Committee on Health, Education, Labor, and Pensions. Dr. Canada[19] noted the disparity in spending resources for African American youth incarcerated and for schools in New York City. He stated:

> As today's poor children enter tomorrow's economy, under-educated and ill-prepared, the cost to America's future competitiveness in the world marketplace is incalculable ... In America's inner cities, more than half of all black men do not finish high school. ... By their mid-30s, 6 in 10 black men who had dropped out of school had spent time in prison.
>
> ... The HCZ model is not cheap. We spend an average $5,000 per child each year to ensure children's success. But compare this to the costs of not spending this money:

- New Yorkers spend roughly $210,000 per youth on detention annually. A recent report from New York State Governor David Paterson's Task Force on Transforming Juvenile Justice highlighted the fact that three-quarters of those released from detention were arrested again within three years and 45% were reincarcerated.
- In the 97 square blocks that constitute the HCZ project, the government will spend $42 million incarcerating some residents of our community.[20]

The HCZ Promise Academy Charter School has taken 12 years to get to its present high academic standards. HCZ schools have longer school days and a longer school year, merit pay and bonuses, data-driven decision making, and school leaders with the ability to hire and fire employees. The HCZ schools have produced some remarkable programs. HCZ established the Baby College, a program for parents of children aged zero to three, where parents have increased the time they spend reading to their children. The school's four-year-old children are now school-ready. Young people are taught concepts rather than just facts. One evaluation of the Promise Academy stated: "Taken at face value, the effects in middle school are enough to close the black-white achievement gap in mathematics and reduce it by nearly half in English Language Arts. The effects in elementary school close the racial achievement gap in both subjects."[21]

I mention Dr. Canada's Promise Academy to show that it takes commitment and hard work to develop the strengths of students and of the schools that they attend. Schools that want quick improvements without doing the necessary work with parents and the surrounding communities are just setting themselves and their students up for failure. To improve students' academic achievement, Canada recommends some of the very steps I have mentioned in this book: (1) serve an entire neighborhood comprehensively; (2) create a pipeline of high-quality programs; (3) build community among residents, institutions, and stakeholders for children's healthy development; (4) evaluate programs; and (5) cultivate a culture of success.

According to the Center for American Progress, poverty now costs the United States about 4 percent of its gross domestic product

---

BLOOMING WHERE YOU ARE

Schools can bloom wherever they are—even in the midst of poverty. Educational gardens can be planted in every community.

annually in lost production, reduced economic output, and increased social expenditures.

Yet for considerably less money than the costs of poverty or what we are already spending on incarceration, the United States can educate its children, have them graduate from college, and bring them back to our communities ready to be success, productive citizens."

Sometimes I think about the young lady who left the university because she did not measure up. Her entire community, however financially strapped it was, was proud of her. It celebrated her. Who could replace the feeling that she had when her entire neighborhood of a few blocks came out to honor her efforts in school? The celebration not only said a great deal about the young lady but also said something about the neighborhood and the value that some of its residents placed on education—even though their education may have been lacking.

Would it not be nice if we could visit that school and change its curriculum to really focus on students' strengths—instead of falsely leading students to believe that they were stronger in some areas than they actually were? Even students in poorly functioning schools do not want to be told for 12 years that they have strengths that they do not really have in certain areas.

A year or two ago, I ran into the young lady who had dropped out of the university because she did not have the skills. She said: "The As I got on all those dittoed sheets and tests did not mean a thing." She informed me that she had worked for a year and then she went to a community college to get training in health care—as a personal assistant to the disabled and to the elderly left by sons and daughters who had moved away years ago to pursue their dreams.

"You know, Dr. Smith," she said. "I'm doing all right. I make on average $25 an hour. I have so much work that I have to turn it down sometimes. When I work on the weekend, I get between $35 and $50 an hour—not bad for someone without a college education. I like my work. I like helping people."

What if—just what if—the school had identified and focused on her true strengths instead of trying to convince her that she was strong in academics when she really was not? What if so many of America's low-achieving schools told the truth rather than graduating kids from high school who can barely read? The school never dealt with my former student's strengths or weaknesses. It just lied to her for 12 years and failed to either correct her academic weaknesses or build on any strength that she had. Clearly, one strength that she had was her ability to nurture others. She also had good survival strengths, as evidenced by the fact that she was faring much better than some people who have graduated from college.

WHAT ARE BARRIERS TO THE STRENGTHS APPROACH IN SCHOOLS?

Our attitude toward change is one of the greatest barriers against implementing a strengths-based approach in our schools. Critics of the strengths approach have labeled it as "fluff." They argue that education is not about fun and feeling good about oneself. There is pain, real pain in learning, and we might as well face the fact that not all people can learn easily.

A strengths-based approach does not ignore genuine concerns about students; nor does it fabricate strengths that do not exist.[22] Those against strengths-based schools maintain that the focus in our schools should be on reading, writing, and arithmetic rather than on building youths' strengths. I agree that the focus should be on creating academic excellence in youth, and I also believe that academic excellence alone will not make this world a better place to be.

The primary barriers to the widespread implementation of the strengths-based approach to education fall into one of three categories:

- Ignorance that strengths-based strategies exist and are effective
- Institutional or cultural resistance to focusing on empowering youth or changing our educational practices
- Challenges of changing the paradigm regarding how our educational system is organized and delivers services to youth

A large number of educators have formed an attachment to the traditional way of educating youth. It is far easier to focus on test scores than on trying to educate the whole person. Learning how to educate youth using a strengths approach may require some educators to take new courses and to rethink their educational practices. While change can be exhilarating, it can also be very challenging.

Schools unintentionally create a world of limits for students. We know far more about identifying and labeling students' weaknesses than we do about nurturing and developing their strengths. A change is needed throughout our entire educational system if the United States is to produce high-achieving, capable young students. Our strengths make life meaningful. Using them gives us purpose and direction for our lives. We stand the greatest chance of making important contributions to society when we focus on our strengths. It takes a village to raise a child—partnerships between schools, families, and communities. The culture of a school must provide a learning environment in which young people feel safe, supported, listened to, respected, and valued.

SUMMARY

This chapter focused on getting a garden vision for strengths-based schools. Each school must establish its own vision for initiating a strengths-based educational program, depending upon the needs of its students, community, and faculty. The process of creating and communicating a strengths-based school vision was examined. Differences between a mission statement and a vision statement were analyzed. Five principles to be considered in establishing a school vision were identified.

Notes

Chapter 1: Emergence, Growth, and Current Uses of Strengths-Based Educational Systems

1. K. Menninger, *A Psychiatrist's World: Selected Papers* (New York: Viking Press, 1959).

2. E. C. Anderson, *StrengthsQuest: Curriculum Outline and Learning Activities* (Princeton, NJ: Gallup, 2003).

3. K. Bowers, "Making the Most of Human Strengths," in *Positive Psychology: Exploring the Best in People: Discovering Human Strengths*, ed. S. J. Lopez, 23–36 (Westport, CT: Praeger, 2009).

4. R. Liesveld and J. A. Miller, *Teach with Your Strengths: How Great Teachers Inspire Their Students* (New York: Gallup Press, 2005).

5. A. Coulson, "A Fair Comparison: U.S. Students Lag in Math and Science," accessed October 8, 2010, http://www.educationreport.org/article.aspx?ID=6998&print=yes.

6. "Diplomas Count 2010: Graduation by the Numbers—Putting Data to Work for Student Success", *Education Week*, EPE Research Center, accessed June 10, 2010, http://www.edweek.org/ew/toc/2010/06/10/index.html.

7. NAS/NAE/IOM, *Rising above the Gathering Storm: Energizing and Employing America for a Brighter Economic Future* (Washington, DC: National Academies Press, 2005); also National Academies Press, 2007. The initial report release was in 2005, with the final, edited book issued in 2007.

8. NAS/NAE/IOM, *Rising above the Gathering Storm, Revisited: Rapidly Approaching Category 5* (Washington, DC: National Academies Press, 2010).

9. Ibid.

10. National Center for Education Statistics, *Digest of Education Statistics, 2009* (NCES 2010-013), chapter 6; NCES, Fast Facts, accessed October 7, 2010, http://nces.ed.gov/fastfacts/display.asp?id=1.

11. NCES, *Highlights from PISA 2006: Performance of U.S. 15-Year -Old Students in Science and Mathematics Literacy in an International Context* (NCES 2008-016) (Washington, DC: U.S. Department of Education, 2008).

12. M. Schmoker, *Results Now: How We Can Achieve Unprecedented Improvements in Teaching and in Learning* (Alexandria, VA. Association for Supervision and Curriculum Development, 2006), 7.

13. Diplomas Count 2010.

14. Ibid.

15. Ibid.

16. Ibid.

17. Ibid.

18. C. Rouse, "Labor Market Consequences of an Inadequate Education" (Paper, symposium on the Social Costs of Inadequate Education, New York, October 24, 2005); Alliance for Excellent Education, *The High Cost of High School Dropouts: What the Nation Pays for Inadequate High Schools* (Washington, DC: Alliance for Excellent Education, 2008).

19. Alliance, *Savings Futures, Saving Dollars: The Impact of Education on Crime Reduction and Earnings* (Washington, DC: Alliance for Excellent Education, 2006).

20. Alliance, *Demography as Destiny: How America Can Build a Better Future* (Washington, DC: Alliance for Excellent Education, 2006).

21. Accessed October 10, 2010. http://articles.conn.com/2009-05-05/us/dropuout.rate.study_1_1dropouts-enrollment-graduation.

22. ABC's *This Week with Christiane Amanpour*, August 15, 2010, http://blogs.ABC.News.com/pressroom/2010/15.

23. NCES, *Numbers and Types of Public Elementary and Secondary Local Education Agencies, From the Common Core of Data: School Year 2007–08*, accessed August 23, 2010, http://nces.ed.gov/pubs2010/2010306.pdf.

24. Ibid.

25. Ibid.

26. NCES, *Highlights from PISA 2006: Performance of U.S. 15-Year -old students in science and mathematics literacy in an international context* (NCES 2008-016) (Washington, DC: U.S. Department of Education, 2008).

27. NCES, *International Outcomes of Learning in Mathematics Literacy and Problem Solving: PISA 2003 Results from the U.S. Perspective* (NCES 2005–003) (Washington, DC: U.S. Department of Education, 2005).

28. Highlights from PISA 2006: Performance of U.S. 15-year-Old Students in Science and Mathematics Literacy in an International Context, U.S. Department of Education, NCES-2008-016, Retrieved on October 9, 2010 at http://nces.ed.gov/pubs2008/2008016.pdf.

29. Ibid.

30. Ibid.

31. Ibid.

32. Ibid.

33. NCES, *International Outcomes*.

34. National Association of Manufacturers, *The Manufacturing Institute, and Deloitte Consulting LLC 2005 Skills Gap Report: A Survey of the American Manufacturing Workforce* (Washington, DC: National Association of Manufacturers, 2005).

35. U.S. Department of Education., National Center for Education Statistics 2007, http://nces.ed.gov/timss/results07.asp

36. OECD, *PISA 2006: Science Competencies for Tomorrow's World* (Paris: OECD, 2007); OECD, *Problem Solving for Tomorrow's World: First Measures of Cross-Curricular Competencies from PISA 2003* (Paris: OECD, 2007).

37. I. Kirsch, H., Braun, K. Yamamoto, and A. Sum, *America's Perfect Storm: Three Forces Changing Our Nation's Future* (Princeton, NJ: Educational Testing Service, 2007).

38. National Center for Education Statistics, *Numbers and Types of Public Elementary and Types of Public Elementary and Secondary Local Education Agencies, 2007–2008* (Washington, DC: U.S. Department of Education, 2008).

39. *The Global Competitiveness Report 2010–2011*, accessed October 8, 2010, http://www.weforum.org/en/initiatives/gcp/Global%20Competitiveness%20Report/index.html.

40. *The Global Competiveness Report 2010-2011*, published by the World Economic Forum, printed in Switzerland by SRO-Kundig; see also *The Global*, accessed October 8, 2010, http://www.weforum.org/en/initiatives/gcp/Global%20Competitiveness%20Report/index.html.

41. Ibid.

42. NAS/NAE/IOM, *Rising above the Gathering Storm, Revisited*.

43. Ibid.

44. See the ACT website: http://www.act.org/news/releases/2008/crr.html.

45. R. M. Solow, "Technical Change and the Aggregate Production Function," *Review of Economic and Statistics 39* (1957): 312–20.

46. NAS/NAE/IOM (2010). *Rising above the Gathering Storm, Revisited*.

47. Ibid.

48. Recovery.gov, accessed October 5, 2010, http://www.whitehouse.gov.issues/education/.

49. Ibid.

50. NCES, *The Condition of Education 2010 in Brief*, NCES 2010-029 (Washington, DC: U.S. Department of Education, 2010).

51. Coulson, *A Fair Comparison*.

52. C. R. Greenwood, "Longitudinal Analysis of Time Engagement and Academic Achievement in At-Risk and Non-Risk Students," *Exceptional Children 57* (1991): 521–35.

53. J. B. Carroll, "A Model of School Learning," *Teachers College Record 64* (1963): 723–33; Carroll, "The Carroll Model: A 25-Year Retrospective and Prospective View," *Educational Researcher 18*, no. 1 (1963: 26–31.

54. M. E. Seligman, "Teaching Positive Psychology," *APA on Psychology* 30, no. 7 (July–August 1999), http://www.apa.org.

55. M. Buckingham, *Go Put Your Strengths to Work: 6 Powerful Steps to Achieve Outstanding Performance* (New York: Free Press, 2007).

56. J. Stanley, *The Millionaire Mind* (Kansas City, MO: Andrew McMeel, 2000).

57. D. O. Clifton and P. Nelson, *Soar with Your Strengths* (New York: Dell, 1992).

58. P. Drucker, *Effective Executive* (New York: HarperCollins, 2006; first published in 1966).

59. D. Restuccia and A. Bundy, "Positive Youth Development: A Literature Review," accessed October 13, 2010, http://www.mypasa.org/failid/positive_youth-dev.pdf.

60. D. Saleebey, *The Strengths Perspective in Social Work Practice* (New York: Longman, 1992).

61. E. J. Smith, "The Strength-Based Counseling Model," *The Counseling Psychologist* 34 (2006): 13–79.

62. M. Gladwell, *The Tipping Point: How Little Things Can Make a Difference* (Boston: Little, Brown, 2002).

63. New Freedom Commission on Mental Health, *Achieving the Promise: Transforming Mental Health Care in America: Final Report*, DHHS Pub. No. SMA-03-3832 (Rockville, MD: New Freedom Commission on Mental Health, 2003), http://www.mentalhealthcomission.gov or www.mentalhealth.samhsa.gov.

64. K. Maton, C. Schellenbach, B. Leadbeater, and A. Solarz, *Investing in Children, Youth, Families, and Communities: Strengths-Based Research and Policy* (Washington, DC: American Psychological Association, 2003).

65. M. Sellars, "The Role of Intrapersonal Intelligence in Self-Directed Learning," *Issues in Educational Research* 16 (2006), accessed October 8, 2010, http://www.iier.org.au/iier16/sellars.html.

66. H. McGrath and T. Noble, *Bounce Back! Classroom Resiliency Program* (Sydney: Pearson Education, 2003).

67. H. Gardner, *Frames of Mind: The Theory of Multiple Intelligences* (New York: Basic Books, 1993).

68. D. Austin, "The Effects of a Strengths Development Intervention Program upon the Self-Perceptions of Students' Academic Abilities" (Unpublished doctoral dissertation, Azusa Pacific University, Azusa, CA, 2005).

69. L. Cantwell, "Creating the Teaching-Learning Environment You've Always Dreamed of," *Educational Horizons* 84, no. 3, pp. 161-169 (Spring 2006).

70. D. O. Clifton and E. C. Anderson, *StrengthsQuest: Discover and Develop Your Strengths in Academics, Career, and Beyond* (Princeton, NJ: Gallup Organization, 2002).

71. W. M. Gillum, "The Effects of Strengths Instruction on Underperforming High School Students in Mathematics" (unpublished doctoral dissertation, Azusa Pacific University, Azusa, California, 2005).

72. K. Norwood, "Strengths-Based Leadership Training of Prospective Public School Leaders: A Comparative Study of a Professional Development Program" (unpublished doctoral dissertation, Azusa University, Azusa, California, 2005).

73. E. C. Anderson, L. A. Schreiner, and P. Shahbaz, Research and Evaluation of Strengths Counselors in a New Beginnings Course (unpublished raw data, 2003); Anderson, Schreinter, and Shahbaz, Research and Evaluation of Strengths Counselors in a New Beginnings Course (unpublished raw data, 2004).

74. J. L. Turner, *StrengthsQuest Counseling Applied to High School Freshmen* (Los Angeles: CASP Scientist-Practitioner Grant, 2004).

75. J. W. Williamson, "Assessing Student Strengths: Academic Performance and Persistence of First-Time College Students at a Private Church-Affiliated College" (unpublished doctoral dissertation, University of Sarasota, 2002).

76. Austin, "The Effects of a Strengths Development Intervention Program."

77. T. D. Hodges and D. O. Clifton, "Strengths-Based Development in Practice," in *International Handbook of Positive Psychology in Practice: From Research to Application*, ed. P. A. Linley and S. Joseph, 256–68 (New York: Wiley, 2004).

78. Cantwell," Creating the Teaching-Learning Environment."

79. M. C. Louis, "A Comparative Analysis of the Effectiveness of Strengths-Based Curricula in Promoting First-Year College Student Success" (Dissertation Abstracts International, 69 [06A], UMI No. AAT 3321378).

80. Michigan Committee on Juvenile Justice, "2003–2005 Report," August 2006, http://www.michigan.gov/documents/dhs/DHS-BJJMCJJ Report_222993_7.pdf.

81. W. H. Barton, "Incorporating the Strengths Perspective into Intensive Juvenile Aftercare," *Western Criminology Review* 7, no. 2: 48–61.

82. "Principal Unites School Around Strengths," accessed October 14, 2010, http://www.education-world.com/a_issues/chat180.shtml.

83. Ibid.

84. Purnell School, http://www/purnell.org.

85. Key Learning Community, http://www.city-data.com/school/key -learning-community-in.html.

86. Gallup, "Student Engagement," http://www.gallup.com/consulting/ education/141290/Student-Engagement.aspx.

Chapter 2: The Strengths Mindset: Understanding the Nature of Strengths

1. L. G. Aspinwall and U. M. Staudinger, *A Psychology of Human Strengths: Fundamental Questions and Future Directions for a Positive Psychology* (Washington, DC: American Psychological Association, 2003).

2. D. O. Clifton and E. C. Anderson, *StrengthsQuest: Discover and Develop Your Strengths in Academics, Career, and Beyond* (Washington, DC: Gallup Organization, 2002).

3. M. Buckingham and D. O. Clifton, *Now, Discover Your Strengths* (New York: Free Press, 2001), 28.

4. Ibid.

5. Clifton and J. K. Harter, "Strengths Investment," in *Positive organization scholarship*, ed. K. S. Cameron, J. E. Dutton, and R. E. Quinn, 111–21 (San Francisco: Berrett-Koehler, 2003).

6. Ibid.

7. P. G. Dodgson and J. V. Wood, "Self-Esteem and the Cognitive Accessibility of Strengths and Weaknesses," *Journal of Personality and Social Psychology* 75 (1998): 178–97.

8. Ibid., 194.

9. E. J. Smith, "The Strength-Based Counseling Model," *The Counseling Psychologists* 34 (2006): 13–79.

10. E. C. Chang, "Cultural Influences on Optimism and Pessimism: Differences in Western and Eastern Conceptualizations of the Self," in *Optimism and Pessimism: Theory, Research, and Practice*, ed. Chang, 257–80 (Washington, DC: American Psychological Association, 2001).

11. U. M. Staudinger, M. Marsiske, and P. B. Baltes, "Resilience and Reserve Capacity in Later Adulthood: Potentials and Limits of Development Across the Life Span," in *Developmental Psychopathology: Vol. 2. Risk, Disorder, and Adaptation*, ed. D. Cicchetti and D. Cohen, 801–47 (New York: Wiley, 1995).

12. Staudinger and M. Pasupathi, "Lifespan Perspectives on Self, Personality, and Social Cognition," in *Handbook of Cognition and Aging*, ed. T. Salthouse and F. Craik, 633–88 (Hillsdale, NJ: Erlbaum, 2000).

13. J. S. Lyons, N. D. Uziel-Miller, F. Reyes, and P. T. Sokol, "Strengths of Children and Adolescents in Residential Settings: Prevalence and Associations with Psychopathology and Discharge Placement," *Journal of the American Academy of Child & Adolescent Psychiatry* 39 (2000): 176–81.

14. C. Darwin, *The Origin of the Species* (New York: Gramercy, 1995).

15. A. Masten and M. Reed, "Resilience in Development," in *Handbook of Positive Psychology*, ed. C. Snyder and S. Lopez, 74–88 (New York: Oxford University Press, 2002).

16. A. Masten and J. Coatsworth, "The Development of Competence in Favorable and Unfavorable Environments: Lessons from Research on Successful Children," *American Psychologist* 53 (1998): 205–20.

17. Smith, "The Strength-Based Counseling Model."

18. Ibid.

19. Ibid.

20. Buckingham, M. (2007). *Go put your strengths to work: 6 powerful steps to achieve outstanding performance.* The Free Press: New York.

21. P. F. Drucker, *The Effective Executive* (New York: Harper and Row, 1966).

22. Ibid.

23. C. Dweck, *Mindset: The New Psychology of Success* (New York: Random House, 2006).

24. R. F. Jevene and J. E. Miller, *Finding Hope: Ways to See Life in a Brighter Light* (Fort Wayne, IN: Willowgreen, 1999).

25. C. R. Snyder and S. J. Lopez, eds., *Handbook of Positive Psychology* (New York: Oxford University Press, 2002).

26. J. Gillham and K. Reivich, "Resilience Research in Children," http://www.ppc.sas.upenn.edu.

27. Ibid.

28. A. Bandura, "Self-Efficacy: Toward a Unifying Theory of Behavioral Change," *Psychological Review* 84 (1977): 191–215.

29. Robert L. Fulghum. *All I Really Need to Know I Learned in Kindergarten.* Ballantine Books, 2003 (1986, 1988).

30. A. Weick, C. Rapp, W. P. Sullivan, and S. Kisthardt, "A Strengths Perspective for Social Work Practice," *Social Work* 34 (1980): 350–54.

31. J. Loehr and T. Schwartz, *The Power of Full Engagement* (New York: Free Press, 2003).

32. R. M. Ryan and E. L. Deci, "Self-Determination Theory and the Facilitation of Intrinsic Motivation, Social Development, and Well-Being," *American Psychologist* 55 (2000): 68–78.

33. T. Rath and D. O. Clifton, *How Full Is Your Bucket?* (New York: Gallup Press, 2004).

34. T. Kuhn, *The Structure of Scientific Revolutions* (Chicago: University of Chicago Press, 1962).

35. Clifton and P. Nelson, *Soar with Your Strengths* (New York: Dell, 1992).

Chapter 3: Brain Development, Emotion, and Learning

1. R. N. Caine, "Building the Bridge from Research between the Neurosciences and Education: Cautions and Possibilities," *NASSP Bulletin* 82, no. 598 (2000): 1–8.

2. E. Jensen, *Teaching with the Brain in Mind* (Alexandria, VA: ASCD-Association for Supervision and Curriculum Development, 1998); Jensen, *Brain-Based Learning* (San Diego: Brain Store, 1998).

3. G. Caine, R. Nummela-Caine, and S. Crowell, *Mindshifts: A Brain-Based Process for Restructuring Schools and Renewing Education*, 2nd ed. (Tucson, AZ: Zephyr Press, 1999).

4. M. Diamond, *Enriching Heredity* (New York: Free Press/Simon and Schuster, 1988).

5. M. D'Arcangelo, "How Does the Brain Develop? A Conversation with Steven Peterson," *Educational Leadership* 58, no. 3 (2000): 68–71.

6. Caine, Nummela-Caine, and Crowell, *Mindshifts*.

7. J. LeDoux, *The Emotional Brain: The Mysterious Underpinnings of Emotional Life* (Boston: Touchstone, 1998).

8. Diamond, *Enriching Heredity.*

9. Ibid.

10. R. A. Mueller et al., "Brain Mapping of Language and Auditory Perception in High-Functioning Autistic Adults: A PET Study," *Journal of Autism and Developmental Disorders* 29 (1999): 19–31.

11. C. Coffman and M. Gonzalez, *Follow This Path: How the World's Greatest Organizations Drive by Unleashing Human Potential* (New York: Warner Books, 2002).

12. J. Hams, *How the Brain Talks to Itself* (Binghamton, NY: Haworth Press, 1998).

13. Caine, Nummela-Caine, and Crowell, *Mindshifts.*

14. Jensen, *Teaching with the Brain in Mind*; Jensen, *Brain-Based Learning.*

15. *Dorland's Medical Dictionary for Health Consumers* (Philadelphia: Saunders, 2007).

16. B. Lipton, *The Biology of Belief: Unleashing the Power of Consciousness, Matter, and Miracles* (Carlsbad, CA: Hay House, 2008).

17. Jensen, *Teaching with the Brain in Mind*; Jensen, *Brain-Based Learning.*

18. Diamond, *Enriching Heredity.*

19. H. Gardner, *Frames of Mind: The Theory of Multiple Intelligences* (New York: Basic Books, 1983); Gardner, *Intelligence Reframes: Multiple Intelligences for the 21st Century* (New York: Basic Books, 2000).

20. Caine, Nummela-Caine, and Crowell, *Mindshifts.*

21. Jensen, *Brain-Based Learning*; Jensen, "Moving with the Brain in Mind," *Educational Leadership* 58, no. 3 (2000): 34–37.

22. Gerald Edelman and Jean-Pierre Changeux, eds., *The Brain* (Piscataway, NJ: Transaction, 2000).

23. Diamond, *Enriching Heredity.*

24. Gardner, *Frames of Mind*; Gardner, *Intelligence Reframes.*

25. Gardner, H. (1983/2003). *Frames of mind. The theory of multiple intelligences.* New York: Basic Books.

26. LeDoux, *The Emotional Brain.*

27. University of Southern California, Institute for Creative Technologies, http://ict/usc.edu/projects.

28. J. F. Morie and J Williams, "Emotional Sensory Learning Systems," report from the Visual Learning Campfire, Snowbird, UT, accessed October 30, 2010, http://people.ict.usc.edu.

29. P. Wolfe, *Brain Matters: Translating Research into Classroom Practice* (Alexandria, VA: Association for Supervision and Curriculum Development, 2001).

30. LeDoux, *The Emotional Brain.*

31. C. P. Pert, *Molecules of Emotion: The Science Behind Mind-Body Medicine* (Boston: Touchstone, 1997).

32. C. Hannaford, *Smart Moves: Why Learning Is Not All in Your Head* (Arlington, VA: Great Ocean, 1995).

33. D. A. Sousa, "Is the Fuss about Brain Research Justified?," *Education Week* 18, no. 16 (1998): 35, 52, accessed January 29, 2004, http://www.edweek.org/ew/1998/16sousa.h18/.

34. D. Goleman, *Emotional Intelligence* (New York: Bantam, 1995).

35. R. Caine, G. Caine, C. McClintic, and K. Klimek, *12 Brain/Mind Learning Principles in Action* (Thousand Oaks, CA: Corwin Press, 2005).

36. M. E. P. Seligman, "Teaching Positive Psychology," *APA Monitor on Psychology* 30, no. 7 (July–August 1999), http://www.apa.org.

37. Wolfe, *Brain Matters*.

38. M. Buckingham and D. O. Clifton, *Now, Discover Your Strengths* (New York: Free Press, 2001).

39. Caine, Caine, McClintic, and Klimek, *12 Brain/Mind Learning Principles*.

40. D. O. Clifton and C. E. Anderson, *StrengthsQuest: Discover and Develop Your Strengths in Academics, Career, and Beyond* (Washington, DC: Gallup Organization, 2002).

41. K. Braun, "Emotional Experience and the Synaptic Development of Limbic Circuits," *FENS Abstract 3* (2006): A171–72.

42. Ibid.

43. M. Katz, *On Playing a Poor Hand Well* (New York: Norton, 1997), 76.

44. Buckingham and Clifton, *Now, Discover Your Strengths*.

45. B. L. Frederickson, "The Role of Positive Emotions in Positive Psychology: The Broaden-and-Build Theory of Positive Emotions," *American Psychologist* 56 (2001): 218–26.

46. Ibid.

47. Ibid., 224.

48. A. Desetta and S. Wolin, *The Struggle to Be Strong: True Stories by Teens about Overcoming Tough Times* (Minneapolis, MN: Free Spirit Press, 2000).

49. A. Maslow, *Motivation and Personality* (New York: Harper and Row, 1954); Maslow, *Toward a Psychology of Being* (New York: Van Nostrand, 1962); Maslow, *The Farther Reaches of Human Nature* (New York: Penguin, 1971).

50. E. L. Deci and R. M. Ryan, "The 'What' and 'Why' of Goal Pursuits: Human Needs and the Self-Determination of Behavior," *Psychological Inquiry* 11 (2000): 227–68.

51. Maslow, *Motivation and Personality*; Maslow, *Toward a Psychology of Being*; Maslow, *The Farther Reaches*.

52. V. E. Frankl, *Man's Search for Meaning: An Introduction to Logotherapy* (New York: Washington Square, 1963).

53. M. Greenstein and W. Breitbart, "Cancer and the Experience of Meaning: A Group Psychotherapy Program for People with Cancer," *American Journal of Psychotherapy* 54 (2000): 487.

54. E. J. Smith, "Ethnic Identity Development: Toward the Development of a Theory within the Context of Majority/Minority Status," *Journal of*

Counseling & Development 70 (1991): 181–88; Smith, "The strength-based counseling model," *The Counseling Psychologist* 34 (2006): 13–79; B. Benard, *Fostering Resiliency in Kids: Protective Factors in the Family, School, and Community* (San Francisco: Far West Laboratory for Educational Research and Development, 1991, Eric Document Reproduction Service No. ED335781).

55. U. Bronfenbrenner, *A Report on Longitudinal Evaluations of Preschool Programs, Vol. II: Is Early Intervention Effective?* (Washington, DC: Office of Development, Department of Health, Education, and Welfare, 1974, ERIC Document Reproduction Service No. ED093501); Bronfenbrenner, "Ecological Systems Theory," *Annals of Child Development* 6 (1989): 185–246.

56. C. Darwin, *The Origin of Species* (New York: Gramercy, 1995); A. Masten and J. Coatsworth, "The Development of Competence in Favorable and Unfavorable Environments: Lessons from Research on Successful Children," *American Psychologist* 53 (1998): 205–20.

57. C. S. Carver and M. F. Scheier, "Principles of Self-Regulation: Action and Emotion," in *Handbook of Motivation and Cognition*, Vol. 2, *Foundations of Social Behavior*, ed. E. T. Higgins and R. M. Sorrentino, 3–52 (New York: Guilford, 1990).

58. Maslow, *Motivation and Personality*; Maslow, *Toward a Psychology of Being*; Maslow, *The Farther Reaches*.

59. A. Bandura, *Self-Efficacy: The Exercise of Control* (New York: Freeman, 1997).

60. C. Rogers, *On Becoming a Person* (Boston: Houghton Mifflin, 1961); Rogers, "The Concept of the Fully Functioning Person," *Psychotherapy Theory, Research and Practice* 1 (1964): 17–26.

61. K. F. Riegel, "The Dialectics of Human Development," *American Psychologist* 31 (1976): 689–700.

62. P. B. Baltes, U. Lindenberger, and U. M. Staudinger, "Life-Span Theory in Developmental Psychology," in *Handbook of Child Psychology*, Vol. 1, *Theoretical Models of Human Development*, 5th ed., ed. R. M. Lerner, 1029–43 (New York: Wiley, 1998).

63. M. E. Seligman, *Learned Optimism* (New York: Knopf, 1991); Seligman, "The President's Address," *American Psychologist* 54 (July–August 1998): 559–62; Seligman, "Teaching Positive Psychology"; Seligman, *Authentic Happiness* (New York: Free Press, 2002); G. Vailant, "The Mature Defenses: Antecedents of Joy," *American Psychologist* 55 (2000): 89–98.

64. Bandura, *Self-Efficacy*.

65. D. Saleebey, "The Strengths Perspective in Social Work Practice: Extensions and Cautions," *Social Work* 41 (1996): 296–305.

66. H. Goldstein, "Strength or Pathology: Ethical and Rhetorical Contrasts in Approaches to Practice," *Families in Society* 71 (1990): 267–75.

67. C. R. Snyder, *Handbook of Hope: Theory, Measures, and Applications* (San Diego, CA: Academic Press, 2000); Snyder, D. Ilardi, S. Michael, and J. Cheavens, "Hope Theory: Updating a Common Process for Psychological

Change," in *Handbook of Psychological Change: Psychotherapy Processes and Practices for the 21st Century*, ed. C. R. Snyder and R. E. Ingram, 128–53 (New York: Wiley, 2000); Snyder and S. Lopez, eds., *Handbook of Positive Psychology* (New York: Oxford University Press, 2002); Snyder, D. McDermott, W. Cook, and M. A. Rapoff, *Hope for the Journey: Helping Children Through Good Times and Bad* (Boulder, CO: Westview, 1997).

68. L. G. Aspinwall and U. M. Staudinger, *A Psychology of Human Strengths: Fundamental Questions and Future Directions for a Positive Psychology* (Washington, DC: American Psychological Association, 2003).

69. P. B. Baltes and U. M. Staudinger,. "Wisdom: A Metaheuristic, Pragmatic to Orchestrate Mind and Virtue towards Excellence," *American Psychologist* 55 (2000): 122–36.

70. Gardner, *Frames of Mind*; Gardner, *Intelligence Reframed*.

71. C. Peterson and M. E. P. Seligman, "Values in Action (VIA) Classification of Strengths Manual," http://www.positivepsychology.org/taxonomy.htm; Peterson and Seligman, *Character Strengths and Virtues: A Handbook and Classification* (Washington, DC: American Psychological Association, 2004).

72. A. Masten and M. Reed, 2002. Resilience in development. In C. Snyder, and S. Lopez (Eds.), *Handbook of Positive Psychology* (pp. 74–88). New York: Oxford University Press.

73. R. Carter (1999). *Mapping the mind*. Los Angeles: University of California Press.

Chapter 4: The Strengths-Based School's Component 1: A Strengths-Building Pyramid

1. D. Saleebey, *The Strengths Perspective in Social Work Practice* (New York: Longman, 1992).

2. M. J. Elias et al., "The School-Based Promotion of Social Competence: Theory, Research, and Practice," in *Stress, Risk, Resilience, in Children and Adolescents*, ed. R. Haggerty, L. Sherrod, N. Garmezy, and M. Rutter, 268–316 (New York: Cambridge University Press., 1994); Bruene-Butler, Kress, and J. Norris, "Institutionalizing Social and Emotional Learning Programs in Elementary Schools," in *E.Q. and I. Q = How to build a smart, nonviolent, emotionally intelligent school*, ed. M. J. Elias, H. Arnold, and C. C. Hussey (Thousand Oaks, CA: Corwin Press, 2002); M. J. Elias, L. Bruene-Butler, L. Blum, and T. Schuyler, "Voices from the Field: Identifying and Overcoming Roadblocks to Carry Out Programs in Social and Emotional Learning/Emotional Intelligence," *Journal of Educational and Psychological Consultation* 11, no. 2 (2000): 253–72.

3. K. Kafer, "Student Misbehavior Impedes Learning, Drives Out Teachers," *School Reform News*, July 2004, accessed November 24, 2010, http://

www/heartland.org/policybot/results/15211/Student_Misbehavior_Impedes_Learning_Drives_Out_Teachers.html. The May 2004 Public Agenda report, "Teaching Interrupted: Do Discipline Policies in Today's Public Schools Foster the Common Good?," is available online at http://www/publicagenda.org/research/research_reports_details.cfm?list=3.

4. D. Goleman, *Emotional Intelligence* (New York: Bantam, 1995).

5. Goleman, *Working with Emotional Intelligence* (New York: Bantam Books, 1998).

6. P. MacLean, *The Triune Brain in Evolution: Role in Paleocerebral Functions* (New York: Springer, 1990).

7. J. LeDoux, "Sensory Systems and Emotion: A Model of Affective Processing," *Integrative Psychiatry* 4 (1986): 237–48.

8. LeDoux, "Emotion and the Limbic System Concept," *Concepts of Neuroscience* 2 (1991): 169–99.

9. Goleman, *Working with Emotional Intelligence*.

10. B. Raychaba, *Pain, Lots of Pain: Violence and Abuse in the Lives of Young People in Care* (Ottawa, Ontario: National Youth in Care Network, 1993).

11. J. Anglin, *Pain, Normality, and the Struggle for Congruence: Reinterpreting Residential Care for Children and Youth* (Binghamton, NY: Haworth Press, 2002).

12. L. K. Brentro, "From Coercive to Strength-Based Intervention: Responding to the Needs of Children in Pain," *Reclaiming Children and Youth, Executive Summary,* http://www.cyc-net.org/features/ft-strengthbased.html.

13. Ibid.

14. N. Eisenberger, M. Lieberman, and K. Williams, "The Pain of Social Exclusion," *Science* 302 (2003): 290–92.

15. Elias and Clabby, *Building Social Problem Solving Skills: Guidelines from a School-Based Program* (San Francisco: Jossey-Bass, 1992); Elias, ed., *Social Decision-Making and Life Skills Development: Guidelines for Middle School Educators* (Piscataway, NJ: Rutgers University Center for Applied Psychology, 1993).

16. Social Decision Making/Problem Solving Program, accessed November 4, 2010, http://www.ubhcisweb.org/sdm/research/evidence.htm.

17. Jessica O'Brien Tyler, "*The Impact of Strengths-Based Development on Student Engagement* (Texas Christian University, Fort Worth, 2006, 3218187).

18. "Calming Techniques," accessed November 4, 2010, http://www.mediate.com/articles/ford16.cfm?nl-156.

19. A. Ellis and W. Dryden, *The Practice of Rational-Emotive Behavior Therapy,* 2nd ed. (New York: Springer, 1998).

20. Elsie J. Smith, "The Strength-Based Model," *The Counseling Psychologist* 34, no. 1 (2006): 13–79.

21. N. Henderson and M. Milstein, *Resiliency in Schools: Making It Happen for Students and Educators* (Thousand Oaks, CA: Corwin Press, 1996).

22. R. J. Davidson et al., "Alterations in the Brain and Immune Function Produced by Mindfulness," *Psychosomatic Medicine* 65 (2003): 564–70.

23. J. Suttie, "Mindful Kids, Peaceful Schools," *Greater Good* 4, no. 1 (2007) http://greatergood.berkeley.edu/article/item/mindful_kids_peaceful_schools/#

24. L. Lantieri, *Building Emotional Intelligence: Techniques to Cultivate Inner Strength in Children* (Boulder, CO: Sounds True, 2008).

25. P. Thomas, *The Power of Relaxation* (St. Paul, MN: Redleaf Press, 2003).

26. R. Kriete, *The Morning Meeting Book* (Greenfield, MA: Northeast Foundation for Children, 1999).

Chapter 5: Component 2: Improving Instruction—The Academic Curriculum

1. NAS/NAE/IOM, *Rising above the Gathering Storm, Revisited: Rapidly approaching Category 5* (Washington, DC: National Academies Press, 2010).

2. "U.S. Kids Mediocre in Math and Science," *USA Today*, November 21, 1996.

3. "4th and 8th Graders in U.S. Still Lag Many Peers," *New York Times*, December 15, 2004.

4. Center for Public Education., "More Than a Horse Race: A Guide to International Tests of Student Achievement," accessed December 29, 2008, http://www.centerforpubliceducation.org/Main-Menu/Evaluating-performance/A-guide-to-international-assessments-At-a-glance/International-tests-at-a-glance.GMEditor.html.

5. Ibid.

6. Ibid.

7. Ibid.

8. Ibid.

9. Ibid.

10. P. E. Jose and C. S. Huntsinger, "Moderation and Mediation Effects of Coping by Chinese American and European American Adolescents," *Journal of Genetic Psychology* 166 (2005): 16–43; C. S. Huntsinger, P. E. Jose, D. Rudden, Z. Luo, Z., and D. B. Krieg "Cultural Differences in Interactions Around Mathematics Tasks in Chinese American and European American Families," in *Research on the Education of Asian and Asian Pacific Americans*, ed. C. Park, A. L. Goodwin, and S. J. Lee, 75–103 (Greenwich, CT: Information Age, 2001).

11. Programme for International Student Assessment, *The High Cost of Low Educational Performance: The Long-Run Economic Impact of Improving PISA Outcomes* (Paris: OECD, 2010). The authors of the report are Prof. Eric. A. Hanushek from the Hoover Institution at Stanford University and Prof. Ludger Woessmann from the IFo Institute for Economic Research and the University of Munich.

12. Ibid.

13. Ibid., 10.

14. B. Auguste, P. Kihn, and M. Miller, *Closing the Talent Gap: Attracting and Retaining Top-Third Graduates to Careers in Teaching: An International and Market Research-Based Perspective* (New York: McKinsey & Company, 2010).

15. Ibid.

16. J. Sivin-Kachala and E. R. Bialo, *1999 Research Report on the Effectiveness of Technology in Schools*, 6th ed. (Washington, DC: Software and Information Industry Association, 1999).

17. S. M. Ross and J. W. Strahl, "Evaluation of Michigan's Freedom to Learn Program," (September 6, 2005), accessed November 10, 2010, http://www.techlearning.com/techleaerning/events/techforum.

18. S. Judge, "The Impact of Computer Technology on Academic Achievement of Young African American Children," *Journal of Research in Childhood Education* (December 2005), accessed January 3, 2009, http://www.access mylibrary.com/ocmsite5/bin/aml_landing_tt.pl?purchase_typeITM&item_id.

19. L. Bostrom and L. M. Lassen, "Unraveling Learning, Learning Styles, Learning Strategies, and Meta-Cognition," *Education and Training* 48 (2006): 178–89.

20. R. Kenyon, *Facts and Statistics on Learning Disabilities and Literacy* (Tallahassee: State of Florida, Office of Work Force Education, September 2003).

21. M. Levine, *A Mind at a Time* (New York: Simon and Schuster, 2002).

22. Benjamin Bloom and David R. Krathwohl, *Taxonomy of Educational Objectives: The Classification of Educational Goals, by a Committee of College and University Examiners—Handbook 1: Cognitive Domain.* (New York: Longmans, 1956).

23. T. Gravois and E. Gickling, "Best Practices in Curriculum-Based Assessment," in *Best Practices in School Psychology*, ed. A. Thomas and J. Grimes, vol. 4, 1–13 (Washington, DC: National Association of School Psychologists, 2002).

24. M. H. Epstein and J. M. Sharma, *Behavioral and Emotional Rating Scale: A Strength-Based Approach to Assessment* (Austin, TX: PRO-ED, 1998), http://www.cecp.air.org/interact/expertonline/strength/transition/8.asp.

25. S. M. Donovan, J. D. Bransford, and J. W. Pellegrino, eds., *How People Learn: Bridging Research and Practice* (Washington, DC: National Academy of Sciences, 1999). The authors are listed as the Committee on Learning Research and Educational Practice and the National Research Council.

26. J. Flavel, "Metacognition and Cognitive Monitoring: A New Area of Cognitive-Developmental Inquiry," *American Psychologist* 34 (1979): 906–11; Flavel, "Speculations about the Nature and Development of Metacognition," in *Metacognition, Motivation and Understanding*, ed. F. E. Weinert and R. H. Kluwe, 21–29 (Hillsdale, NJ: Erlbaum, 1987).

27. M. Sellars, *Using Students' Strengths to Support Learning Outcomes* (Berlin: Springer Verlag, 2008).

28. Gravois and Gickling, "Best Practices in Curriculum-Based Assessment."

Chapter 6: Component 3: Caring and Empathic Classrooms

1. L. A. Schreiner and E. Hulme, "A comprehensive strengths approach to the first year experience," accessed November 13, 2010, http://www.scedu/ fye/events/presentation/annual/2006.

2. D. Goleman, *Working with Emotional Intelligence* (New York: Bantam Books, 1998).

3. Howard Gardner, *Frames of Mind: The Theory of Multiple Intelligences* (New York: Basic Books, 1983); Gardner, *Multiple Intelligences: The Theory in Practice* (New York: Basic Books, 1993); Gardner, *Intelligence Reframed: Multiple Intelligences for the 21st Century* (New York: Basic Books, 1999); Gardner, "A Reply to Perry D. Klein's 'Multiplying the Problems of Intelligence by Eight,'" *Canadian Journal of Education* 23, no. 1 (1998): 96–102.

4. H. Gardner (1983/2003). *Frames of mind. The theory of multiple intelligences, p. 238.* New York: BasicBooks.

5. R. W. Blum, C. A. McNeely, and P. M. Rinehart, *The Untapped Power of Schools to Improve the Health of Teens* (Minneapolis: Center for Adolescent Health and Development, University of Minnesota, 2002).

6. Ibid.

7. "School Connectedness and Meaningful Student Participation," accessed November 13, 2010, http://www2.ed.gov/admins/lead/safety/ training/connect/school_pg3.html.

8. Blum and H. P. Libbey, "Executive Summary," *Journal of School Health* 74, no. 7 (September 2004): 231–32.

9. M. D. Resnick et al., "Protecting Adolescents from Harm: Findings from the National Longitudinal Study on Adolescent Health," *Journal of the American Medical Association* 278, no.10 (September 10, 1997), 823–32.

10. Blum, McNeely, and Rinehart, *Improving the Odds*.

11. Libbey, "Measuring Student Relationships to School: Attachment, Bonding, Connectedness and Engagement," *Journal of School Health* 74, no. 7 (September 2004): 274–83.

12. M. Watson, *Learning to Trust: Transforming Difficult Elementary Classrooms through Developmental Discipline* (San Francisco: Jossey-Bass, 2003).

13. J. Whitlock, *Places to Be and Places to Belong: Youth Connectedness in School and Community* (Ithaca, NY: Family Life Development Center, Cornell University, 2004).

14. Sue Bredekamp and Teresa Rosegrant, eds., *Reaching Potentials: Appropriate Curriculum and Assessment for Young Children*, vol. 1 (Washington, DC: NAEYC, 1992).

15. H. L. David and R. M. Capraro, "Strategies for Teaching in Heterogeneous Environments while Building a Classroom Community," accessed February 20, 2005, http://www.findarticles.com/p/articles/mi_qa3673/ is_200110/ai_n8996767.

16. R. Brooks, "The Search for Islands of Competence: A Metaphor of Strength and Hope," accessed November 14, 2010, http://www.drrobert brooks.com/writings/articles/0506.html.

17. J. Saphier and R. Gower, *The Skillful Teacher: Building Your Teaching Skills* (Acton, MA: Research for Better Teaching, 1997).

Chapter 7: Component 4: Preventing Failure

1. G. D. Gottfredson, D. C. Gottfredson, and E. R. Czeh, *National Study of Delinquency Prevention in Schools: Appendix D—Taxonomy of School-Based Prevention Activities and Prevention Objectives, Final Report* (Ellicott City, MD: Gottfredson Associates, 2000).

2. R. Rumberger, "Why Students Drop Out of School," in *Dropouts in America: Confronting the Graduation Rate Crisis,* ed. G. Orfield (Cambridge, MA: Harvard Education Press, 2004), 131–55.

3. "Prevention: Home, Community, and School Connections," accessed November 14, 2010, http://www.edjj.org/focus/prevention/phcsc.html.

4. Alliance for Excellent Education, Fact Sheet, "High School Dropouts in America," updated February 2009, http://www.all4ed.org.

5. Rumberger, "Why Students Drop Out of School."

6. Ibid.

7. M. Dynarski, L. Clarke, B. Cobb, J. Finn, R. Rumberger, and J. Smink, *Dropout Prevention: A Practice Guide* (NCEE 2008-4025) (Washington, DC: National Center for Education Evaluation and Regional Assistance, Institute of Education Sciences, U.S. Department of Education, 2008), http://ies.ed.gov/ncee/wwc.

8. R. F. Catalano, R. Loeber, and K. C. McKinney, *School and Community Interventions to Prevent Serious and Violent Offending* (Washington, DC: Office of Juvenile Justice and Delinquency Prevention, October 1999).

9. "Prevention and Early Intervention," accessed November 19, 2010, http://www.edjj.or/focus/prevention/phcsc.html.

10. B. Hart and T. Risley, *Meaningful Differences in the Everyday Experiences of Young American Children* (Baltimore: Brookes, 1995).

11. K. A. Graham and D. Hardy, "In Reading, Dick Lags Far Behind Jane," *Philadelphia Inquirer,* April 2, 2006, A02.

12. M. A. Clark, K. Flower, J. Walton, and E. Oakley, "Tackling Male Underachievement: Enhancing a Strengths-Based Learning Environment for Middle School Boys," *Professional School Counseling, y* (December 1, 2008), vol. 12, pp. 127–132.

13. U.S. Department of Education, "Study Shows Educational Achievement Gender Gap Shrinking," 2004, accessed May 10, 2008, http://www.ed.gov/news/pressreleases/2004/11/11192004b.html.

14. National Center for Educational Statistics, "The Condition of Education 2006," accessed August 2009, http://nces.ed.gov/pubsearch/pubsinfo .asp?pubid=2006071.

15. M. A. Clark, E. Oakley, and H. Adams, "The Gender Achievement Gap Challenge," *ASCA School Counselor* 43, no. 3 (2006): 20–25.M. A. Clark, P. Thompson, and W. Vialle, "Examining the Gender Gap in Educational Outcomes in Public Education: Involving Pre-Service School Counsellors and Teachers in Cross-Cultural and Interdisciplinary Research," *International Journal for the Advancement of Counselling* 30 (2008): 52–66.

16. National Center for Educational Statistics, "Student Effort and Educational Progress: The Condition of Education 2005," accessed June 9, 2009, http://nces.ed.gov/pusearch/pubsinfo.asp?pubid=2005094.

17. J. C. Carey and I. Martin, *What Are the Implications of Possible Selves Research for School Counseling Practice?*, School Counseling Research Brief 5.2, (Amherst, MA: Center for School Counseling Outcome Research, 2007); D. Oyserman, D. Bybee, and K. Terry, "Possible Selves and Academic Outcomes: How and When Possible Selves Impel Action," *Journal of Personality and Social Psychology* 91 (2006): 188–204.

18. J. A. Clark, K. Flower, J. Walton, and E. Oakley, "Tackling Male Underachievement: Enhancing a Strengths-Based Learning Environment for Middle School Boys," *Professional School Counseling* 12, no. 2 (2008): 127–32.

19. J. P. Galassi and P. Akos, *Strengths-Based School Counseling: Promoting Student Development and Achievement* (Mahwah, NJ: Erlbaum, 2007).

20. K. A. S. Howard and V. S. H. Solberg, "School-Based Social Justice: The Achieving Success Identity Pathways Program," *Professional School Counseling*, 9 (2006): 278–87.

21. M. E. Walsh, M. E. Kenny, K. M. Wieneke, and K. R. Harrington, "The Boston Connects Program: Promoting Learning and Healthy Development," *Professional School Counseling* 12, no. 2 (2008), 166–69.

22. Ibid., 166.

23. Ibid, 167.

24. Walsh, J. G. Barrett, and J. DePaul, "Day-to-Day Activities of School Counselors: Alignment with New Directions in the Field and the ASCA National Model," *Professional School Counseling* 10 (2007): 370–78.

25. W. L. Logan and J. L. Scarborough, "Connections through Clubs: Collaboration and Coordination of a Schoolwide Program," *Professional School Counseling* 12, no. 2 (2008): 157–61.

26. M. J. Karcher, "The Cross-Age Mentoring Program: A Developmental Intervention for Promoting Students' Connectedness across Grade Levels," *Professional School Counseling* 12, no. 2 (2008): 137–43; C. D. Ryff and B. Singer, "The Contours of Positive Human Health," *Psychological Inquiry* 9 (1998): 1–28.

27. M. F. Steger, P. Frazier, S. Oishi, and M. Kaler, "The Meaning in Life Questionnaire: Assessing the Presence of and Search for Meaning in Life," *Journal of Counseling Psychology* 53 (2006): 80–93.

28. E. Erickson, *Childhood and Society* (New York: Norton, 1963); Erikson, *Identity: Youth and Crisis* (New York: Norton, 1968).

29. L. H. Eilers & C. Pinkley (2006). Metacognitive strategies help students to comprehend text. *Reading Improvement, 46,* pp. 13–29.

Chapter 8: Component 5: Increasing Home, School, and Community Partnerships

1. A. T. Henderson and N. Berla, eds., *A New Generation of Evidence: The Family Is Critical to Student Achievement* (a report from the National Committee for Citizens in Education) (Washington, DC: Center for Law and Education, 1994).

2. G. Olsen and M. L. Fuller, *Home-School Relations: Working Successfully with Parents and Families* (New York: Pearson Education, 2003).

3. http://www.education.com/definition/background/?_module=Deep Link&hit&id=10037.

4. http://www.education.com/topic/classroom-behavior/?_module= DeepLink&hit&id=41278.

5. http://www.education.com/topoic/child-adolescent-development/? _module=DeepLink&hit&id-11363.

6. E. J. Smith, "The Strength-Based Counseling Model," *The Counseling Psychologist* 34, no. 1 (2006): 13–79.

7. J. L. Epstein, *School, Family, and Community Partnerships: Preparing Educators and Improving Schools* (Boulder, CO: Westview Press, 2001); A. T. Henderson and K. L. Mapp, *A New Wave of Evidence: The Impact of School, Family, and Community Connections on Student Achievement* (Austin, TX: Southwest Educational Development Laboratory, 2002); S. B. Sheldon, "Linking School-Family-Community Partnerships in Urban Elementary Schools to Student Achievement on State Tests," *Urban Review* 35, no. 2 (2003): 149–65.

8. Epstein, M. G. Sanders, B. S. Simon, K. C., Salinas, M. R. Jansorn, and F. L. van Voorhis, *School, Family, and Community Partnerships: Your Handbook for Action,* 2nd ed. (Thousand Oaks, CA: Corwin Press, 2002).

9. M. Tschannen-Moran, J. Parish, and M. F. DiPaola, "School Climate: The Interplay between Interpersonal Relationships and Student Achievement," *Journal of School Leadership* 16 (2006): 386–415.

10. J. Bryan, "Fostering Educational Resilience and Academic Achievement in Urban Schools through School-Family Partnerships," *Professional School Counseling* 8 (2005): 219–27.

11. J. P. Kretzmann and J. L. McKnight, *Building Communities from the Inside Out: A Path toward Finding and Mobilizing a Community's Assets* (Chicago: ACTA Publications, 1993).

12. S. Catsambis, "Expanding Knowledge of Parental Involvement in Children's Secondary Education: Connections with High School Seniors' Academic Success," *Social Psychology of Education* 5 (2001): 149–77; B. S. Simon,

"High School Outreach and Family Involvement," *Social Psychology of Education* 7 (2004): 185–89.

13. Sheldon and Epstein, "Involvement Counts: Family and Community Partnerships and Math Achievement," *Journal of Educational Research* 98 (2005): 196–206.

14. Epstein and S. B. Sheldon, "Present and Accounted For: Improving Student Attendance through Family and Community Involvement," *Journal of Educational Research* 95 (2002): 308–18; Sheldon and Epstein, "Getting Students to School: Using Family and Community Involvement to reduce Chronic Absenteeism," *School Community Journal* 4, no. 2 (2004): 39–56.

15. Sheldon and Epstein, "Improving Student Behavior and Discipline with Family and Community Involvement," *Education in Urban Society* 35, no. 1 (2002): 4–26; Sheldon and Epstein, "Involvement Counts: Family and Community Partnerships and Math Achievement," *Journal of Educational Research* 98 (2005): 196–206.

16. Sheldon and Epstein, "School Programs of Family and Community Involvement to Support Children's Reading and Literacy Development across the Grades," in *Literacy Development of Students in Urban Schools: Research and Policy*, ed. J. Flood and P. Anders (Newark, DE: International Reading Association, 2005), 107–38.

17. Epstein and K. C. Salinas, "Partnering with Families and Communities," *Educational Leadership* 61, no. 8 (2004): 12–18.

18. Ibid.

19. Ibid.

20. Accessed November 24, 2010, http://www.ncrel.org/sdrs/areas/issues/envronmnt/famncomm/pa400.htm.

21. S. G. Peters, *Inspired to Learn: Why We Must Give Children Hope* (Marietta, GA: Rising Sun, 2001).

22. J. Bryan and L. Henry, "Strengths-Based Partnerships: A School-Family-Community Partnership Approach to Empowering Students," *Professional School Counseling* 12 (2008): 149–56.

23. D. Weiler, A. LaGoy, E. Crane, and A. Rovner, *An Evaluation of K–12 Service-Learning in California: Phase II Final Report* (Emeryville, CA: RPP International and the Search Institute, 1998).

24. P. Scales and D. Blyth, "Effects of Service-Learning on Youth: What We Know and What We Need to Know," *The Generator* Winter (1997): 6–9; F. O'Bannon, "Service-Learning Benefits Our School," *State Education Leader* 17 (1999): 3.

Chapter 9: Assuring Teachers Understand Their Own Strengths

1. K. Lizotte, "Recalling Your Favorite Teacher," November, 25, 2005, accessed November 26, 2010, http://ezinearticles.com/?Recalling-Your-Favorite-Teacher&id=10234.

2. E. Werner and R. Smith, *Overcoming the Odds: High-Risk Children from Birth to Adulthood* (New York: Cornell University, 1992).

3. J. K. Rice, *Teacher Quality: Understanding the Effectiveness of Teacher Attributes* (Washington, DC: Economic Policy Institute, 2003).

4. B. Berry, "What It Means to Be a 'Highly Qualified' Teacher," Southeast Center for Teaching Quality, 2003, accessed November 26, 2010, http://umatilla.k12.or.us/NCLB/definingHQ520teachers.

5. D. R. Cruickshank, D. B. Jenkins, and K. K. Metcalf, *The Act of Teaching* (New York: McGraw-Hill, 2003), 329.

6. N. Noddings, *Caring: A Feminine Approach to Ethics and Moral Education* (Berkeley: University of California Press, 1984, pp. 100-101).

7. S. Thompson, J. G. Greer, and B. Greer, "Highly Qualified for Successful Teaching: Characteristics Every Teacher Should Possess," accessed November 24, 2010, http://usca.edu/essays/vol102004/thompson.pdf.

8. R. F. Ferguson, "Teachers' Perceptions and Expectations and the Black-White Test Score Gap," in *The Black-White Test Score Gap*, ed. C. Jencks and M. Phillips (Washington, DC: Brookings Institution Press, 1998), p. 483. R. F. Ferguson. Teachers' Perceptions and Expectations and the Black-White Test Score Gap. *Urban Education, vol. 38 (4), July 2003, pp. 460-507.*

9. R. D. Stanton-Salazar and S. Spina, "The Network Orientations of Highly Resilient Urban Minority Youth: A Network-Analytic Account of Minority Socialization and Its Educational Implications," *Urban Review* 32, no. 3 (2000): 227–61.

10. Ferguson, "Teachers' Perceptions and Expectations and the Black-White Test Score Gap," *Urban Education* 38, no. 4 (2003): 460–507.

11. T. L. Strayhorn, "Teacher Expectations and Urban Black Males' Success in School: Implications for Academic Leaders," *Academic Leadership: The Online Journal* 6, no. 2 (May 2008).

12. D. Saleebey, "The Strengths Approach to Practice," in *The Strengths Perspective in Social Work Practice*, 4th ed., ed. D. Saleebey (Boston: Allyn & Bacon, 2006), 77–92.

13. B. Benard, *Resiliency: What We Have Learned* (San Francisco: WestEd, 2004).

14. A. Masten, "Ordinary Magic: Resilience Processes in Development," *American Psychologist* 56 (2001): 227–38.

15. C. Dweck, *Mindset: The New Psychology of Success* (New York: Random House, 2006).

16. S. M. Donovan, J. D. Bransford, and J. W. Pellegrino, eds., *How People Learn: Bridging Research and Practice* (Washington, DC: National Academy of Sciences, 1999). The authors are listed as the Committee on Learning Research and Educational Practice and the National Research Council.

17. B. L. Fredrickson, "The Role of Positive Emotions in Positive Psychology: The Broaden-And-Build Theory of Positive Emotions," *American Psychologist* 56 (2001): 218–26; Fredrickson and T. Joiner, "Positive Emotions

Trigger Upward Spirals toward Emotional Well-Being," *Psychological Science* 13 (2002): 172–75.

18. Fredrickson, K.E. Maynard, M. J. Helms, T. L. Haney, I. C. Seigler, and J. C. Barefoot, "Hostility Predicts Magnitude and Duration of Blood Pressure Response to Anger," *Journal of Behavioral Medicine* 23 (2000): 229–43; J. J. Gross, B. L. Fredrickson, and R. W. Levenson, "The Psychophysiology of Crying," *Psychophysiology* 31 (1994): 460–68.

19. Fredrickson and R. W. Levenson, "Positive Emotions Speed Recovery from the Cardiovascular Sequelae of Negative Emotions," *Cognition and Emotion* 12 (1998): 191–220; Fredrickson, R. A. Mancuso, C. Branigan, and M. Tugade, "The Undoing Effect of Positive Emotions," *Motivation and Emotion* 24 (2000): 237–58.

20. Fredrickson, *Positivity: Groundbreaking Research Reveals How to Embrace the Hidden Strength of Positive Emotions, Overcome Negativity and Thrive* (New York: Crown, 2009).

Chapter 10: Creating and Communicating a Strengths-Based School Vision: Getting Involved

1. The Thoreau quotation is taken from http://inspire-edu.com/2008/03/02 and from http://www/leadership-with-you.com/vision-quotes.html.

2. The Helen Keller quotation is taken from http://www/brainyquote.com/quotes/authors/h/helen-keller.

3. The Calvin Coolidge quotation is taken from http://www.brainyquote.com/quotes/authors/c/calvin_coolidge_3.html.

4. B. L. Fredrickson, *Positivity: Groundbreaking Research Reveals How to Embrace the Hidden Strength of Positive Emotions, Overcome Negativity and Thrive* (New York: Crown , 2009); Fredrickson, "The Role of Positive Emotions in Positive Psychology: The Broaden-and-Build Theory of Positive Emotions," *American Psychologist* 56 (2001): 218–26.

5. S. Covey, A. R. Merrill, and R. Merrill, *First Things First* (New York: Simon and Schuster, 1994).

6. M. C. Louis, "Optimizing Strengths Development Initiatives in the Classroom," Gallup Organization, 2010, 1–2, http://api.ning.com/files/cgh3w fl3j7wQ3gRo61CM42I5xZWX*j8fw4qEJ6VWJVpCh6te3Lq5SSCxBnFVIJB9-fEUznO25LRdSvEeczESrUCdtFEHeJwj/LouisOptimizingStrengthsDevelopment_SQ_PRES_021010_bp.pdf . See also http://strengths.gallup.com.

7. Fredrickson, "The Role of Positive Emotions."

8. C. Dweck, *Mindset: The New Psychology of Success* (New York: Random House, 2006).

9. R. M. Ryan and E. L. Deci, "Self-Determination Theory and the Facilitation of Intrinsic Motivation, Social Development, and Well-Being," *American Psychologist* 55, no. 1 (2000): 66–78.

10. S. J. Lopez and M. C. Louis, "The Principles of Strengths-Based Education," *Journal of College and Character* 10, no. 4 (2009), http://journals.naspa.org/jcc/vol10/iss4/3/.

11. R. Liesveld and J. A. Miller, *Teach with Your Strengths: How Great Teachers Inspire Their Students* (New York: Gallup Press, 2005).

12. J. P. Kretzmann and J. L. McKnight, *Building Communities from the Inside Out: A Path toward Finding and Mobilizing a Community's Assets* (Chicago: ACTA, 1993).

13. National Middle School Association, *This We Believe: Keys to Educating Young Adolescents* (Westerville, OH: NMSA, 2010). Also available at http://www.nmsa.org.

14. H. E. Gardner, *Frames of Mind: The Theory of Multiple Intelligences* (New York: Basic Books, 1983); Gardner, *Intelligence Reframed: The Theory of Multiple Intelligences* (New York: Basic Books, 2000).

15. D. Goleman, *Emotional Intelligence* (New York: Bantam, 1995); Goleman, *Working with Emotional Intelligence* (New York: Bantam Books, 1998).

16. P. R. Pintrich, "The Role of Metacognitive Knowledge in Learning, Teaching, and Assessing," *Theory into Practice* (Fall 2002), http://findarticles.com/p/articles/mi_m0NQM/is_4_41/ai_94872708/.

17. Ibid.; J. Bransford, A. Brown, and R. Cocking, *How People Learn: Brain, Mind, Experience, and School* (Washington, DC: National Academy Press, 1999); R. Snow, L. Corno, and D. Jackson, "Individual Differences in Affective and Cognitive Functions," in *Handbook of Educational Psychology*, ed. D. Berliner and R. Calfee (New York: Macmillan, 1996), 243–310.

18. J. P. Comer, *Leave No Child Behind: Preparing Today's Youth for Tomorrow's World* (New Haven, CT: Yale University Press, 2004).

19. Testimony of Geoffrey Canada, president/CEO, Harlem Children's Zone, and president, Harlem Children's Zone Promise Academy Charter Schools, before the Senate Committee on Health, Education, Labor and Pensions, April 22, 2010.

20. Ibid. Some of the reference sources cited by Dr. Canada include: E. Eckholm, "Plight Deepens for Black Men," *New York Times*, March 20, 2006; "Charting a New Course: A Blueprint for Transforming Juvenile Justice in New York State," a report of Governor David Paterson's Task Force on Transforming Juvenile Justice, (2009).

21. W. Dobbie and R. G. Fryer, Jr., "Are High-Quality Schools Enough to Close the Achievement Gap? Evidence from a Social Experiment in Harlem" (NBER working paper no. 15473, National Bureau of Economic Research, Cambridge, MA, 2009).

22. E. J. Smith, "The Strength-Based Counseling Model," *The Counseling Psychologist* 34 (2006): 13–79.

Index

About the Author

ELSIE JONES-SMITH, PhD, is a licensed clinical psychologist with doctoral degrees in clinical psychology and counselor education. She is also president of the Strengths-Based Institute (SBI), which is a consulting, training, and coaching organization that integrates best practices in strengths-based education, counseling, and corporate team building. Her published works include Praeger's *Nurturing Nonviolent Children: A Guide for Parents, Educators, and Counselors, Counseling and Psychotherapy: Toward an Integrative Approach* from Sage Publishing, and coauthor of *Group Counseling: Theory and Process* from Houghton Mifflin. Jones-Smith is a Fellow of two divisions of the American Psychological Association, a Diplomate of the American Board of Professional Psychology, and former professor at Temple University, Philadelphia; Michigan State University, East Lansing; University ofBuffalo, Buffalo, NY; and Boston University, Boston. She is the creator of the strengths-based therapy model, a new approach for providing therapy for individuals seeking to build upon their strengths. She is currently writing a book, Strengths-Based Therapy: Theory and Process.

ELSIE JONES-SMITH, PhD

There are some 60 million students in the United States, but the rate for graduation from high school in 2007 was 68.6 percent—a proportion below that of most developed nations. Strengths-based systems could help American students better compete against their peers in an increasingly globalized and challenging world.

Many American schools use an educational model that focuses on remedying students' academic deficits. It's a familiar and seemingly logical model: to improve performance, identify weaknesses and target these problem areas. Could doing the opposite be a better way? Licensed clinical psychologist Elsie Jones-Smith argues that strengths-based systems are indeed more effective—not just in social work, where the philosophy became popular; or in the business world, where the concept is increasingly being embraced—but in the academic setting as well.

Spotlighting the Strengths of Every Single Student: Why U.S. Schools Need a New, Strengths-Based Approach explains how and why a system that focuses on students' strengths enables kids to be self-confident, goal-directed, and to possess a stronger sense of self-efficacy, self-control, and academic achievement.